T0244311

TO BE A HOLY PEOPLE

TO BE A HOLY PEOPLE

Jewish Tradition and Ethical Values

EUGENE KORN

URIM PUBLICATIONS
Jerusalem · New York

To Be a Holy People:
Jewish Tradition and Ethical Values
By Eugene Korn

Typeset by Ariel Walden

Printed in Israel

First Edition

ISBN 978-1-60280-455-5

Urim Publications
P.O. Box 52287,
Jerusalem 9152102
Israel

www.UrimPublications.com

Cover image: "Exodus" by Marc Chagall. Israel Knesset, Jerusalem, 1969
Photographer: Shai Halevi

Cover design by the Virtual Paintbrush

Library of Congress Cataloging-in-Publication Data

Names: Korn, Eugene, 1947- author.
Title: To be a holy people : Jewish tradition and ethical values / Eugene Korn.
Description: First edition. | Jerusalem ; New York : Urim Publications, [2021] | Includes bibliographical references and index. | Summary: "Can Jewish tradition face our modern understanding of justice, equality, and human progress? The author addresses ancient and modern moral questions. Building on biblical and rabbinic traditions, he analyzes how Jewish ethics relates to Jewish law, fairness, equality, and compassion, as well as the challenge of religious violence. This provides food for thought on subjects ranging from gender, freedom, and military ethics to Jewish particularism and contemporary universalism"— Provided by publisher.
Identifiers: LCCN 2021037136 | ISBN 9781602804555 (hardcover)
Subjects: LCSH: Jewish ethics—21st century.
Classification: LCC BJ1285.2 .K67 2021 | DDC 296.3/6—dc23
LC record available at https://lccn.loc.gov/2021037136

To Lila,
Life partner, teacher and inspiration

Contents

Introduction

Holiness and Ethics

Jewish tradition faces a spiritual and existential crisis today, one unlike any other in the past. The source of this sharp new challenge is modern ethics. In the Middle Ages, Maimonides wrote *Guide of the Perplexed* to answer the intellectual challenges that Greek philosophy and metaphysics posed for Jewish belief. How could the Bible and Talmud compete with the claims of human reason? How could a Jew understand the Torah in a way that was consistent with the canons of rationality? At the beginning of modernity, it was scientific knowledge that unsettled Jewish tradition: Could tradition continue to hold in the face of the overwhelming evidence for natural causality, evolution and empirical history?

Those issues have lost their urgency today, but in their place stand contemporary ethical values and unprecedented visions that demand bold responses from Jewish tradition. Can age-old Jewish practices be justified in the face of our modern understanding of justice, equality and human flourishing? How can "commandedness" and *mitsvot* be defended in light of personal autonomy and modernity's relentless attack on authority? Will Jewish tradition's particularism be able to co-exist with contemporary universalism? And now that Jews have sovereignty and military power, how can their religious fervor be tamed so that it doesn't lead to violence and fanaticism, the way it has in some other religions?

Judaism cannot survive without a deep commitment to ethics, both in action and thought. The medieval rabbinic authority, Naḥmanides (Moses ben Naḥman/Ramban), observed in his commentary on Leviticus 19:1 ("Thou shall be holy") and Deuteronomy 6:18 ("You shall do the right and the good in the eyes of the Lord") that these two commandments are intimately linked. The Torah text itself testifies to this inseparable linkage: Of the initial 21 *mitsvot* in Leviticus 19 spelling out how holiness is realized, 18 of them are indisputably ethical, i.e., they are imperatives regarding interpersonal relations that affect the interests of others and that demand fairness, concern and sensitivity.

As a result, living a holy life entails doing what is ethically right and morally good. Without ethics there cannot be holiness. If Jews are to fulfill their biblical covenantal mission of becoming "a kingdom of priests and a holy people," the Jewish people must be committed to moral goodness and justice. The centrality of ethics for modern Jewish life is true also as a fact. According to the 2020 PEW study, 72% of American Jews believe that leading a moral life is essential to their Jewish identity. So unless Jewish tradition remains passionately dedicated to ethical integrity, most of these Jews will cease leading Jewish lives.

Yet what is the Jewish idea of morality, and what is the place of ethics in Jewish thought? How does Jewish ethics differ from Jewish law (*halakhah*), which plays an essential role in rabbinic tradition and Jewish life? And most importantly, how should ethics and moral values influence the lives of Jews today in Israel and the Diaspora, whether religious or secular, traditional or modern?

This book explores how Jewish tradition can address many of these modern and post-modern ethical challenges. It is written for rabbis, scholars and knowledgeable laypersons alike. The interconnected chapters examine biblical, talmudic, rabbinic and contemporary Jewish texts along with their implications for Jewish ethics and life. It is my hope that they weave a seamless tapestry out of the major moral issues confronting Jews and Jewish tradition today.

Some of the essays were written years ago, and I have updated them to include recent changes in Jewish life, thought and culture. Yet while reviewing them I was struck by how many age-old fundamental moral questions still loudly resonate with us: What is the relationship of ethical values to Jewish law? How can we ensure that halakhic decisions are just and do not violate moral norms? What roles should compassion and fairness play in our thinking and action? Are Jews essentially different from gentiles and do we have different foundational moral values? How can we prevent our religious commitments from making us insensitive and committing injustice? Is there a place for freedom in a world dominated by religious commandments revealed from a transcendent "beyond"? How can we extend full human and ethical consideration to all persons, including women and gentiles who have been marginalized in rabbinic tradition? How do we understand and prevent religious violence?

In Chapter One, "Jewish Ethics: Foundations, Development & Future," I outline the structure of Jewish ethics by examining the subject's basic values, evolutionary process and future challenges. It describes three layers of Jewish values in attempting to reconstruct Jewish ethics as a coherent structure and rational process. After outlining the dynamic relation between those levels, it suggests specific areas posing challenges for Jewish ethics today and in the future.

Because *halakhah* is prominent in Jewish thought and life, there is a need to clarify the relationship between halakhic thinking and correct moral reasoning, between legal concepts and fundamental ethical values. Chapter Two, "What Makes Halakhic Thinking Moral?" examines this relationship, pointing out specific halakhic areas that are in tension with moral values. The chapter analyzes the form of correct ethical arguments, and sets out fundamental moral standards for future halakhic discourse. "Reflections on a Jewish Tragedy: The Image of God and Jewish Morality" was originally written in the aftermath of Prime Minister Yitzhak Rabin's assassination by a religious fanatic. This shocking event occurred more than two decades ago, but religious extremism still haunts us. Not long ago a few rabbis justified violence in a book. Some traditional Jews preach intolerance and others have even murdered innocent Arabs – all under the guise of religious ideals. In this chapter I try to understand how a religious person can come to commit violence and murder, and I analyze the problem of Jewish extremism that continues to stain the Jewish body politic and sully our souls. Grounded in the biblical principle that every human being is created in the Divine Image (*Tselem Elokim*), I argue that the intrinsic sanctity of human life needs to function as the corrective for religious tendencies toward extremism and violence.

Chapter Four, "Moralization in Jewish Law: Divine Commands, Rabbinic Reasoning and Waging a Just War," contends that justice and the intrinsic value of human life were the controlling factors in the creative rabbinic interpretations of the problematic *mitsvot* to exterminate the Amalekite and Canaanite peoples. It recommends these considerations in the ongoing evolution of Jewish military ethics, and more generally, whenever contemporary Jews confront a conflict between the literal meaning of traditional commandments and moral values.

If divine law is comprehensive and absolute, what place is there for human freedom? "On Liberty and *Halakhah*" examines the tension between traditional authority based on divine law and the modern value of autonomy expressed as political liberty. It demonstrates that in both the Talmud and post-talmudic rabbinic tradition, the ideal of observance is freely chosen religious commitment, not externally imposed behavior. In Chapter Six, "Receiving but not Donating Organs: Ethical and Jewish

Considerations," I analyze the moral contradiction and communal consequences of recent halakhic decisions forbidding Jews to donate vital organs for transplantation while permitting Jews to receive such organs from others. It argues that Jewish ethics cannot allow technical *halakhah* to be oblivious to fundamental concepts of fairness, objectivity and reciprocity. Nor can it remain blind to the human and political costs of pursuing such an unjust halakhic ruling.

"The Open Torah of Maimonides" parses a critical passage of Maimonides' legal code, *Mishneh Torah*, noting his distinction between formal Jewish law (*din*) and ideal religious behavior. The essay also examines the universalistic dimensions of Maimonides' ethics present in this text, his consistent principle that Jews and non-Jews are the same in essence, and the central role that he placed on *ḥesed* (lovingkindness) in correct Jewish behavior.

In Chapter Eight, "Religious Violence, Sacred Texts and Theological Values," I return to the problem of religious extremism, examining the methods of interpreting violent sacred Jewish texts. The discussion analyzes how normative rabbinic tradition sought to bring these texts into line with ethical values in order to limit religious violence. I urge that this classic approach to sacred texts be determinative in all investigations of future Jewish ethics.

"Judaism and the Religious Other" considers the principles and limitations of legitimate Jewish pluralism. It examines the universal and particularist themes in Jewish thought, demonstrating that Jews gave different priorities to those orientations in different periods in Jewish history. Those conceptual orientations have broad consequences in real life: Jews in Israel today find themselves in an unprecedented situation in Jewish history. They are a powerful majority in their society and can choose universalist or particularist values relatively free from non-Jewish culture and politics. Whether the emerging Israeli experience opts for universal values or particularist values has fateful implications not only for Israelis, but will greatly influence all future Jewish life and ethics.

If it is true that ethics is essential to both holiness and Jewish identity, then all people committed to the integrity of the Jewish people and the survival of Jewish tradition need to reflect anew about Jewish ethics and the novel moral challenges in today's Jewish life. My aim in this book is to help clarify those challenges and contribute to finding solutions necessary for Jews to realize their age-old aspiration to become a "holy people."

Throughout the book I have used the masculine "His" in reference to God as a linguistic convention only, and do not want to imply any gender or gender-preference to God. In both *halakhah* and Jewish philosophy, God transcends gender, and any literal understanding that God is "male" – or "female" – is heretical as well as philosophically untenable and morally unacceptable. I have also adopted the traditional convention of spelling the name of God as *Elokim* rather than in its pure form.

All translations of Tanakh throughout the books are taken from the *JPS Hebrew-English Tanakh,* second edition (Philadelphia: Jewish Publication Society, 1999).

I am indebted to the following for granting permission to publish in this volume revised versions of essays that appeared previously:

Conversations for "What Makes Halakhic Thinking Moral?"

Tradition for "Reflections on a Jewish Tragedy: The Image of God and Jewish Morality," which appeared originally as "*Tselem Elokim* and the Dialectic of Jewish Morality" and "On Liberty and *Halakhah*," which originally appeared as "Tradition Meets Modernity: On Liberty – and the *Halakhah*."

The Edah Journal for "Moralization in Jewish Law: Divine Commands, Rabbinic Reasoning and Waging a Just War."

The International Rabbinic Fellowship for "Receiving but Not Donating Organs: Jewish and Moral Considerations," which originally appeared in *Halakhic Realities:*

Collected Essays on Organ Donation, edited by Zev Farber.

KTAV for "The Open Torah of Maimonides," which originally appeared in *Black Fire on White Fire,* edited by Daniel Goodman.

Brill Publishers for "Judaism and the Religious Other," which originally appeared in *Religious Perspectives on Religious Diversity,* edited by Robert McKim.

Readers will easily detect the profound influences on this book of many great rabbis, philosophers and other thinkers past and present, among them Isaiah Berlin, Eliezer Berkovits, Yuval Cherlow, Yitz Greenberg, David Hartman, R. M. Hare, Abraham Heschel, Immanuel Kant, Jacob Katz, Menachem Kellner, Soren Kierkegaard, Norman Lamm, Maimonides (Rambam), Naḥmanides (Ramban), Nahum Rabinovitch, Shlomo Riskin, Jonathan Sacks, Daniel Sperber, and Joseph B. Soloveitchik.

I am indebted to many people who read parts of this book and shared their wisdom with me: Rabbis Hayyim Angel, Michael Harris, Anthony Knopf, Aharon Lichtenstein, Shlomo Riskin, Walter Wurzburger, Professors Aviva Freedman, Yehuda Gellman, Robert Jenson, Menachem Kellner, Robert McKim, Louis Newman, Aviezer Ravitsky, Don Seeman, David Shatz, Shubert Spero, and Dr. Joel Wolowelsky, and of course my students in America and Israel from whom I have learned so much over the years.

Tzvi Mauer, publisher of Urim Publications, encouraged this project from its inception, and I thank his staff at Urim, particularly Pearl Friedman, the superb copy editor whose keen professional eye was essential to the final production of this book.

I would also like to thank Ohr Torah Stone Educational Network and the many friends and colleagues who helped support the publication of this book.

Lastly, I dedicate this book to my wife Lila, who has been a source of wisdom, comfort and inspiration to me throughout all the years of our marriage.

– Eugene Korn
Jerusalem, 2021

Chapter One

Jewish Ethics: Foundations, Development & Future

Until modern times no one attempted a systematic account of Jewish ethics. Rabbinic authorities were generally not philosophers who attempted systematic constructs. They were committed to more practical endeavors: working out the details of Jewish law (*halakhah*) and guiding the actual behavior of Jews in their daily lives.

On a deeper level, the absence of systematic Jewish ethics is probably attributable to the fact that Jewish tradition never considered ethics an autonomous subject matter or mode of inquiry. In fact, there is no indigenous Hebrew word for "ethics." The word was originated by Greek thinkers to signify the subjects of the development of human character, social responsibilities and personal duties. Yet while the word and the independent study of ethics is Greek, classical and rabbinic texts are often devoted to describing character development, responsibilities and personal obligations. Ethics, then is part of the core of traditional Judaism. Jewish ethics is embedded in traditional *halakhah* and theology, and only a modern person would see Jewish ethics as isolated. In describing Jewish ethics therefore, I will attempt to formulate what philosophers call a "rational reconstruction," i.e. a logical tapestry weaved from many different strands of Jewish literature, law, liturgy and theology. Systematizing Jewish ethics is made more difficult by the fact that Jewish ethics (and law) is strongly pluralistic and consequently it cannot be formulated as a universal apodictic system similar to logic or mathematics, as Spinoza and many contemporary ethical systems have attempted to do.

Presenting Jewish ethics systematically contains great value to Jews and gentiles alike. It can help guide Jews toward correct behavior in the new situations and dilemmas that modern life presents. It also helps shed light on the relation between formal legal obligations and those duties and responsibilities that transcend *halakhah*. For Christians, it can assist in correcting the traditional polemical notions of Judaism and Jewish values. For Moslems, it may help counter anti-Jewish political rhetoric that has arisen around the tragic Israeli-Palestinian conflict. And for thinkers of all backgrounds, it can assist in resolving the age-old problem of defining Judaism and Jewish culture.

I. THE ESSENTIAL COMPONENTS OF JEWISH ETHICS

Jewish ethics can be seen as having three fundamental structural components.[1] The first level are explicit biblical imperatives. These are usually detailed prohibitions or prescriptions of specific behavior in particular circumstances. Sometimes the Bible is a bit too general, so the talmudic rabbis had to flesh out the specific situations and behavior to which these imperatives apply. Honoring one's father and mother (Exodus 20:12) and not infringing on a neighbor's property or business (Deuteronomy 27:17) are cases in point. Just how does one display honor? How much competition is fair when it reduces another's profits? The Talmud proceeded to define in careful detail how one can fulfill these imperatives.

The second level is that of overarching values. Examples of

1. See Eliezer Berkovits, *Essential Essays on Judaism*, ed. David Hazony (Jerusalem: Shalem Press, 2002), Introduction.

these generic values are *Tselem Elokim*, the Divine Image implanted in all human beings (Genesis 1:26), peace (Isaiah 57:19), holiness (Leviticus 19:2), justice (Deuteronomy 16:20), love of neighbor (Leviticus 19:18) and a general concept of moral rightness and goodness (Deuteronomy 6:18). In later chapters I will analyze each of these values in detail, but it is important now to recognize that these values run throughout specific behavioral *mitsvot* (commandments), and constitute the intermediate purposes of the implementation of these commandments.[2]

The last level, which can be understood as the final objective (the *summum bonum*) of Jewish ethics, is the ultimate vision that animates the entire system. This is the messianic vision of a society suffused with peace, justice and knowledge of God, and is the dream that Jews are obligated to help realize within human history by virtue of their covenant with God.

The structure of Jewish ethics, therefore, is similar to a tree. Its branches are specific positivist laws, its trunk is formed by overarching values, and its roots are the ultimate messianic dream that nurtures the entire living body.

II. POSITIVIST IMPERATIVES

Legal imperatives constitute the first level of Jewish ethics. "Commandment" (*mitsvah*) is the central category of Jewish life, religion and culture, giving Jewish ethics a strong emphasis on duty and a deontological character. These positivistic imperatives flow from the sacred biblical covenant contracted between God and the Jewish people, and hence there is very little influence – if any at all – of natural law considerations in formal *mitsvot*. For example, in contrast to Catholic teaching on sexuality and reproduction, Jewish sexual ethics are driven by the value of

2. This is the position of the medieval rabbinic authority, Naḥmanides. See his commentary on Deut. 6:18. Chapter Three discusses his conception in more detail.

fulfilling the *mitsvah* imperative to procreate (*pru u'vu u'milu ha-arets*) found in Genesis 1:28, not how God designed nature. Since Jews have a legal duty to procreate, if a woman has blocked fallopian tubes it is a religious duty to seek artificial reproductive methods (e.g. IVF). If nature poses a problem, it is a religious imperative to "get around" the natural blockage. If pregnancy would endanger the life of a woman, then birth control is warranted since preserving life is a penultimate value and Judaism seeks to avoid sexual abstinence, seeing it as injurious to mental and spiritual health. The fact that such methods deviate from the way that pre-scientific humans reproduced or engaged in sexual activity is irrelevant for Jewish law and ethics. I believe these examples are representative within the entire system of *mitsvot.*

Jewish ethics is consequently behavior and act oriented. "Give to the poor," "Do not murder," "Do not stand idly by while your neighbor is in danger," "Do not work others on the Sabbath," are hallmark forms of Jewish ethics. The system does not strive for contemplation, as did Plato's or Aristotle's ethics, metaphysical unity (*ala* mystics) or intention/authenticity (*ala* existentialists), but for empirical action that has beneficial effects on society and its individuals.

It is important to stress that while traditional Jews take scriptural imperatives most seriously, traditional Jewish ethics is not fundamentalist or literalist. Even Orthodox Jews who insist that the Bible is divine and inerrant, understand that its interpretation is given over to human judgment and reason. The Talmud goes so far as to claim that the Sages of the Talmud aggressively told God to "stay out" of a debate on a point of Jewish law, since after revelation at Sinai "the Torah no longer resides in Heaven."[3] Jewish exegesis always employs rationality and considerations of the above guiding values to determine the normative meaning of

3. Babylonian Talmud (henceforth "BT") *Baba Metsi'a* 59b based on Deut. 30:12.

biblical imperatives. This means that Judaism is not necessarily committed to a literal interpretation of biblical texts.

In fact sometimes a literalist interpretation constitutes heresy. The famous *lex talionis*, "An eye for an eye. . . ." (Exodus 21:23) best illustrates this principle. The Talmud reasoned that the value of one person's eye is not always equal to the value of another person's eye, and that the pain suffered by one person in losing his eye is not necessarily equivalent to the pain suffered by another losing his eye. It would therefore be a violation of justice if the court were to apply the verse literally. Instead, normative Jewish teaching demanded that monetary compensation equivalent to the value of the lost eye be paid by the aggressor to the victim.[4] Note that it is considerations of justice that guided the normative application of the verse, not the literal meaning.

Capital punishment is another case in point. The Bible enumerates a large number of capital crimes, yet the intrinsic sanctity of each human person derived from his or her *Tselem Elokim* established a bias against taking any life. Hence the rabbis of the Talmud established elaborate judicial procedures that for all practical purposes ruled out the actual legal implementation of execution.[5] The towering talmudic authority, Rabbi Akiva, even maintained that if he were the head of the Jewish court, he would rule out capital punishment in principle. One last example is the prohibition of charging interest. Biblically, this prohibition applies to all loans – whether business or personal. If applied literally, however, there would be little incentive to issue loans on property or for business purposes, causing all but the wealthy to be deprived of a livelihood. As a result, Jewish law found a way to permit charging interest indirectly on commercial loans, while retaining the prohibition on loans for personal reasons to the poor. In other words, biblical imperatives mean what

4. BT *Baba Qama* 83b–84a.
5. BT Sanhedrin 81b.

authoritative rabbinic interpretation says they mean, not what the words literally connote.

III. OVERARCHING VALUES

There are a number of major guiding values that run through all Jewish ethical judgment, sometimes referred to as "meta-halakhic values." Most important is the doctrine that every human being is created *b'Tselem Elokim,* in God's Holy Image. This invests all human life with intrinsic sanctity and immeasurable value. A famous talmudic dictum (that later found its way into the Koran)[6] claims, "One who saves a single life is [i.e. morally equivalent to] as if he saves the entire world; one who destroys a single life is as if he destroys the entire world."[7] Mathematically these equivalencies hold only if human life has no value or if it possesses immeasurable value. Obviously Judaism opted for the latter solution, and this means that all life/death ethical dilemmas cannot be solved by finite utilitarian calculations. Human life has intrinsic non-finite value that is independent of any social or intellectual utility. Hence Jewish ethics insists that all human life is worth living, and that one may not destroy one innocent life to save another – even to save many other lives. Moral utilitarianism now found in academic circles as well as the supremacy of the pleasure principle that are now pervasive in modern society are, from the point of view of Jewish ethics, thoroughly unacceptable and sometimes are regarded as little more than old paganism in new garb.

The intrinsic value of human life derived from *Tselem Elokim*

6. Sura 5, verse 32.

7. *Mishna Sanhedrin* 4:5. While there are textual variants that include "one life in Israel," it is clear that the original text did not include this qualification. See Ephraim E. Urbach, "'All who Save One Life' – Development of the Version, Vicissitudes of Censorship and the Manipulations of Printers" [Heb.], *Tarbiz* 40:3, (1971), 268–284.

– which later became known by the Latin, *Imago Dei* – is the governing consideration in nearly all Jewish prescriptions for interpersonal relations,[8] and creates an absolute axiological dichotomy between physical objects and human beings. Well before Immanuel Kant formulated his Categorical Imperative as the fundamental principle of philosophical ethics in the 18th century, Jewish ethics understood that the worst violation of ethics is to dehumanize a person and treat him as a finite object whose worth is measured by his usefulness to another.[9] Jewish rabbis and philosophers have interpreted *Tselem Elokim* differently, including metaphysical freedom/moral sensibility, glory, conceptual powers, and creativity,[10] but all these interpretations converge on the principle that *Imago Dei* confers upon every human being sanctity and intrinsic dignity. In fact, the foremost Orthodox theologian and prominent halakhic authority in the 20th century, Rav Joseph B. Soloveitchik, maintained that the halakhic category of *kevod ha-beriyot* (the dignity owed to all human beings) was nothing other than the rabbinic formulation of the biblical doctrine of *Tselem Elokim*.[11] Thus the sanctity of human life is the starting axiom of Jewish ethics.

There is another critical implication of the doctrine of *Tselem Elokim*. Commenting on the Biblical prohibition against leaving

8. Chapter Three extensively analyzes this idea.

9. The non-finite value of every human being is the origin of the popular Jewish custom of not counting persons. Counting presupposes both finitude and commensurability of that which is counted, thus implying that the countables are "objects." Hence the Jewish custom is to indirectly number persons by associating a word of a scriptural verse to assimilate the holiness of the person to the holiness of the Torah scripture.

10. Meir Simcha Ha-Kohen, *Meshekh Ḥokhmah*, Gen. 1:26; Naḥmanides, commentary on the Torah, Gen. 1:26; Moses Maimonides, *Guide of the Perplexed*. (Chicago: University of Chicago, 1963), 1:1–2; Joseph B. Soloveitchik, *Halakhic Man*, trans. Lawrence Kaplan (Philadelphia: JPS, 1983), Part II, respectively. See Chapter Three.

11. *Days of Remembrance* [Heb.] (Jerusalem: World Zionist Organization), 9–11.

the corpse of an executed criminal hanging over night (Deut. 21:23), the rabbinic *Midrash* states:

> There were once twin brothers who were identical in appearance. One was appointed king, while the other became a brigand and was hanged. When people passed by and saw the brigand hanging, they exclaimed, "The King is hanging. The King is hanging."[12]

This parable tells us that *Tselem Elokim* constitutes an essential bridge between ethics and theology. To abuse a human being – even a human body that has lost its soul – is *ipso facto* to defame or blaspheme God. This means that God is present in all human relationships. In effect, there are no bilateral human relations because how one treats another human being necessarily reflects on God. One cannot be ethically impure and religiously pious. Thus in Jewish terms, ethics always has theological consequences and cannot be isolated from one's relationship with God.

Although *Tselem Elokim* confers infinite value on human life, Jewish ethics are not pacifist. Life – not suicide – is a religious *desideratum*, and Jewish ethics teaches that if someone attempts to kill you, you have the moral right to defend yourself by killing him first, if necessary.[13] Both Jewish values and Jewish history have taught Jews that while the abuse of power is sinful, so is powerlessness. There is no glory in martyrdom, and allowing evil to reign unopposed by physical force only promotes slaughter and greater evil, thus plunging the world back into primordial darkness. Jews today make no excuse for possessing sovereignty and defending their legitimate security interests with physical force when necessary. Neither unbridled power nor complete powerlessness is a virtue. The Jewish ideal is to have power and use it within moral limits.[14]

12. *Midrash Tanhuma*, ad loc.
13. BT *Berakhot* 58a.
14. Chapter Nine analyzes this principle.

A second foundational value of Jewish ethics is justice, or *tsedeq*. This is articulated as a broad judicial and moral value by the commandment in Deuteronomy, *Tsedeq, tsedeq tirdof* – "Justice, justice you shall surely pursue." (Deut. 16:20) More fundamentally, at the very beginning of the Jewish people, God establishes "teaching justice and righteousness" as an objective for Jewish covenantal identity. (Gen. 18:19) Again there is a nexus here with Jewish theology. Pursuit of justice is not only a *sine qua non* of Jewish behavior, but as the continuation of that biblical passage indicates, Jews understand it as an essential attribute of God and His[15] relationship with the world. When Abraham challenges God with the rhetorical question, "Shall not the Judge of all the world act justly" (Gen. 18:25), he indicates that the Jewish idea of God requires that God abide by the demands of the human concept of justice. An unjust God is no God at all, and certainly not the God of the covenant. As such, there can be no contradiction between morality and *mitsvah*, the divine command.

Jews never interpreted the story of the binding of Isaac as did Soren Kierkegaard, namely a conflict between the demands of faith and ethics. Kierkegaard's entire dilemma is incomprehensible to people with a Jewish conception of God and what He wants of them. No matter how lovesick Jews are in their romance with God, Judaism insists that faith never transgress the boundaries of the moral.[16] Additionally, the majority of

15. As explained in the introduction. I do not wish to imply any gender preference in using the masculine "His" in reference to God. God is neither male nor female in any literal sense. Yet in attempting to understand God, rabbinic literature found it helpful to ascribe to God traits traditionally associated both with masculinity (e.g., authority and punishment) and femininity (e.g., compassion and nurturing) in relating human beings. This has significant moral and pedagogical implications: The imperative to imitate God demands, then, that human beings also strive to develop a combination of personality traits as an ideal religious and ethical model. According to Jewish mystical thought, in the *eschaton* all these traits will merge into a perfect unity – both in God and in His creatures.

16. Joseph B. Soloveitchik, "Lonely Man of Faith." *Tradition* 7:2, (1965),

talmudic rabbis and medieval Jewish philosophers, would have been equally perplexed by Tertullian's famous phrase, "*credo quia absurdum est*," ("I believe *because* it is absurd") which celebrates violating rationality to achieve religious goals. The classic Jewish understanding of the relation between faith and reason was best articulated by Sa'adya Gaon in the 10th century: Reason is a God-given gift and God would be a sadist if He required humans to deny this gift in order to attain faith.[17] Hence Jewish ethical discussion typically contains a minimum of dogma and a maximum of practical reason.

A third fundamental guiding value of Jewish ethics is the imperative to imitate God (Heb: *v'halakhta b'derakhav;* Latin: *Imitatio Dei*). Here the Jewish concept differs essentially from the Greek philosophic idea of *Imitatio Dei* as contemplation, and the Christian understanding of *imitatio* as suffering that mirrors the passion of Jesus.[18] Again, the Talmud supplies the key to the Jewish concept.[19] The discussion begins, "Who can walk after God? Is He not a consuming fire?" How can a mortal human being emulate "The Perfect and Wholly Other"? Philosophically, it is only because a person shares something with God, namely *Imago Dei,* that he is able to engage in *Imitatio Dei.* What religious obligations do the rabbis derive from the power of divine emulation within human grasp? The ethical imperatives to clothe the naked, feed the poor, visit the sick, comfort mourners and others in pain, extend mercy and compassion to those in need, and perform acts of voluntary *ḥesed* (loving-kindness) – because Jewish tradition understood God to have so acted in the narratives of the Bible.[20] God as transcendent infinitude is beyond

footnote on 61–62.

17. Sa'adya Gaon, *Book of Beliefs and Opinions*, trans. Samuel Rosenblatt (New Haven: Yale U., 1955), Treatise III.

18. See David Shapiro, "The Doctrine of the Image of God and *Imitatio Dei.*" *Judaism* 13:1, 1963.

19. BT *Sotah* 14a.

20. This is the message of perhaps the most philosophic text of the Pentateuch,

human understanding, but we can know God through his moral attributes and ethical behavior. God is immanent through His relations with others, and as such is the archetype for deepening existence by relating to the Other. This is the source of Emanuel Levinas' contemporary Jewish ethical philosophy of being. A corollary to this is that the Jewish concept of holiness is essentially social and moral, realized in community with others.[21] The monastic life is holy for some, but to Jews, leaving the community bespeaks of sin that is devoid of any trace of *kedushah* (holiness).

Another corollary of *Imitatio Dei* is the notion of going beyond the requirements of law *(lifnim meshurat ha-din)*, and acting with loving-kindness out of voluntary motive. Just as God is not constrained by outside forces, *imitatio* demands that Jews develop virtuous characters that impel natural love and giving. If legal imperatives are the floor for Jewish ethics, acts of *ḥesed* are the ceiling. From the virtue of *ḥesed* flow compassion and a general sense of moral goodness that cannot be legislated.[22] The succeeding chapters further analyze each of these overarching values of Jewish ethics, examining their moral implications and discussing their roles in correct Jewish moral thinking.

Ex. 33:12–34:7. Moses' plea of "Show me Your Glory" (34:18) is refused on grounds that no living human can fathom the Divine Essence. Moses' request to understand God's behavior, "Teach me Your ways" (33:13) is granted by God revealing the divine moral attributes of compassion, slowness to anger, abundant mercy and truth, etc. (34:7). See Maimonides, *Guide of the Perplexed* 1:54.

21. The clearest exposition of this is found in Lev. Chapter 19, which details holiness in terms of social relationships.

22. Naḥmanides commentary on Deuteronomy 6:18. For an exposition for the extra-legal character of *ḥesed* and the relationship of formal law to Jewish ethics, see Eugene Korn, "Legal Floors and Moral Ceilings: A Jewish Conception of Law and Ethics." *The Edah Journal, Tammuz* 7562 (2002) at https://library.yctorah.org/files/2016/09/Legal-Floors-and-Moral-Ceilings-A-Jewish-Understanding-Of-Law-and-Ethics.pdf; accessed 28 January, 2020. See Chapter Two for the discussion of the place of *ḥesed* in Jewish and general ethics.

IV. THE GUIDING VISION

The global enterprise of Jewish ethical and religious life is messianic. That is, the vision of a messianic era is the endpoint of history that supplies direction and purpose to normative Jewish behavior. The messianic ideal is not a mere theoretical idea, but a practical goal to be worked toward. Unlike some other religions and mystical concepts, the Jewish messianic era occurs within empirical history. This means that taking the messianic vision seriously entails assuming moral responsibility for building a better future, indeed for repairing the world, which has become known by the popular Hebrew phrase, *Tikkun Olam.* Jewish ethics therefore is activist, and resists impulses to historical passivity or determinism. All acts – either ritual or interpersonal – are designed to produce the ultimate *telos* that is the vision of the Jewish Prophets:

> In the days to come, the Mount of the Lord's House shall stand firm above the mountains; and shall tower above the hills. And all the nations shall gaze on it with joy. And the many peoples shall go and say, "Come, Let us go up to the Mount of the Lord, to the House of the God of Jacob; that He may instruct us in His ways and that we may walk in His paths." For instruction shall come forth from Zion, and the word of the Lord from Jerusalem. . . . And they shall beat their swords into plowshares and their spears into pruning hooks. Nation shall not take up sword against nation; They shall never again know war; But every man shall sit under his vine or his fig tree with no one to disturb him. (Micah 4:2–4)[23]

As the neo-Kantian Herman Cohen noticed in the early 20th century, postulating the messianic dream not only supplies vision

23. The same vision is found in Isaiah 2:2–4, with some variations.

and inspiration, it also provides practical motive for ethical commitment since it ensures the ultimate efficacy of moral action.

V. THE PROCESSES, METHODS AND FUTURE OF JEWISH ETHICS

If the above schema of three dimensions of Jewish ethics is accurate, then Jewish ethics is a dialectical process balancing law, values and vision. Because of this balance, Jewish ethics tends to be casuistic – reasoning about a specific case in a detailed context – and therefore variable and pluralistic, leaving room for competing opinions. There are very few absolutes ("categorical imperatives") in Jewish ethical discussion. In fact there are only three *mitsvot* that must be preserved even at the cost of sacrificing one's life. These are the prohibitions against taking an innocent life, idolatry, and adultery/incest – and the Talmud makes clear that there are exceptions even to these seemingly ironclad imperatives.[24] Priorities, operative imperatives and decisions are most often dependent upon the particulars at hand.

It is crucially important to understand Jewish ethics as developmental. Again because of the balance of biblical law with human reason and its understanding of values, different applications of the same *mitsvah* can evolve and normative behavior can change over time. This is best demonstrated by the biblical command to destroy the tribe of Amalek. According to the Bible, Jews are obligated to blot out all traces of the Amalekite people.[25] Taken literally, this means killing each and every Amalekite – not only adult male combatants, but also women and children. In other words, on a biblical level there is an imperative to commit genocide. Thus Jewish authorities were faced with a morally dangerous, yet authoritative, text. This is the "dark side" that all

24. BT *Sanhedrin* 74a.
25. Ex. 17:14–15 and I Samuel 15:2–3.

revelatory religions need to honestly admit. Do religions follow the literal authority of the text and disregard the moral voice or do they acknowledge the darkness, face the problems and somehow refashion new normative understandings consistent with moral consciousness?[26]

There is no historical evidence that Jews in fact ever tried to fulfill this imperative literally, but even the potential and the theory are quite disturbing. Recognizing the morally problematic nature of the *mitsvah*, the talmudic rabbis ensured that the prescribed genocide never take place by announcing that the Assyrian king Sennacherib forced his conquered nations to intermarry as a way of subjugating them and undermining the threat of their own nationalisms.[27] Hence, concluded the rabbis, it is in principle impossible to know that any specific person is descended from Amalek and the imperative to annihilate Amalekites is *per force* inoperative.

One thousand years later, Maimonides went further and interpreted this commandment to apply only to those persons who do not accept the basic moral principles of civilization, i.e. the prohibitions against murder, theft, anarchy and adultery/incest.[28] It is important to note that these developments were not done by unimportant Jewish voices in the wilderness, but by authorities who determined the normative understanding of Jewish law and the normative behavior of Jews.[29] The history of Jewish ethics indicates that similar conceptual and behavioral developments took place regarding polygamy, and the biblical institutions of

26. Chapter Four charts the development of talmudic and rabbinic interpretation of this problematic biblical commandment.

27. *Mishna Yada'im* 4:4, and BT *Berakhot* 28a, *Yebamot* 17b, *Yoma* 84b. For normative codification, see Maimonides; *Mishneh Torah* (henceforth "MT"); *The Laws of Kings and their Wars*, 5:4. (Jerusalem: Mossad Ha-Rav Kook); see Chapter Four for more details of the rabbinic treatment of this topic.

28. MT, *Laws of Kings and their Wars*, 6:4 and commentary of *Kesef Mishnah ad loc.*

29. Naḥmanides, for example, clearly followed Maimonides lead. See his commentary on Deuteronomy 20:10.

servitude and monarchy, among others.[30] Here again we see a resistance to fundamentalism, and the thrust of progress dictated by the primacy of the ethical in Jewish tradition.

If indeed Jewish ethics is developmental, then there will be challenges for the future of that spiritual and intellectual discipline. Obviously, the rapid pace of technology – particularly in the bio-medical sciences and cyber-technology – changes our current existential reality and offers new possibilities for the future. These give rise to profound ethical questions around the subjects of extending life, genetic engineering, transplanting vital organs, pregnancy, disease prevention and privacy. Jewish ethics will have to grapple with these new areas based on its traditional methodologies and guiding values, when scientific breakthroughs are thrown into the mix. Another major area of required rethinking is gender equality, the status of women and their rights in Jewish life. There is no gainsaying the fact that traditional Jewish ethics was structured around a patriarchal dominance in domestic life, political and social roles, authority, scholarship, marriage, divorce, and ritual performance. Jewish ethics needs to find a way to honor tradition while taking into account a modern sensibility of justice and equality for women's rights and roles. This is a difficult – almost Solomonic – dilemma, whose gradual resolution requires wisdom, sensitivity, patience, change and practical compromise, to both tradition and absolute egalitarian considerations. A parallel challenge exists with respect to the changing conceptions of gender identity and orientations. Should these new conceptions give rise to new policies with regard to persons who do not have traditional heterosexual orientations? What does Jewish ethics demand in this area?

The new-found status of Jews as full citizens in Western

30. Nahum Rabinovitch, "*Darkhah shel Torah*," [Heb.]. *Me'aliyot*. (Ma'ale Adumim: Yeshivat Birkat Moshe, 1988). In English: "The Way of Torah." *The Edah Journal*, Tevet 5763 (2002) at https://library.yctorah.org/files/2016/09/The-Way-of-Torah.pdf; accessed on 28 January, 2020.

pluralistic societies combined with the reality of a secure Jewish homeland affords Jews the possibility to relate to gentiles as political and social equals. Today is perhaps the first opportunity to do this since the destruction of the Second Commonwealth in the first century and the subsequent Jewish exilic experience as a minority population in the Diaspora. Jews were often victimized but always vulnerable in this arrangement, and their condition of weakness tended to generate "an ethic of suspicion" toward the Other. Today when the State of Israel has an army and possesses significant power, new questions have arisen in the fields of military and diplomatic ethics. How can this power be used legitimately for self-defense but not for domination and exploitation? Where is the line between the moral and immoral use of that power? Chapters Two and Nine discuss aspects of this "ethics of power" dilemma.

The new reality gives rise to another general set of ethical questions: Jews have now established relations as equals with Christians in most of the West (but not yet with Moslems in the Middle East), and Christianity and Judaism are no longer their physical and spiritual enemies. In effect, modern tolerance and Jewish independence constitute an experiment in transforming Jewish culture: Can Israeli sovereignty liberate Jews from the image of being a victim? Can Jews generate an ethic of partnership and equality with the gentile world? Certainly the universal guiding values of Jewish religious teachings about human beings created in the Image of God, and the dignity and sanctity of all persons can be the foundation for this ethic, but psychological and intellectual transformations born of a new sense of security will also be required. Obviously, both Christians and Muslims will play essential roles in this experiment.

VI. CONCLUSION: WHAT WE SHOULD TEACH ABOUT JEWISH ETHICS

What then should people teach regarding the essential characteristics of Jewish ethics? First and foremost, Jewish religion, ethics and culture cannot be reduced to "Law," as many previous Christian and Western polemics referred to them. Jewish ethics is a dialectic of law, values and vision, all captured by the term that Jews themselves use, namely *Torah*. Torah is best translated literally as "teaching," and not as "law" by way of the Greek, *nomos*.

Second, Jewish ethics is interpretative and an ongoing process of bringing traditional values and imperatives into confrontation with evolving moral consciousness and sensibilities.

Third, redemption *within* history is the dream for which Jewish ethics – and hopefully Jews – work relentlessly. This will be achieved through concrete acts, some obligated and some out of voluntary motive, in the physical and social world. Jewish ethics rejects any spiritual flight from the messiness of human affairs. Human bodies and biology, a particular people, and a particular homeland are all essential agents in this movement toward redemption and they become sanctified in the process. There is tension between the empirical present and the spiritual dream, but no Platonic motif of *soma sema*, which seeks release from physical reality and the problematics of history. Jewish holiness is the penetration of the spiritual into the physical.[31]

Lastly, the doctrine that all human beings are created *b'Tselem Elokim*, in God's Image, necessitates that there is no cleavage between moral and religious duties, between Jewish ethics and theology. Some modern thinkers like Kant strove to separate

31. Even fervently Orthodox Jews (*ḥaredim*), who are more ascetic and spiritually attuned than modern Jews, have not rejected the physical world and its challenges. They reject hedonism, modernity and many of its values, not physicality.

ethics from religion. They may have succeeded on philosophic or systematic grounds, but no faithful account of Jewish ethics can succeed in such an enterprise. This is because the intrinsic value of human life as the beginning of Jewish ethics is fundamentally theological, and the messianic dream as the end-point of Jewish ethics is a fusion of moral perfection and theological knowledge. Here is the way Maimonides formulated the prophetic vision:

> At that time (the Messianic Era) there will be no starvation; there will be no hunger, no war; nor will there be any jealousy, nor any strife. Blessings will be abundant, comforts within the reach of all. The single preoccupation of the entire world will be to know the Lord. . . . great sages will attain an understanding of the Creator to the utmost capacity of the human mind, as it is written: "The earth will be filled with the knowledge of God, as waters cover the sea." (Isa. 11:9)[32]

Note here how peace and social perfection are the natural consequences of "the full knowledge of God." Neither the prophets nor Maimonides were social workers. They were God-intoxicated personalities, passionate theocentric visionaries.[33] In their religious understanding, the knowledge of God necessarily leads to ethical progress, because the ideal moral state of affairs is a world where every person fully recognizes the Image of God of others, thereby making God felt with clarity and immediacy.

I mentioned earlier that there is no Hebrew word for ethics. In fact there is no indigenous Hebrew word for religion either. The term most often used is *dat*, whose more accurate connotation is law or edict.[34] This is because both Jewish ethics and religion are incomprehensible in isolation from each other. Jewish ethics

32. MT, *The Laws of Kings and their Wars*, 12:5.

33. See Abraham Heschel, *The Prophets* (New York: Burning Bush Press, 1962), Introduction.

34. See Book of Esther 1:8, 13, 15.

and religion are inextricably intertwined – not only linguistically and conceptually, but in the actual experiences of religious Jews.

The messianic dream is Jewish in origin, but all who have a vision and commitment to historical and ethical progress can play a role in this prophetic process. It obligates each of us to become moral agents, to take responsibility for our future and that of humankind by creating good and defeating evil. In the conceptualization of the ancient Jewish teaching, when we do this we not only imitate God, we become partners with The Holy One to help Him perfect creation.

Chapter Two

What Makes Halakhic Thinking Moral?

"*You shall do what is right and good in the eyes of the Lord*" (Deut. 6:18)

A number of years ago I delivered a lecture in an Orthodox synagogue that I carefully titled, "The Ethics of Receiving but not Donating Organs." Before the presentation a sizable number of interested listeners approached me in protest under the mistaken assumption that I deemed this practice to be moral. Their collective instinctive response to me was, "You must be joking. It is ridiculous to think that this could be ethical." These people were neither philosophers, nor ethicists, nor experts in any field of abstruse logic, just people with healthy moral instincts.

The lecture came on the heels of a study on the halakhic definition of death published by the (Orthodox) Rabbinical Council of America in June 2010.[1] The subject is enormously important because it has, quite literally, life and death consequences. The possibility of successfully transplanting hearts and lungs depends upon the transplant taking place prior to cardiac cessation, and

1. Rabbinical Council of America. Halachic Issues in the Determination of Death and in Organ Transplantation Including an Evaluation of the Neurological "Brain Death" Standard, Sivan 5770 – June 2010, found at http://www.rabbis.org/pdfs/Halachi_%20Issues_the_Determination.pdf. Accessed on February 16, 2020.

thus saving a recipient's life depends on the removal of the brain-dead donor's vital organ while his/her heart is still beating aided by artificial means. While not intended as a formal legal ruling (*p'saq halakhah*), the RCA analysis relied on halakhic authorities who employed technical halakhic reasoning in their arguments. No mere theoretical study, the report was intended to influence practicing Orthodox rabbis whose congregants seek guidance from them regarding the halakhic (im)permissibility of donating and receiving transplanted organs.

The RCA study rejected clinically certified brain death as a sufficient condition for halakhic death, leading to the conclusion that extracting a heart of a brain-dead person for the purpose of transplantation constitutes illicit bloodshed (*shefikhat damim*) against the donor. It therefore ruled that a person (or his family) is forbidden to donate such a vital organ. Yet while forbidding donation, the study also concluded that it is permissible to be the recipient of a heart transplant. In other words, it ruled that it is right to benefit from another's benevolence but wrong to provide that same benefit to others, that one may be a taker from others, but not a giver to others.[2]

The audience at the lecture was not alone in their moral judgment: Permitting a person to be a recipient of a vital organ transplant but forbidding him to be a donor (hereafter "RBND") is widely considered a violation of ethical principles by transplant specialists, the broader medical community, philosophers, professional ethicists, the European Network of Organ Sharing, and nearly all people committed to fairness and equality. Perhaps because of the widespread criticism of RBND, the RCA has not given much prominence to the report after its release, although it is not known if the RCA *poseqim* (halakhic decisors) who

2. In Israel the prominent halakhic authority Rabbi Shlomo Zalman Auerbach also ruled in 1993 that a Jew in the Diaspora may receive but not donate a heart. See *Minḥat Shlomo*, II, section 86, letter of 17 *Adar*, 5753. Chapter Six analyzes this in detail.

supported RBND have since altered their halakhic conclusions in any way.

The RCA study provides a prime example of halakhic reasoning that violates ethical standards and reasoning.[3] There are other *halakhot* that also seem morally problematic, such as the obligation to return the lost object of a Jew but not of a gentile, the principle of saving a Jewish life on the Sabbath but not a gentile life, the permission to indiscriminately kill civilians in war, and the advocacy of harmful therapy for homosexual persons, to name but some. Should we dismiss the moral qualms of halakhic Jews regarding these halakhot as mere chimeras, or should we better regard this disquiet as real and consider it a call to further religious thinking and action?

I do not wish to explore whether these problematic *halakhot* are correct *qua halakhah*, but why these *halakhot* pose ethical problems. More generally, I wish to ask, "What values and principles must be part of halakhic reasoning to render it moral?"

I. THE CONCEPTUAL INDEPENDENCE OF *HALAKHAH* AND ETHICS

There is an argument that must be addressed before identifying which values and principles make halakhic arguments moral. Some Jews maintain that *halakhah defines* correct morality (the strong thesis),[4] while others insist that halakhic decisions by themselves are sufficient grounds for moral correctness (the

3. See Chapter Six for the full formal analysis demonstrating how RBND contravenes ethical principles and reasoning.

4. This position is a variant of the second option expressed by Socrates in Plato's *Euthyphro* (10a): "Is the pious loved by the gods because it is pious, or is it pious because it is loved by the gods?" and expressed much later by Gottfried Wilhelm Leibnitz in the opening of his essay, *Reflections on the Common Concept of Justice*: "There remains the question whether it is good and just because God wills it or whether God wills it because it is good and just; in other words, whether justice and goodness are arbitrary or whether they belong to the necessary and eternal truths about the nature of things."

weaker thesis). According to each of these theses it is impossible for Jewish law and morality to conflict with each other, and one need not consult anything outside of *halakhah* to ensure an ethical conclusion. For these Jews engaging in such extra-legal inquiry is not merely superfluous, but may even be dangerous and indicative of flagging religious conviction.

While these dogmatic positions are popular beliefs among some Orthodox Jews today, in fact they are new ideas in rabbinic thought,[5] ones easily disproven by both logical arguments as well as rabbinic tradition itself. To my knowledge no talmudic sage or medieval rabbinic authority maintained either of these positions. To the contrary, we shall see that many were convinced of their opposites.

All of us make ethical judgments and use terms like "good" and "right." But what do we mean by these terms? The 20th century British philosopher G.E. Moore devised an elegant proof to show that however we attempt to define "good" by identifying it with any non-moral idea or object, we fail.[6] If we define "good" as some particular natural entity like pleasure or law (for the sake of discussion let's call it "X"), we can always ask the question, "This is X, but is it good?" Even if the answer to the question is "yes," the question remains coherent and "open", i.e. it is at least possible to conceive of the answer being "no." This is unlike asking, "He is a bachelor, but is he unmarried?"

5. See Avi Sagi, "The Punishment of Amalek in Jewish Tradition: Coping with the Moral Problem. *Harvard Theological Review* 87:3 (1994), 323–346, and A. Sagi & Daniel Statman, "Dependency of Ethics on Religion in Jewish Tradition," in *Between Religion and Ethics*, [Heb.] (Ramat Gan, Israel: Bar Ilan University, 1993), 116–144. In English: "Divine Command Morality and the Jewish Tradition." *Journal of Religious Ethics* 23 (1995), 49–68. The authors contend that the stronger thesis appears explicitly for the first time in rabbinic material only in the writings of R. Kalonymus Shapiro, who lived through the Holocaust. This late break with Jewish tradition suggests the possibility of some conceptual assimilation with Christian and Moslem theology, or as Sagi and Statman put it, the thesis "is a foreign shoot that cannot grow in the vineyard of Israel" (140).

6. G.E. Moore, *Principia Ethica* (London: Cambridge University, 1903), §13.

where it is impossible to think that the answer is "no" when we understand what the words mean. The openness of the question about goodness indicates that "X" is not analytically identical with "good." In the halakhic context we can ask, "This action is required by *halakhah*, but is it morally good? Is it morally right? Is it just?"[7] These questions are non-tautologous and remain open, which indicates that *halakhah* is not identical with our notions of "good" or "right" and it cannot accurately define moral goodness and ethical rightness.

Moreover, people with no knowledge of *halakhah* or even awareness of the existence of *halakhah* make moral arguments and form moral judgments. If *halakhah* indeed defined morality we would never be able to agree or even disagree about ethical issues with these non-halakhic people, for we would be talking about completely different ideas in our discussions with each other. I could not claim that I am correct in believing that abortion is morally wrong and another is incorrect in his belief that abortion is morally right, since we would not at all have in mind the same thing when we use the term "moral." Yet obviously we do engage in real moral discussion, agreement and disagreement with people who have no idea of *halakhah*.

Rabbinic tradition agrees fully with this conceptual independence of *halakhah* and ethics. According to the rabbis of the talmudic era (*Ḥazal*), "Civility [i.e., patterns of correct behavior] preceded the Torah itself" (*Derekh erets kadmah l'Torah*), which clearly implies that standards for correct behavior existed independently of the formal Torah. The talmudic rabbis and later authorities go still further: They point to situations where formal *halakhah* not only fails to define ethical action, it falls short of correct moral standards. The classic concept of *lifnim meshurat*

7. Abraham challenged God with a similar question: "Will the judge of all the Earth not act justly?" (Gen. 18:25) Clearly Abraham's convictions about justice transcended what God then commanded.

ha-din (going beyond the strict *halakhah*) illustrates just that truth. Consider the important statement in Babylonian Talmud, *Baba Metsi'a* 30b:

> R. Yohanan said, "Jerusalem was destroyed only because [Jews] judged according to the law (*din*) of the Torah." [But] should they have judged according to the laws of tyranny? [No.] Rather say, "They insisted on the law of the Torah and did not act above and beyond the strict requirement of the law (*lifnim mishurat ha-din*)."

The talmudic rabbis understand the destruction of Jerusalem as the divine punishment for the Jewish people's violation of its sacred covenant with God. According to R. Yohanan, this violation existed at the very same time that Jews were observing formal *halakhah* impeccably. ("Jews judged according to the law [*din*] of the Torah.") Yet God called the Jewish people to account and imposed on them the harshest punishment known in Jewish history. Thus according to R. Yohanan Jews were morally culpable even though they had no legal liability. While there are other talmudic opinions about the cause of the Temple's destruction, no talmudic opinion challenges the intelligibility of the category of *lifnim mishurat ha-din* or the conceptual presuppositions of Rabbi Yohanan's statement, i.e. that the highest Torah standards are beyond the boundaries of strict *halakhah*. This is impossible if *halakhah* defines or satisfies all moral requirements. Nor can the concept of *lifnim meshurat hadin* be understood as formal *din* without entailing infinite regress and/or incoherence.

Another passage in the Palestinian Talmud (*Baba Metsi'a* 2:5; 8c) demonstrates even more graphically the ethically unsatisfactory nature of some halakhic rules:

> Shimon ben Shetach was in the flax trade. One day his students said to him, "We will buy you a donkey so you won't have to work so hard." They bought a donkey for him from a non-Jewish trader, and it happened that a precious gem was hanging from its neck.

> The students came to him and said, "From now on, you won't have to work anymore!" He replied, "Why not?"
>
> They explained, "We bought you a donkey from a gentile trader and we found a precious gem hanging from its neck."
>
> R. Shimon said, "And did its owner know (about the gem)?" "No," they replied. He then said, "Go and return it."
>
> But his students argued, "Is it not permitted to keep a lost article of an idolater?"
>
> Shimon ben Shetach answered them: "Do you think that Shimon ben Shetach is a barbarian?"

Note that there is no dispute about the halakhic requirements in this case. It is clear that strictly speaking *halakhah* allows Shimon ben Shetach to keep the jewel. Yet Rabbi Shimon knew that confining his behavior to the halakhic minimum was morally wrong, that as a moral agent he was required to "go beyond the strict line of the law." He understood the intrinsic value of doing what was ethically right, independent of the halakhic standard. His use of the term "barbarian" is shocking, indicating Rabbi Shimon's moral outrage – and it is important to note that this outrage stands independent of his motive to bring honor to the God of Israel by dint of his exemplary moral behavior.

The talmudic sages were not the only authorities who understood the difference between halakhic requirements and moral norms; medieval rabbinic authorities did also. Naḥmanides claimed that a person can be a "loathsome person [*naval*] within the bounds of Torah law," and therefore there is an independent religious obligation to "do what is right and good" in our interactions with other people, an obligation that requires us to sometimes desist from what is halakhically permitted. Naḥmanides understood that there is conceptual continuity between the *mitsvot* of being holy and living the ethically good life.[8] And

8. Commentary on Lev. 19:2 and Deut. 6:18, which form one continuous unit.

no one less than the greatest halakhic authority in the history of the Jewish people, Maimonides, insisted that hewing exclusively to the letter of the *halakhah* can produce behavior that is cruel and that befits only "idolators," not pious Jews. Maimonides stressed that while *halakhah* points in one direction, good Jews must sometimes behave differently.[9] He never saw *halakhah* as more than a floor on which to build a more robust Jewish ethic.[10]

Modern halakhic authorities also admit that *halakhah* is sometimes insufficient to satisfy the demands of morality. Here are the words of Rabbi Aharon Lichtenstein:

> Who has not found that the fulfillment of explicit halakhic duty could fall well short of exhausting clearly felt moral responsibility? . . . the full discharge of one's formal duty as defined by *din* often appears palpably insufficient.[11]

It is clear, then, that morality, and the ideas of what is good, right and just extend beyond *halakhah*, even if halakhic behavior and moral behavior frequently overlap.

Some halakhic authorities contend that the methods of halakhic argumentation and intrinsic halakhic norms are logically independent from the methods of correct moral reasoning and

9. MT, end Laws of Servants; *Guide of the Perplexed*, III:17.

10. Among other medieval rabbinic thinkers who recognized that halakhic norms do not exhaust moral obligations are Paquda, Baḥya ibn. *Duties of the Heart*, Introduction, and Me'iri, Menaḥem, *Bet HaBeḥirah*, BT *Shabbat* 105b.

11. Rabbi Aharon Lichtenstein, "Does Jewish Tradition Recognize an Ethic Independent of Halakha," in *Contemporary Jewish Ethics,* ed. Menachem Marc Kellner (New York: Sanhedrin Press, 1978), 107. Among other modern authorities who also explicitly affirmed this position are R. Samson Raphael Hirsch (Commentaries to Leviticus 18:4 and Deuteronomy 6:18, and *Ḥoreb*, paragraphs 219 and 325), R. Shmuel Glasner, *Dor Revi'i*, Introduction, R. Avraham Yitzhḥak Hakohen Kook, *Orot Ha-kodesh*, 3:318 and *Iggerot Re'iyah*, Vol. 1, letter 89; and R. Yehuda Amital, *Jewish Values in a Changing World*, Ch. 2, and *Commitment and Complexity: Jewish Wisdom in an Age of Upheaval*, 48. I thank Anthony Knopf for pointing out these rabbinic references. See his "Moral Intuition and Jewish Ethics." *Hakirah* 23 (2017), 197–222 for further discussion on the topic.

fundamental ethical concepts. The total independence of halakhic axioms, rules of inference, values and method was stressed by Lithuanian analytic talmudic scholars, and it was best described by the Brisker school of the nineteenth and twentieth centuries, whose leading proponents were Rabbi Hayyim Soloveitchik and his grandson, Rav Joseph B. Soloveitchik. Both fiercely insisted on the autonomy and the internal coherence of halakhic thinking. For them *halakhah* was a rigorous "closed" logical system: "To whom may he [the halakhic man] be compared? To a mathematician," proudly announced the grandson Rav Soloveitchik. In the Brisker understanding, *halakhah* is an ideal system analogous to pure mathematical systems, which are the archetypes of objective rational inquiry. *Halakhah* is a science that molds and imposes interpretations on empirical reality, rather than being influenced by it.[12] In other words, ideal *halakhah* is abstracted from the flux of human experience – the very meaning of the term *apriori*, which Rav Soloveitchik was so fond of using when describing *halakhah*.

As an independent and autonomous system, *halakhah* is value-neutral, similar to mathematics, whose methodological guides are solely consistency, coherence and simplicity. Like differential equations, it is largely removed from human emotions, sensibilities and desires. And like the autonomous sciences, halakhic logic is amoral – sometimes yielding ethically neutral conclusions (as in ritual law), sometimes yielding conclusions consistent with

12. *Halakhic Man*, trans. by Lawrence Kaplan (New York: JPS, 1983), section VI, 19–23. Also, R. Soloveitchik wrote: "R. Hayyim fought a war for of independence on behalf of halakhic reason and demanded for it complete autonomy. . . . R. Hayyim provided for the halakhah specific methodological tools, created a complex of halakhic categories and an order of *apriori* premises through a process of pure postulatization." "*Mah Dodeikh Midod*" in *B'sod Hayaḥid Vehayaḥad* (Heb.) Pinchas Peli, ed. (Orot, Jerusalem), 224. Elsewhere, "Not only *halakhot* but also the *chazakot* [legal presumptions] [that *Ḥazal*] introduced are indestructible . . . [Even] the *chazakot* are based on permanent ontological principles rooted in the very depths of the metaphysical human personality, which *is as changeless as the heavens above*." "Surrendering to the Almighty," address to the RCA, November, 1998.

ethical reasoning, and potentially sometimes yielding rulings contrary to ethical values, rules and judgments. This is why halakhic geniuses can sometimes arrive at rulings like RBND and other morally problematic conclusions. In Rav Soloveitchik's words, "the sole authority [of *halakhah*] is logic,"[13] and thus some halakhists simply go wherever their value-neutral logic takes them. This is not to imply that Rav Soloveitchik himself was deaf to the call of ethical values. He certainly was not.[14]

II. THE FUNDAMENTAL VALUES OF ETHICS

There are two fundamental moral concepts that form the foundation of all sound moral reasoning: justice and compassion. Morally sensitive people display a commitment (even if sometimes unconsciously) to these values, and nearly every good ethical judgment is derived from some variation of these concepts. These values are the foundations of our moral sense, and they go to the heart of what we mean by ethics.[15] Certainly we would

13. *From There You Shall Seek* (*U'bikashtem Mi-sham*), beginning Ch. 15.

14. See *Abraham's Journey*, for Rav Soloveitchik's understanding of the Abraham as the archetypical yet pre-halakhic Jew: "Avraham was the model Jew because he substituted the ethical life for the immoral one" and "possessed an ethical system to be carried out and implemented." In that work R. Soloveitchik also claimed that the experience of slavery in Egypt was necessary to create a *ḥesed* people of the emerging Jewish nation. His commitment to ethical integrity also moved him to demand that the Israeli government investigate the role the Israel Defense Forces in the Sabra and Shatila massacres in 1982. Rav Soloveitchik called the National Religious Party officials and told them that he could not continue as President of the Religious Zionist of America if the National Religious Party did not vote in favor of the investigation. Given Rav Soloveitchik's statements on the importance of elemental fairness, justice and ethical integrity, it is inconceivable that he would have agreed with the cited unethical halakhic positions. Nevertheless some of his prominent students have led in advocating these positions because the Brisker formalist *theory* of *halakhah* as a value-neutral apodictic system to which they were exposed sometimes conduces to unethical conclusions in practice when not tempered by considerations of justice and *ḥesed*.

15. This is elegantly and cogently explained by Yitzchok Block, in "G-d and Morality" presented at the Third Miami Conference on Torah and Science, December 15, 1999, and published in *B'Or Ha'Torah* (12). Shamir, (2006), 129–136.

not consider a person who is indifferent to injustice or one who remains stone-cold to human suffering to be a moral person. Being blind to justice and compassion are the surest indications that such a person is not in our moral universe.[16]

Justice and compassion are the natural sensibilities that God has implanted in our unique human consciousness to enable us to be moral beings – and they require no further defense or justification. When Abraham challenges God by asking rhetorically, "Will the Judge of all the earth not act justly?", both Abraham and the Torah assume that if God is the moral ruler of the universe, God *must* act according to the standards of justice. When the Torah announces "Justice, justice you shall pursue" (Deut. 16:20), the value of justice itself needs no proof. When Maimonides rails against insensitivity to the hardship and suffering of others,[17] it is self-evident that compassion (*ḥesed*) itself is a moral good requiring no further validation.

Justice here means fairness and impartiality. In a just social system people are not granted unfair advantage over others and those benefiting from the system's privileges must also accept its duties. Justice expresses itself in the principles, "treat similar people similarly," and "do not give one individual preferential treatment over others who are in the same situation." These generalization rules give ethical judgments their objectivity, enable us to reason from one case to another, and they ensure that moral claims are logical principles rather than mere expressions of personal interest.[18]

When I say "you ought to pay your taxes," the "ought" signals

16. The philosopher Isaiah Berlin claimed that if you meet someone who doesn't recognize the difference between sticking a pin into a cushion and putting a knife into a person's stomach, you should cease ethical conversation with him, since that person lacks all empathy and does not share your moral universe.

17. MT, *ibid.*

18. Chapter Six discusses this in detail. For a full analysis of prescriptivity and how this generalization principle works in moral reasoning, see R.M. Hare, *Freedom and Reason* (New York: Oxford University, 1965).

an ethical principle if I agree that all people like you – including me – ought to pay their taxes too. If I reject this generalization and claim that you ought to pay your taxes, but although I am just like you I am not obligated to pay my taxes, my claim is not a moral principle at all, just a subjective preference. The best way to test the objectivity of a moral judgment and the ethical legitimacy of any statement I make about your obligations is to reverse our positions: If I don't accept that I too have that obligation when I am in your shoes, then I am not really making a moral claim. If I claim that "everyone ought to be kind to me when I am in need, but I have no obligation to be kind to others when they are in need," no clear-thinking person would deem this a legitimate moral position. This generalization test is sometimes referred to as "moral imagination," since it requires a person to see himself as the other person.

Of course this generalization principle of ethics and its reasoning appears in the Torah as "Love your fellow as yourself" (Lev. 19:18), as well as in other formulations, but it is not a uniquely Jewish idea. It is not only "the great general principle of the Torah," as Rabbi Akiva claimed (*Sifra* 2:16:11), it is also the essential characteristic of justice that is found in the literature, laws and correct reasoning of all moral religions and ethical societies.[19]

Compassion is the second foundation of morality. There is enormous difference between analytic intelligence – the ability

19. S. Blackburn, *Ethics, A Very Short Introduction* (Oxford, UK: Oxford U., 2001), 101. Examples abound: "Love your neighbor as yourself" in Christian scriptures (Matthew 22:39), Kant's first formulation of the Categorical Imperative, "Act only on principles you could will as a universal law," "Justice is blind," and of course the colloquial, "What is good for the goose is good for the gander." Other instances in Jewish literature are Hillel's "Do not judge your fellow until you have reached his place." (*Avot* 2:4) The famous biblical dialogue between King David and Nathan (II Samuel 12:1–7) most dramatically illustrates this principle's moral power: David condemns a rich man who takes a sheep from a poor man, and then understands that if it is a principle, the moral condemnation must apply equally to him after Nathan announces, "You are the man!"

to see logical connections and make deductive inferences – and emotional intelligence, the capacity to understand the human condition of another and to think about other people as subjects like ourselves, not mere objects of cognitive or halakhic inquiry.

Compassion is *raḥamim* and *ḥesed* – feeling what others feel, empathizing with them when they are in distress, and extending ourselves into the lives of others.[20] Rabbi Samson Raphael Hirsch explained this beautifully, emphasizing its importance for being fully human:

> Compassion is the feeling of empathy, in which the pain of one person of itself awakens in another. The higher and more human the beings are, the more keenly attuned are they to re-echo the note of suffering. Like a voice from heaven, it penetrates the heart.[21]

Compassion is not only the ability to see another person as equal to yourself, but it is to sense – even if only in a small way – how that person feels, what s/he wants and how s/he wants to be treated. When we apply this moral sense we feel the responsibility to accord others dignity and respect (as we ourselves naturally want to be respected), to avoid causing them emotional and physical pain (as we naturally want to avoid pain), and help others flourish (as we ourselves naturally wish to flourish).[22]

In fact both these fundamental elements of justice and compassion are often opposite sides of the same moral coin, and when we employ them correctly they frequently yield the same

20. Maimonides defines *ḥesed* as "*haflagah*" (excess or overflow) – i.e., the extension of one substance into another. *Guide of the Perplexed*, III:53.

21. *Horeb*, 17:125.

22. This is why Kant requires the second formulation of the Categorical Imperative ("Act such that you always treat humanity, whether in your own person or in the person of any other, never simply as a means, but always at the same time as an end"), which stresses treating others with compassion as subjects rather than as objects, to complement the Imperative's first formulation stressing justice achieved by universality.

conclusions: Justice as fairness and impartiality is moral reasoning's cognitive dimension, while compassion is the emotive component of a healthy moral sense that moves us to treat others the way we wish for others to treat us. This emotive component is critical to both ethical logic and moral motivation, as a strictly cognitive rule-dominated approach to ethics, be it halakhic or philosophical, proves sometimes cruel and usually impotent.[23]

Examining these two root moral concepts reveals why RBND and some other *halakhot* are morally problematic. Is it fair to take from others, but not give to them? Is it just to return the lost articles of other Jews, but not of gentiles – as the simple *halakhah* allows?[24] Is it compassionate to intentionally kill helpless infants and infirmed elderly people who pose no direct threat during war – as the commandments to wipe out Amalek and the Canaanite nations require and the halakhic guidelines of *milḥemot mitsvah* (obligatory wars) allow?[25] Can these latter *halakhot* really be moral and just, particularly when we correctly judge the intentional killing of innocent civilian Jews by Palestinian terrorists to be abhorrent?

We will fully analyze the moral problems with RBND in Chapter Six, but a brief summary suffices here. Heart transplants create an ethical symmetry between donor and recipient, and a unique one-to-one causal relationship between them.[26] Because of this relationship, if it is wrong for me to donate my heart because I contend it is murder, it must also be wrong for to me to be a recipient because in receiving another's heart I am an agent in

23. See Jonathan Haidt, *The Righteous Mind* (New York: Random House, 2012), who demonstrates the weaknesses and failures of strictly rational ethics. In the end justice and compassion need to exercise a dialectical balance on each other to create a temperate and healthy ethical system.

24. Deut. 22:3 and BT *Bava Kamma* 113b.

25. Deut. 20:16–18, and MT, Laws of Kings 6:4.

26. This is unlike organs stored in an organ bank for future use by an unidentified recipient at the time of donation. For a detailed analysis of this causal relationship, see Chapter Six, footnote 23.

that donor's murder. And if it is permissible for me to receive the transplanted heart, then it must be permissible for me to donate my heart to a recipient.[27] Justice rules out the morally untenable position of my having a privileged status over others by receiving someone else's heart when the other person could not receive my heart due to my refusal to donate. Because the values of fairness and impartiality are fundamental to our moral thinking, if we assume that heart transplants constitute possible murder, *there is no legal technicality or casuistic distinction within halakhah that can succeed in morally justifying a person to receive an organ while he refuses on principle to donate.* Such action violates the moral consistency and reversibility tests, asserting that transplants are wrong when I am a donor and another is the recipient, but right when I am a recipient and another is the donor. As such, RBND reasoning is morally illogical and ethically unprincipled, and acting on it is morally wrong.

As we will soon see, many rabbinic authorities have noticed that this moral logic is at play regarding returning lost objects. Shimon ben Shetach realized that it is unethical – to the point of barbarism – to expect others to return my lost object, yet not be under any obligation to return the lost objects of others. This is logically akin to demanding that others pay their taxes so I benefit from state services, but permitting myself to evade the corresponding obligation to pay my own taxes. Halakhic authorities also employed comparable moral reasoning in interpreting other morally problematic *halakhot.*

III. THE ETHICS OF TORAH

Of course both justice and compassion are critical to Judaism and rabbinic writing. They cut to the core of proper Jewish life and the ideal religious Jewish personality, as the previous

27. *Ibid.*

citations of R. Yohanan, Shimon ben Shetach, Maimonides[28] and Naḥmanides insist.

The Torah implores Jews to strive after these generic values in Deut. 6:18. Yet they appear prominently in other explicit and implicit forms as well as in other derivative ethical concepts contained in the Torah and in rabbinic writings.

The fundamental imperative for Jews to follow the requirements of justice and legislate objectively appears explicitly in Deut. 1:16–17 and Deut. 16:18–20:

> You shall decide justly between an [Israelite] man and his fellow Israelite and between an Israelite and a stranger. You shall not take note of the individual in judgment; [rather] you shall hear a small person the same as you do a great person.
>
> Judges and officers shall you appoint in all your gates, which the Lord your God gives you, throughout your tribes; and they shall judge the people with just judgment. You shall not pervert judgment; you shall not take note of persons, nor take a bribe; for a bribe blinds the eyes of the wise, and perverts the words of the righteous. Justice, justice shall you pursue, that you may live, and inherit the land which the Lord your God gives you.

Although these imperatives appear in a judicial context, the value of justice for general Jewish behavior is undeniable. Note here the focus on fairness in administering justice, i.e. treating everyone equally and prohibiting favoring one person over another.

Justice as equality and fairness is also an implicit value underlying Lev. 19:18: "You shall love your fellow as yourself: I am the Lord." According to Abraham Ibn Ezra,[29] this equality applies to every human person because all persons are created

28. In the passage of MT just cited (Laws of Servants 9:8), Maimonides explicitly mentions these two values as the foundations of ideal Jewish behavior: "A person should always be a *raḥaman* [compassionate person] and a pursuer of *tsedeq* [justice]." Chapter Seven analyzes this passage in detail.

29. Commentary on Lev. 19:18.

the same way by God. Hillel's talmudic negative formulation of this verse[30] has as its thrust the moral reversibility test for correct Jewish behavior, i.e. "if you do not want others to do a specific act toward you, you ought not to do it towards others." Hillel's standard is nothing other than a precise reformulation of the generalization principle of moral reasoning.

As Ibn Ezra understood, justice and the Jewish moral imperative to act with justice flow directly from two central principles of Jewish theology: First, that all persons are created in the Image of God (*Tselem Elokim)*, and derivatively that human beings are capable – nay obligated – to imitate the Divine (*Imitatio Dei)*. Because God is exalted, dignified and worthy of respect, so too all persons endowed with the Divine Image are owed intrinsic dignity and respect. As Rav Soloveitchik incisively observed, respect for every human being (*kavod ha-beriyot*) is merely the rabbinic expression of the Bible's concept of *Tselem Elokim.*[31] Just as God has intrinsic sanctity, so too must we treat His children as creatures with intrinsic value, and not solely as a means to our own ends or exploited for utilitarian purposes. As such, *Tselem Elokim* is the theological version of the basic principle of rational humanistic ethics.[32]

Justice as fairness also underlies the talmudic statement, "The entire Torah is for the sake of peace." (BT, *Gittin* 59b) Peace, i.e. social order, stability, diminution of strife, is a substantive value that every person pursues for himself. If so, he has a moral obligation to promote it in the lives of all others. The same logic obtains regarding the Torah value of *darkhei no'am* – ways of pleasantness. If one wishes to pursue a pleasant life where he can flourish, the logic of justice implies that he must extend that opportunity to others and allow them to flourish.

30. BT *Shabbat* 31a: "Do not do unto others what is hateful to you."

31. *Yimei Zikhron* [Heb.] (Jerusalem, World Zionist Organization), 9–11.

32. The most concise formulation of the foundational principle of ethical reasoning is Kant's Categorical Imperative, as cited in footnote 22.

The second moral pillar, compassion, plays an essential role in our understanding of the Divine. *Ḥesed* is the primary attribute of God and hence is central to our own human religious behavior:

> R. Hama son of R. Hanina further said: What is the meaning of the text: Ye shall walk after the Lord your God? Is it possible, then, for a human being to walk after the *shekhinah*? . . . . But [the meaning is] to walk after the attributes of the Holy One, blessed be He. As He clothed the naked . . . so you must clothe the naked. The Holy One, blessed be He, visited the sick . . . so you shall also visit the sick. The Holy One, blessed be He, comforted mourners . . . so you shall also comfort mourners. The Holy one, blessed be He, buried the dead . . . so you must also bury the dead. (BT *Sotah* 14a)

For Rabbi Eliyahu Dessler also, *ḥesed* is a primary attribute of God, and therefore a religious imperative for humans:

> The power of giving is a Divine power, one of the traits of the Creator of all things, may He be blessed, Who shows compassion, is beneficent and gives, without receiving anything in exchange. . . . In this way, God made man, as it is written: "God made humankind in His own image," so that humans would be able to show compassion, be beneficent and give.[33]

And the empathy towards others and moral imagination that are required for correct ethical reasoning are primary in the Torah's understanding of the covenant and correct Jewish behavior:

> You shall not oppress the stranger, for you know the feelings of the stranger, having yourselves been strangers in the land of Egypt. (Ex. 23:9)

33. *Mikhtav Eliyahu* I, [Heb.] 32.

As Naḥmanides explained this verse:

> [The Torah] added this reason: for you know what it feels like to be a stranger, because you were strangers in the land of Egypt. That is to say, you know that every stranger feels depressed, and is always sighing and crying, and his eyes are always directed towards G-d, therefore He will have mercy upon him even as He showed mercy to you.

The Talmud beautifully illustrates the necessity for empathy and moral imagination when deciding how to treat others:

> There were captive women who were brought to Neharde'a by their captors so that the local residents would redeem them [with ransom money]. Shmuel's father posted guards with them to ensure that they would not enter into seclusion with gentiles [and be sexually defiled]. Shmuel said to him: Until now who guarded them? If there is concern about their status, it should be with regard to the possibility that they engaged in intercourse while in captivity before they were brought to Neharde'a. He [the father of Shmuel] said to Shmuel: "*If they were your daughters, would you treat them with such contempt?* They are no longer captives and deserve to be treated like any Jewish woman of unflawed lineage." (BT *Ketubot* 23a)

Shmuel's father insisted that his son rule with compassion and brings home his point with the stinging rhetorical question that demands that Shmuel put himself in the position of the captives' father, i.e. to identify with the captive women, to empathize with their distress and to treat them as human subjects as would their fathers and mothers, not as mere halakhic objects.

If the halakhic principle of imitating God (*v'halakhta b'derakhav*) means anything to Jewish tradition, it is acting toward others with both justice and compassion, since these values are the most prominent attributes of God. The Torah lays this down as the underlying principle of Israel's uniqueness:

> Abraham shall surely become a great and mighty nation, and all the nations of the earth shall be blessed in him? For I have known him, to the end that he may command his children and his household after him, that *they may keep the way of the Lord, to do compassionate righteousness and justice;* to the end that the Lord may bring upon Abraham that which He hath spoken of him. (Genesis 18:18–19)

The prophets Micah and Zachariah focused in on these two moral properties as the essential characteristics of Jewish religious life:

> It hath been told to you, O man, what is good, and what the Lord requires of you: *only to act justly, and to love mercy*, and to walk humbly with your God. (Micah 6:8)
>
> This is what the LORD Almighty said: 'Administer true *justice;* show *mercy* and *compassion* to one another. (Zechariah 7: 8–9)

Jeremiah also understood that justice and compassion pave the path to the religious ideals both of imitating God and living the ethically good life:

> Let not the wise man glory in his wisdom; neither let the mighty glory in his might; let not the rich man glory in his riches. But let him that glory, glory in this: that he understands and knows Me, that I am the Lord who *exercises compassion* [*ḥesed*], *justice* [*mishpat*] *and righteousness* [*tsedakah*] in the earth; for in these things I delight, says the Lord. (Jeremiah 9:22–23)[34]

Jewish tradition denominates the Creator of Heaven and Earth by *Elokim* (the cosmic God of justice) and *Adonai* (the personal

34. These values are so important to Jewish religious life that Maimonides chose to end his classic philosophical treatise, *The Guide of the Perplexed*, with Jeremiah's plea and exaltation of these ethical values in Jewish life. Once more, Maimonides' message to us here is that justice, righteousness and *ḥesed* are the essence of proper religious behavior.

God of love and compassion). In other words, just as God is moral by virtue of the divine attributes of justice and compassion, so we too must be moral by acting with *tsedeq* (justice) and *ḥesed* (compassion).

Finally it is important to note that R. Akiva's "great principle of the Torah," *Ve-ahavta l're'akha kimokha,* is a fusion of the generalizing principle of justice (*kimokha)* with the necessity of feeling toward the other *(ve-ahavta*). This principle, then, is the religious formulation of the ground of good ethical reasoning and behavior.

IV. INTERPRETING *HALAKHAH* MORALLY

Classic rabbinic thinking utilized moral argumentation to determine *halakhah*. The talmudic sages determined the operative interpretation of *lex talionis* ("an eye for and eye")[35] based on a moral argument from retributive justice: "one person's eye may not be equal to another person's eye" and thus they ruled that these verses should be implemented via fair monetary compensation rather than literally. Halakhic tradition similarly interpreted the Biblical laws regarding the idolatrous city (*ir ha-nidaḥat*)[36] and the rebellious son (*ben sorer u'moreh*)[37] to be only theoretical

35. Lev. 24:19–21, Ex. 21:22–25 and Deut. 19:16–21.

36. In accordance with the requirements of retributive justice, numerous rabbinic interpretations of the biblical imperative insisted on judging each person in an idolatrous city individually, rather than the literal collective killing of all residents. R. Meir Afulafiah (Rama) argued strenuously on moral grounds against such literal implementation of killing innocent children of the city, exclaiming, "Heaven forbid that God cause such evil." For full discussion of the rabbinic deliberations on the topic, see Halbertal, M., *Interpretative Revolutions in the Making* [Heb.] (Jerusalem: Magnes, 1997), Ch. 6.

37. See BT *Sanhedrin 71a:* "Said R. Simeon, 'because he ate a *tartimar* of meat and drank a half *log* of wine, do his father and mother take him out and have him stoned?'" R. Simeon's objection to the literal interpretation can be understood as based on considerations of justice: "There can never be an actual case of a stubborn and rebellious son because an act of gluttony can never justly be the difference between guilt and innocence in a capital case."

because of the unjust and overly harsh punishments that literal implementation would entail.

Despite this powerful ethical thrust in biblical, talmudic and rabbinic traditions, there remain halakhic rulings that are in deep, in tension with ethical standards.

Aside from the RBND ruling that violates moral consistency and just standards, the halakhic obligation to return the lost article of a Jew, but not of a gentile is another problematic case. This distinction appears to constitute unjust discrimination, as does the distinction between putting the life of a Jew ahead of Shabbat observance but not doing so for gentile life.

Rabbinic authorities have been troubled by these halakhic claims and sought to interpret them in ways that are consistent with justice and compassion, i.e. render them ethically correct. Examining these approaches are instructive for shaping other aspects of *halakhah* in line with moral standards.

A large number of Orthodox rabbis have rejected RBND in the name of *halakhah*. Many announced early on that this position is ethically untenable due to its lack of moral consistency.[38] In addition, the Halakhic Organ Donor Society (HODS) lists over 300 Orthodox rabbis who accept brain death as halakhic death, thus disagreeing with both RBND and the RCA report. (Importantly, many of the HODS signatories belong to the RCA.) The Israeli Chief Rabbinate accepts clinically certified brain death as halakhic death and thus also rejects RBND.

Rabbis Menachem Meiri, Moshe Isserless (Ramo), Isser Zalmon Meltzer and others interpreted the *halakhah* of returning lost objects to conform with moral standards by confining the dispensation to refrain from returning gentile objects only to immoral pagans who have no respect for property and hence

38. "To adopt a restrictive position regarding donating organs and a permissive position regarding receiving organs is morally untenable," found at http://organdonationstatement.blogspot.com. I am a signatory to this statement, as well as a member of HODS. For HODS, see https://hods.org/about-hods/orthodox-rabbis.

would not return lost objects to other people.[39] In their understanding of Jewish law, when gentiles feel obligated to return lost objects to Jews, Jews are under the obligation to return lost objects to them. In other words, their interpretations reinforce justice and equality based on reciprocity. Rabbi Baruch Halevi Epstein articulated this position most effectively:

> They [those who violate the basic laws of civility] destroy the world, imperil society and destroy both civilization and the establishment of governments. Certainly they are not fit to be considered as inhabitants of civilization and thus subject to a legal order. Therefore they have no monetary rights. In contrast, those who observe the seven Noahide commandments – and they are the majority of people today and all enlightened nations – there is no doubt whatsoever that they are treated like Israelites [with respect to this law of returning lost objects]. In my judgment this is true and logical.[40]

Note R. Epstein's last word: "In my judgment this is true and logical." The truth referred to is his correct ethical conclusion, and the logic to which he referred is valid moral reasoning based on justice as fairness. He has internalized the moral universe built around these moral values, and hence it is self-evident for him that *halakhah* must be interpreted this way.

More generally, R. Menachem Meiri argued extensively in his commentary on the Talmud that all civil halakhic discriminations with respect to rights and responsibilities of gentiles apply only to those gentiles categorized as "not having religion", i.e. those who were immoral uncivilized idolators.[41] In doing so, Meiri was

39. For a thorough analysis of this position and the rabbinical authorities subscribing to it, see Michael Broyde, "Access to Justice in Jewish Financial Law" in *Radical Responsibility: Celebrating the Thought of Chief Rabbi Lord Jonathan Sacks,*" edited by Michael Harris, Daniel Rynhold and Tamar Wright (Jerusalem and New Milford, CT., 2012), 111–123.

40. Commentary on the Torah *(Torah Temimah)* on Deut. 22, note 22.

41. See Meiri's commentary on BT Talmud, *Beit ha-Behirah, Yoma* 84a,

successful in interpreting the *halakhot* governing Jewish-gentile relations as reflecting just and fair standards, where justice means the elimination of arbitrary inequalities.

One of the critical distinctions between halakhic treatment of a Jew and a gentile is the question of whether one may desecrate the Sabbath to save someone in danger of dying. The Talmud and normative halakhic tradition ruled that saving the life of a Jew takes precedence over a particular instance of Sabbath observance,[42] whereas saving a gentile life does *not* take precedence over a Jew's Sabbath observance.[43] Thus there is a clear axiological distinction between Jewish life and gentile life. Rabbinic tradition does grant a Jew the dispensation to violate the Sabbath to save a gentile's life in order to prevent gentile hatred (*mishum aivah*) and the retaliation against Jews that such hatred might engender. This dispensation, however, is prudential and based on self-interest, not on moral principle, justice, compassion or the intrinsic value of gentile life derived from Divine Image. The disparity between the justifications to save a Jew's life on the Sabbath and saving a gentile's life is, at best, morally problematic.

Other than Meiri, a number of contemporary *poseqim* have been troubled by the distinction in this *halakhah*. In the 1960s R. Eliezer Samson Rosenthal, an accomplished halakhic scholar who was a member of the Israeli Chief Rabbinate halakhic committee and *poseq* for the Movement for Torah Judaism in Israel, argued that a Jew is obligated to save the life a of a gentile on the Sabbath as an ideal rooted in the sanctity of the gentile's life, rather than from prudential self-referring reasons.[44] Citing support from then Chief Rabbi Unterman he argued,

---

Sanhedrin 57b, and *Bava Kama* 37b &113b. For explication of Meiri's halakhic position on these cases, see Moshe Halbertal, "Ones Possessed of Religion: Religious Tolerance in the Teachings of the Meiri" *The Edah Journal* 1:1. *Marheshvan* 5761 at: http://edah.org/backend/JournalArticle/halbertal.pdf.

42. BT *Yoma* 85a–b; MT Laws of Shabbat, Ch. 2.

43. BT *Yoma* 85a; *Mishnah Berurah*, 330:8.

44. See Benjamin Lau, "A Reflection of Truth: The Rabbinate and the Academy

> We today have no choice but to act in accordance with the principal of equality, considering all persons fully equal even to the point that the Sabbath may be set aside when they face mortal danger, "because of the ways of peace and as a sort of danger to all!" We Jews in particular have tasted the cruel reality of that danger in almost every generation . . . When they rose up to destroy us, we stood against them in the dark of night, defending ourselves and crying out: "Are we not your brothers, not the sons of the same father or the same mother – how have we differed from every other nation that you persecute us harshly?" But we were not answered, and nothing was of use. So we cannot believe that the law of the Torah requires us, in our present situation, to abandon any person's life, even to preserve the sanctity of the Sabbath.

Note how R. Rosenthal engaged in ethical reasoning by employing Hillel's principle and moral logic's reversibility test: We Jews know how unethical it was for gentiles to refrain from saving us, therefore we are obligated not to commit the same wrong by failing to save them.

R. Jacob Avigdor in R. Rosenthal's era argued this also on the basis of moral considerations,[45] as did the contemporary authority R. Nahum Rabinovitch, who contended that the Torah itself makes no distinction whatsoever between the obligation to save a Jewish life on the Sabbath and saving the life of any civilized gentile (*ger toshav*).[46] He posited that this was

---

in the Writings of A. S. Rosenthal on Violating the Sabbath to Save Gentile Life." *Meorot* 10, Tevet 5773, found at https://library.yctorah.org/files/2016/07/meorot-10-tevet-5773.pdf.

45. R. Jacob Avigdor argued, "Saving a gentile is not a matter of the Torah's law or statute; it is a matter of man's good, human, attributes." In other words, the obligation stems from natural human characteristics of compassion and fairness. See Lau, *op. cit.*

46. *Tradition – A Journal of Orthodox Thought,* (8:3) 1966. Other halakhic authorities who argued similarly based on the value of the gentile life include Rabbis Yehuda Loewe (Maharal), Yehiel Heller, Meir Dan Plotski, Tsvi Hersch Chajes, Yehuda Gershuni, Joseph B. Soloveitchik, Ahron Soloveichik and Aharon Lichtenstein.

Naḥmanides' understanding of the halakhic imperative in Lev. 25:35: "If your brother falls low and cannot maintain himself with you, you shall uphold him; though he be a stranger [*ger*] or a resident [*Toshav*] he shall live with you."[47] Like R. Rosenthal, R. Rabinovitch understood the Torah to naturally reflect the ethical principle of treating human life equally, which must be honored in the era of universal human rights of all non-threatening civilized persons. This is expressed religiously as the intrinsic sanctity and dignity of all human life derived from the universal endowment of *Tselem Elokim*. As such, the distinction between saving a Jewish life and a gentile life on Shabbat cannot be made consistent with the basic assumptions of equality and intrinsic dignity of each human life.

A number of contemporary *poseqim* seem oblivious to – or explicitly reject – principles of just war and contemporary international standards, even though the Israel Defense Forces accepts these ethical principles as their rules of engagement. Contravening the "principle of distinction" that constitutes one of the foundations of just war theory, they reject the distinction between enemy soldiers and enemy non-combatants. Thus just as it is permitted – even necessary – to target enemy combatants, it is in principle permissible to intentionally kill all civilians in the societies of Israel's enemies. Such opinions may even represent the consensus of halakhic decisors today.[48] To quote

---

For the latter three, see: http://www.yuTorah.org/lectures/lecture.cfm/756185/_Dov_Karoll/Laws_of_Medical_Treatment_on_Shabbat.

47. In Rabbi Rabinovitch's own words: "In other words, our obligation to save a life is exactly the same for a *Ger Toshav* as for a Jew and requires that we do everything short of sacrificing our own life to save him." According to Rabbi Shlomo Riskin, Rav Joseph Soloveitchik told him that he believed the imperative to save gentile life on Shabbat is based on this opinion of Ramban.

48. Survey by Howard Jachter, *Halachic Perspectives on Civilian Casualties – Part 3*," *Parashat Toledot*, (24:9) at www.koltorah.org/index2.html. The surveyor concluded that there was only one contemporary *poseq*, Rabbi Aharon Lichtenstein, who demands that Jews consider enemy civilian casualties when fighting according to halakhic standards – and as a lone exception he does not express accepted

one contemporary Israeli halakhic authority, "According to the worldview of Torah, there is no such thing as an innocent person among a hostile population."[49]

The ethical illegitimacy and logical inconsistency of this position is clear. Jews (and all right-thinking people) properly condemn the actions of terrorists who attack, kill and maim Israeli civilians. If the unacceptability of intentional attacks on civilians is a moral principle, then it must be so generally: Both when Palestinians attack Jewish non-combatants, as well as when Israelis (whether in or out of uniform) attack Palestinian non-combatants. Moral consistency demands that if we condemn the former, we must also condemn the latter. Permitting the latter puts Jewish fighters on the same immoral level as cruel terrorists who brutally murder Israeli teens innocently eating pizza in Jerusalem, Jews celebrating a Seder in Netanya and Israeli infants riding quietly in their parents' car.

Of course, permitting the targeting of non-threatening enemy civilians also blatantly violates the second moral value of compassion. Intentionally killing a Palestinian infant or a non-threatening infirmed grandmother, is the very opposite of exercising compassion. It can be done only by rejecting empathy, legitimizing cruelty and considering these targets impersonal objects rather than human subjects.

Rabbinic tradition has long wrestled with the moral problem of targeting civilians in war – even when such action appears to be mandated by explicit verses of the Torah. As previously mentioned, the talmudic and later rabbinic authorities succeeded in "moralizing" the rules of engagement when fighting Amalek, the

---

halakhah. One halakhic scholar in the survey claims that "there is no halakhic source that takes cognizance of the likelihood of causing civilian casualties in the course of hostilities."

49. Dov Lior, "Jewish Ethics" in *Book of Hagi*, 423 [Heb.]. Nor is his *psaq* without historical precedent, as he and others base themselves on the opinion of Maharal (*Gur Ayeh*, Gen. 34–13, and *Parashat Vayishlach*).

Canaanite tribes and enemies in a *milḥemet mitsvah*. Aware of the moral problematics of these imperatives, they engaged in creative interpretations that rendered the imperative to kill innocent non-combatants of enemy nations either as purely theoretical laws that must no longer be acted upon or ones that prohibited *ab initio* intentionally killing innocent non-combatants entirely.[50] In modern times, Rabbis Naftali Zvi Yehuda Berliner (Netziv) and Shlomo Goren restricted targeting the enemy in war to combatants and explicitly forbade targeting non-combatants.[51] R. Goren ruled that according to *halakhah*, contemporary wars must not be fought according to the biblical rules of engagement: "God forbid that those laws are applied to non-biblical wars or wars of our times."[52]

There is one more example of a morally problematic halakhic thinking that bears analysis. As mentioned earlier, there has been considerable rabbinic advocacy for reparative (change) therapy for homosexual persons,[53] no doubt in trying to defend the biblical prohibition against homosexual relations (Lev 18:22). One well known example is the 2011 "Declaration on the Torah Approach to Homosexuality," which continued supporting change therapy until late 2018. Rabbi Tzvi Yehuda Tau, the spiritual leader of the Noam party in Israel and head of Yeshiva Har HaMor, continues to publicly support change therapy on

50. *Mishnah Yada'im* 4:4; BT *Berakhot* 28a and MT, Laws of Kings, 5:4; for prohibition to kill peaceful persons *ab initio*, see MT, Laws of Kings, 6:1 and 6:4. Chapter Four examines in detail the rabbinic argument for this conclusion.

51. Commentary on the Torah, *Ha-Emeq Davar*, Deut. 7:2.

For R. Goren, see *Meshiv Milhamah* [Responsa on Matters of the Military, War and Security] (Hebrew) 1983–1992, 1:14.

52. *Ibid*. See also Yitzchak Blau, "Biblical Narratives and the Status of Enemy Civilians in Wartime," *Tradition* (39:4), 8–28, who also argues against permission to intentionally harm civilians in war.

53. "Declaration on the Torah Approach to Homosexuality" (2011), found at www.torahdec.org, signed by 223 Orthodox rabbis. The declaration advocated "therapy and *teshuvah* [repentance]," where it is clear that the therapy referred to aims to change a homosexual's orientation to "a natural gender identity." The Declaration was removed from the public domain only in late 2018.

religious grounds. In July 2019, then Israeli minister of education and disciple of Rabbi Tau, Rabbi Rafi Peretz, also publicly advocated change therapy. While Peretz was forced to retract his support because of the loud public outcry, a number of rabbis in Israel and the United States still advocate this approach on religious grounds.

This advocacy has persisted long after the American Medical Association, the American Psychological Association, the American Psychiatric Association, numerous other professional medical organizations and many governmental bodies have concluded that there is no credible evidence indicating that change therapy is effective and, worse still, that this therapy is likely to cause physical and psychological damage to the patient.[54] This is also the consensus opinion of medical professionals in Europe and Israel.[55] Because of change therapy's harmful effects a growing number of states and municipalities in America have banned this therapy for minors.[56]

It may well be that the rabbis who signed the 2011 Declaration were not sufficiently informed or convinced of the non-efficacy and harmful effects of change therapy, in which case the advocacy did not indicate a lack of compassion or empathy for gay and lesbian persons. However in light of the well-known persuasive public evidence of the potentially dangerous effects

54. See https://www.hrc.org/resources/the-lies-and-dangers-of-reparative-therapy. For a fuller list of medical and professional organizations opposed to change therapy see https://www.hrc.org/resources/policy-and-position-statements-on-conversion-therapy

55. In 2015 fourteen professional organizations in England (including the National Health Service) pronounced reparative therapy to be "harmful and unethical." See https://www.psychotherapy.org.uk/wp-content/uploads/2016/12/MoU-conversiontherapy.pdf. Malta has outlawed this therapy. Israel's Health Ministry advises against reparative therapy and calls it "scientifically dubious and potentially dangerous." In 2014 Israeli Health Minister Yael German stated "there is no scientific evidence for the success of any method of conversion, and there is testimony on possible damage." See http://awiderbridge.org/health-ministry-against-ex-gay-therapy/

56. https://www.ncbi.nlm.nih.gov/pmc/articles/PMC5040471/

of change therapy prior to 2018, it was morally irresponsible to continue to advocate this course of treatment. Even if this rabbinic advocacy is no longer the majority opinion today, its original support can illuminate why certain halakhic positions are morally problematic.

Let us assume that the consensus of medical professionals is correct and that change therapy is both ineffective and harmful. Given these data, would the rabbinic signatories of the declaration have prescribed such therapy to their own sons and daughters, as they did to others? To paraphrase the father of Shmuel in BT *Ketubot* 23a, "*If they were your sons and daughters, would you treat them this way?*" Yet this is what the generalization and reversibility rules of ethics demands if such a policy is to be moral. Did the signatories fulfill the biblical imperative to "love your peer like yourself?" According to the medical consensus, change therapy is the equivalent of a drug rejected by the FDA because clinical trials failed to satisfy standard efficacy and safety requirements. Would the declaration's signatories have given their loved ones such a questionable medication, particularly when knowing that these loved ones have increased incidents of drug use, depression, suicide ideation and suicide attempts, as do homosexuals?[57] Can advocating this doubtful therapy be accurately described in any way as evincing compassion or empathy? And on strict halakhic grounds, the potential harm to the health of the patient as well as the misuse of his/her assets by ineffective conversion therapy render this therapy highly undesirable, if not explicitly forbidden as R. Daniel Sperber argued in his formal responsum of June 2020.[58]

Halakhic Jews have a moral responsibility to protect the welfare and equality of all non-threatening persons. Correct

57. https://www.healthline.com/health/depression/gay.

58. The responsum was written in response to a formal request from the Israel Society for Sex Therapy on 21 June 2021 for a halakhic opinion on conversion therapy.

ethics require that LGBQT persons be treated by others as full human beings to be understood and treated with compassion, not as problems to be solved. In addition to rejecting scientific judgment, the said rabbinic advocacy of conversion therapy neglected the welfare of individual same-sex oriented persons for the purpose of sustaining a traditional ideology. This is neither just, nor compassionate, nor ethically justifiable.

Similar to each of the other cases, there are halakhic alternatives to this approach, reflected in different statements by rabbis and religious educators regarding policies toward LGBTQ persons.[59] One such statement, written in 2010 and reinforced in 2016, has garnered over 200 signatures of Orthodox rabbis, Talmud scholars and communal leaders including two former presidents of the RCA, demands that homosexuals be treated with full "dignity and respect" and welcomed into Orthodox communities and synagogues.[60] These statements avoid advocating harmful policies, and stress the moral and religious obligations to demonstrate compassion and understanding toward gay, lesbian and gender fluid persons, similar to all other persons. These approaches recommend non-discriminatory policies toward all persons with same sex orientations and the religious obligation to treat them in their full humanity – all without violating the biblical proscription against male homosexual relations.

59. See http://www.beithillel.org.il/show.asp?id=71658#.WqTio-huY2w.; http://www.tabletmag.com/scroll/192649/watch-orthodox-rabbi-benny-laus-powerful-denunciation-of-homophobia-justified-in-the-name-of-god; and http://www.jpost.com/Jerusalem-Report/Choose-life-412588; https://www.facebook.com/Dr.Benny.Lau/photos/a.284667231611370/3338570346221028 and https://m.jpost.com/judaism/rabbi-lau-releases-guide-for-religious-lgbtq-jews-its-not-good-to-be-alone-645358, accessed on October 13, 2020.

60. Statement of Principles NYA, updated April 2016 found at http://statementofprinciplesnya.blogspot.co.il/, accessed on December 1, 2019.

V. "*GAM HAYN NIVR'U B'TSELEM*" – THEY ARE ALSO CREATED IN THE DIVINE IMAGE

There is no doubt that ethical thinking based on the concepts of justice and compassion have a universalizing tendency, and this universalism is sometimes in tension with traditional *halakhah*. It also chafes against the current Orthodox tendencies toward inwardness and parochialism. The most severe ethical challenges to *halakhah* for today and the future require us to think anew about how to justly treat and promote the full humanity of women, heterodox, secular and LGBTQ Jews, Jews of color, *mamzerim* (Jews born out of incestuous or adulterous relationships) as well as gentiles – i.e., persons other than the white Jewish adult religious males, who traditionally dominated halakhic discourse and Jewish leadership. The ongoing project of Jewish ethics entails the continuous expansion of the spheres of justice and compassion to include all human beings. Nor is this progressive growth in our moral awareness inimical to the eternal nature of Torah. Rather, it should be seen as essential to God's plan for the Torah to apply over all different cultures and the entire sweep of human history.[61]

The concept of *Tselem Elokim* is a rich source for sound ethical reasoning built on justice and compassion. No less an authority than Rabbi Joseph Soloveitchik, it considered the obligation to imitate God (*v'halakhta b'derakhav*") to be the basic principle underlying all Jewish ethics.[62] Yet imitating God is only possible for human beings if they possess something in common with God, namely God's Image.[63] The Torah doctrine is clear that

61. This is most explicitly affirmed in Rabbi Nahum Rabinovitch's "*Darkhah shel Torah*," [Heb.], in English, "The Way of Torah," op. cit.

62. Joseph Soloveitchik, *Shi'urim le-zekher Abba Mori* II [Heb.] (Jerusalem, (5745) 1985), 8–9. "*U-vikashtem mi-sham*" [Heb.] (Jerusalem: World Zionist Organization (5739) 1979), 223ff.

63. That is, *Imitatio Dei* presupposes *Imago Dei*, both conceptually and ethically.

all human beings are endowed with this transcendent quality, and hence the ethics flowing from *Tselem Elokim* dictate that we widen our scope of sensitivity and ethical concern toward all human beings, striving to treat each not merely as a means to another end, but as a subject who has emotions, anxieties, interests and needs like ours and who has a unique voice worth hearing, just as we wish to be treated, understood and heard. The endowment of *Tselem Elokim* also implies that we must understand that a person's value, dignity and right to equality reside in his/her personhood, not in his/her gender, theological orientation or ethnic identity. This requires a conceptual shift from the classical halakhic categorization of people as members of a group to evaluating and relating to each as an autonomous individual.[64] This outlook is closely linked to R. Akiva's great principle of the Torah in Lev 19:18 and to achieve highest levels of morality we must interpret *ve'ahavta l're'akha kimokha* to require the full consideration of all non-threatening human beings, as did Avraham Ibn Ezra.

R. Ben Zion Uziel demonstrated this ethical sensitivity in a 1920 responsum dealing with the question of whether women should be afforded both passive and active suffrage and whether they had a right to represent themselves in political matters.[65] His

64. While this shift is typical modern moral and philosophic thinking, Rabbi Joseph Soloveitchik noted that its source is biblical. He observed that in the account of creation God created all animals in groups "according to their species" (*leminayhu*), i.e. without individuality, while Adam and Eve were created singly *qua* individuals. Their defining human characteristic is *Tselem Elokim*, which replaces *leminayhu* in the biblical narrative of the creation of human beings. In other words *Tselem Elokim* implies considering each person as a unique individual subject, rather than a generic group member. See also his *Halakhic Man*, 126–130, and Maimonides, *Guide of the Perplexed* III:18, which stress the value of individuality. *Mishna Sanhedrin* 4:5 is another pre-modern source emphasizing the religious value of each person's uniqueness and individuality. The modern rabbinic thinker, Irving Greenberg, cogently points out the theological connections between this Mishna and *Tselem Elokim* in *The Triumph of Life: A Narrative Theology of Judaism*, Ch. 2 (forthcoming), as well as in *Living in the Image of God*, 31–45 (Jason Aronson, 1998).

65. *Mishpatei Uziel* 44.

argument was stunningly simple: Even if for the sake of argument we concede that strict *halakhah* does not include women in the formal category of the pubic community (*kahal* or *edah*), he asked,

> Are they [i.e. women] not creatures created in the Divine Image who are endowed with intelligence? Do they not have interests that will be affected by a representative government?

Rabbi Uziel insisted that women have the right to vote and to hold public office because he understood that treating people as creatures endowed with *Tselem Elokim* entails granting them full human dignity, including the right to speak for themselves and to defend their own interests. Ovadia Seforno also understood *Tselem Elokim* to mean that people must be allowed to be free to make their own choices,[66] and therefore each adult has the right to a voice in decisions affecting him or her. As such, *Tselem Elokim* foreshadows the principle of justice and requires that we give all Jews including women, heterodox, secular and those with different sexual orientations the right to speak for themselves in communal decisions and policies affecting their interests. To exclude them and presume to speak for them, however well-meaning in intent, is a paternalism that does not square with the demands of fairness and human dignity. In halakhic language, it is a violation of *kevod ha-beriyot*. And certainly to ensure maximal understanding of human realities, the process of halakhic deliberation must entail speaking *to* people affected by a halakhic decision, rather than merely speaking *about* them. Anyone who has read responsa can immediately detect the difference between the *poseq* who is engaged with the people affected by his *pesaq*, and those for whom others comprise only a theoretical or legal category.

66. Commentary on Gen. 1:26–27.

This is a particularly vexing moral problem today in Orthodox rabbinic decisions regarding women, who continue to be excluded from decision-making processes about women's rights as well as communal policies and norms.[67] The logic of justice and compassion dictates that we not marginalize women in voice or decision. And when deciding Jewish policies affecting gentiles, correct ethics demand that we consider them full human beings equal to Jews in both value and rights.

Unfortunately Rabbi Uziel's use of *Tselem Elokim* is an exception in halakhic literature. The use of the general concepts of *tsedeq, ḥesed* and *Tselem Elokim* is rare amid the technicalities of conventional formal halakhic discourse. These concepts are conspicuously absent from the halakhic deliberations of the previously cited cases, yet they and their implications are precisely what is needed if halakhic rulings are to have moral stature. The reasoning of responsa and their resulting halakhic decisions will be moral only to the extent that justice, fairness and human compassion factor into halakhic reasoning in any given situation. Responsa on strictly ritual questions lack moral dimension and have no need for these values. But questions about interpersonal relations and individual interests do, and hence halakhic rulings regarding human affairs can prove immoral if they are oblivious to these values. When halakhic logic emphasizes formalism at the expense of compassion and empathy, when it is reduced to value-neutral mathematical type thinking, when "let the law bore

67. Classic halakhic literature is replete with cases of men making presumptions about, categorizing and rendering decisions affecting women. In these deliberations, women have no voice to speak for themselves or play a role in the decision-making process. It is difficult to see these processes as just, fairly representing women's interests or yielding accurate results. Two prominent contemporary examples are the prosecution of divorce proceedings by exclusively male rabbinic courts and the recent discussion and decisions by the Orthodox rabbinate in America regarding the eligibility of women for religious leadership. Can the exclusion of women from both these procedures be consistent with the full humanity and ontological equality of women created with full *Tselem Elokim*? Can men fairly and accurately represent women's interests and preferences?

through the mountain" becomes the single guiding principle in halachic argumentation, *halakhah* opens itself up to unethical rulings. In the words of one rabbinic sage, "Standing upon strict *din* entails ruin."[68]

Halakhah cannot and should not be reduced to ethics alone. Surely there exist other *desiderata* with valence in the halakhic system, and for *halakhah* to maintain its identity and structural integrity, the justice, compassion and the human sensitivity demanded by *Tselem Elokim* cannot be the only values operative in halakhic reasoning. Yet if *halakhah* is to retain moral integrity, it must function within the bounds of *tsedeq* and *ḥesed.*

To ensure the ethical character of halakhic judgments, halakhic authorities must ask themselves, "Is my legal conclusion just or does it discriminate unfairly?" "Is my *pesaq halakhah* compassionate and empathetic?" "Does my reasoning employ the full meaning of *Tselem Elokim* by treating each person it affects as an end and not merely a means, as a human subject rather than just an object of legal inquiry?" "Does my ruling respect the full dignity of the persons involved?" "Does it allow others to voice their own opinions on issues that affect them?" "Does it allow others to flourish as I wish to flourish?"

VI. A THEOLOGICAL POST-SCRIPT

Not long ago I discussed the military ethics of Israel Defense Forces with someone who helped write the IDF's code of military engagement. I asked him why the IDF insists on following just war principles even when they entail significant risk to Israeli soldiers, make battlefield decisions more difficult and are costly in blood and treasure.

He answered that morality is essential to Jewish identity. It is who we are and who we should be. He then added a more prosaic

68. Yehuda Loewe (Maharal), *Netivot Olam,* Chapter 5, "*Gemilut Hasadim.*"

reason: Israeli soldiers must believe in the justice and rightness of their cause. They must be able to look at themselves in the mirror and know that their sacrifices are for a noble purpose. IDF officials realize that if their soldiers lose conviction in the justice of their cause and the moral integrity of their battlefield behavior, they will not be willing to risk their lives. Many, in fact, will not return to serve when called upon. It is these ethical values that sustain the high morale of the Israeli army.

And so it is with *halakhah*. Should Jewish law lose its ethical moorings, it will devolve into just another set of laws holding no more attraction than any other legal system. As a consequence, *halakhah* will cease to be a rallying point for many Jews, at which point they will deem *halakhah* inferior to more just systems, lose their conviction in it and renounce their halakhic commitment. Only when *halakhah* manifests a deep passion for justice and human sensitivity will it secure the allegiance of most Jews today. Moral integrity is, therefore, an existential imperative for contemporary *halakhah*.

No doubt a small number of Jews will choose to disregard moral logic, broader human wisdom, and anything other than the technical and parochial aspects of *halakhah*. As one radical halakhic decisor claimed: "The morality of gentile nations cannot understand the essence of Judaism. Therefore gentiles have nothing to teach us."[69] No wonder, then, that this *poseq* permits intentionally killing civilians.

It is fallacious to interpret this kind of insular thinking with its dismissal of ethics as authentic to Jewish law or spirit. On the contrary, dismissing ethics in determining formal *halakhah* represents a severe defect in their understanding of Torah, of which justice and compassion are intrinsic elements. At the dawn of God's covenant with the Jewish people, God challenged Abraham and his descendants "to act with compassionate righteousness

69. Lior, *op. cit.*

and justice" (Genesis 18:19) as the necessary characteristics of their covenantal commitment. Moses later commanded the Jewish people to "do what is right and good" (Deuteronomy 6:18), and later still Isaiah challenged the Jewish people in God's name to be "a light for the nations." (Isaiah 42:6 & 49:6) Thus the ethics of justice and compassion have always been intrinsic Jewish values and essential to the sacred Jewish covenantal mission.

Contrary to the contemporary rabbinic opinion just cited, the Torah insists that when Jews observe God's commands correctly, the nations of the world will not be at a loss for understanding. On the contrary, they will conclude about the Jewish people, "Surely this is a wise and discerning people." (Deut. 4:6) The Bible proclaims that Jewish ethics is no esoteric enterprise; rather it is one whose values all people will appreciate when Jews observe Torah correctly. Justice and compassion are fundamental to Jewish religious life, but they are also universal. And so Hebrew Scriptures promise that when Jews live properly their behavior will be exemplary, their wisdom will be understood and their values will be recognized by all God's creatures.

This is true not merely theologically, but also empirically: Nothing falsifies claims to religious truth in human hearts and minds as does unjust and immoral behavior. As Maimonides understood almost 800 years ago, Jews who defy moral logic will cause Jews to be seen only as "a foolish and despicable people," rather than a wise and discerning one.[70]

Nor is this commonality with general human ethical judgment a threat to the unique nature of Jewish religious commitment. The Torah challenges the Jewish people to be a holy people and a kingdom of priests, and when all Jews are priests it can only be gentiles who Jews are bidden to bless, influence and teach.

70. *Introduction to Mishna*, Chapter *Helek*, pt. 2. Maimonides' statement is a play on the original Hebrew. Instead of the Bible's, *am ḥakham v'navon* ("a wise and discerning people"), Maimonides used *am sakhal v'naval* – a foolish and despicable people.

And as Naḥmanides understood, our status as a holy people is dependent on our doing what is morally right and good.

That holiness is analytically tied to the right and the good, and that there can be no holiness without an abiding commitment to ethics may be two of the most important teachings in the entire Torah.

Chapter Three

Reflections on a Jewish Tragedy: The Image of God and Jewish Morality

In the end of the twentieth century and first decades of the twenty first century we have witnessed a world-wide renaissance of religious passion and commitment. Faith was once considered the opiate of the masses destined to be left behind by modern scientific culture, but today it has burst forth as a powerful force in the politics, sociology, and philosophy of events. Although evolving from different causes, the unpredicted success of an Orthodox Judaism in America and Israel, the resurgence of evangelical Christianity in the United States, and the widespread growth of Islamic fundamentalism in Africa and the Middle East all testify to the potency with which the quest for God has recently captured the hearts of individuals, communities, and even entire countries.

For religious Jews, the re-entry of God into human affairs should be cause for celebration. The Torah teaches that the mission of the Jewish people is to sanctify God in the world by testifying to His presence and sovereignty before all His creatures.[1] That is the meaning of Israel's election. Maimonides teaches that, like the return of Jews to *mitsvot,* even the strengthening of Christian and Islamic belief is a step towards the realization of our dream of ultimate redemption when "the earth will be

1. Leviticus 22:32; Deuteronomy 4:5–7; Isaiah 43:9–12.

filled with the knowledge of God as the waters cover the sea."[2]

Yet sadly, modern religious passions have not brought the world closer to the messianic vision of a world free of hunger, war, hatred, or misery.[3] On the contrary, they sometimes motivate extremists and justify their heinous acts: beheadings by radical Islamists in Iraq, bombings by suicidal "martyrs" on Israeli buses, the murder of almost 3,000 people in the September 11, 2001 attack on the World Trade Towers by Al Qaida terrorists, the murder of doctors practicing abortion in the United States, and other "holy wars" that slaughter thousands in the name of Allah, to name but a few.

Historically, Jews have rarely engaged in such extremism. Primarily, we have refrained from violence not because we have lacked the means, but because the Torah has challenged us with the vision to be a holy people. This remains true today for the overwhelming majority of Jews who are committed to the *mitsvot* and ethics of the Torah. Yet the combination of active political Zionism and uncritical religious fervor has led a few to depart grievously from this moral standard. In the last 40 years, we have witnessed the emergence of a Jewish underground that practiced lethal violence, an organization formed by a rabbi dedicated to violence and racism, the murder of 29 Arabs engaged in prayer in Hebron, and the burning of churches in the Galilee, all motivated by a misguided conception of Judaism and God's holy name. In November 1995, this divine madness has turned inward, leading a religious zealot to assassinate Prime Minister Yitzhak Rabin. In attempting to return to God, some religious Jews have become fanatics.[4]

2. Maimonides, MT, *The Laws of Kings and their Wars* (*Hilkhot Melakhim*) 11:4 (See edition of *Mosad Harav Kook* for uncensored text.) He ends *Mishneh Torah* by quoting the cited verse from Isaiah 11:9.

3. Maimonides describes the *halakhic* vision of the messianic era in MT, *The Laws of Kings and their Wars*, (*Hilkhot Melakhim*) 12:5.

4. Nor is this the only instance of fanatical Jews fighting other Jews, mostly on religious grounds. See Ehud Sprinzak, *Brother Against Brother* (New York:

These extremist acts were carried out by isolated extremists not representative of all religious Jews. Yet we must admit with great pain that there are "believers" among the Jewish people who openly try to justify these acts, many who "wink" at them in covert sympathy, and hundreds more who tolerate them with no sense of moral revulsion. Surely these persons are grave warning signals to inherent dangers to the healthy spiritual life of Jewish and Israeli communities.

Judaism and Jewish life now stand at a fateful crossroads. Fanaticism is not merely a tragedy for the ethical humanist; it is also a profound desecration of God's name. According to the medieval rabbinic authority Menahem ha-Meiri, idolatry is a belief system that does not impose moral constraints on its believers.[5] Thus extremist religious fervor has brought some to the gates of Moloch's temple. In response, we need to go beyond our sense of outrage and understand this aberrant problem at its roots. Above all, Jews must ensure that we too do not unwittingly sacrifice at Moloch's pagan altar. The extremism of a few should give pause to the correct religious commitment of the many. The rise of religious extremism indicates that it is not enough to merely be believers. Holiness requires that the faithful live out *correct* belief and couple their faith with an immutable commitment to the sanctity of human life and the centrality of morality within their spiritual world. Theologically, nothing so readily falsifies religious testimony as does the justification of fanaticism with its denial of moral norms; and on the level of experience, nothing

Free Press, 1999). *Inter alia*, Sprinzak documents the religious development and testimony of Yigal Amir, Rabin's assassin.

5. *Meiri* formulated a new definition of non-idolatrous gentiles as, "nations limited by the ways of their religion," i.e. those whose religions impose ethical constraints upon their behavior that conform to conventional moral prohibitions against murder, stealing, etc. (*Beit HaBehirah* on tractate *Avodah Zarah* 20a, Schreiber edition, 39, 46, and 591.) The *Meiri's* conception of idolatry, therefore, is primarily a religion that permits murder and gross immorality.

so effectively "pushes the *Shekhinah* (God's immanent presence) out of the world," as does descent into violence.

I. "AND ABRAHAM AROSE EARLY IN THE MORNING. . . ." (GEN. 22:3)

Jews have often been the victims of the religious fanaticism: holy wars, religious persecutions, and forced conversions among them. How could it happen that throughout history so many men dedicated to making the world holy instead become the agents of bloodshed and hatred? Unfortunately, the potential for fanaticism is rooted in the logic of faith. It follows directly from the essential recognition of God's authority. God is infinite (*ein sof*); His will is perfect and humans are His dependent creatures whose knowledge is limited. Hence divine authority over humans is categorical, the obedience owed God is unlimited. Because God's authority is absolute, His will eclipses human volition, reason and obligations. Without this fundamental posture of radical submission to God, true worship is impossible. Thus the very form of human relationship to God requires that a religious person surrender himself to God's word, disregarding practical concerns and conventional moral judgments.

Yet who is the fanatic if not the unreasonable person who ignores normal considerations and social constraints to pursue an ideal without limit? The religious fanatic is not someone with faulty reasoning – on the contrary, he is the perfectly consistent religious servant because he is unwilling to allow any personal interest or ethical constraint interfere with his understanding of the divine command. Unconditional obedience seems to be built into the very fabric of the human relationship to God, and therefore fanatical extremism is a philosophical difficulty for all theologies and a potential ethical horror for all faith communities.[6]

6. The problem of the relationship of law to morality is a general one, applying

In our times of runaway assimilation when modern culture idolizes personal autonomy, it is understandable why Abraham's virtue of unlimited obedience has become a dominant motif in contemporary religious teaching and practice. Halakhic authorities celebrate it, traditionalist Jewish educators make it the primary objective of their curricula, and communal rabbis preach it to their faithful. So strong has this value become that "obligation" seems to be the defining moment of authentic Jewish religious experience. Deontological ethics have at times become the exclusive way to live God's Torah. For many, the ideal religious personality has become the person who empties himself of any independent moral sense or critical judgment. On a popular level, many view the introduction of independent reason, moral sensibilities or *a priori* values as indicators of weak commitment, ignorance, or rebellious antinomian impulses. Instead of developing the authentic "Halakhic Man,"[7] we run the risk of producing persons who know only surrender and personal resignation, or perhaps more ominously, religious individuals without strong conscience who feel neither a disparity between formal *halakhic* duty and moral responsibility, nor a tension between their intellectual judgments and *halakhic* dictates.

II. "SO GOD CREATED ADAM IN HIS OWN IMAGE" (GEN. 1:26)

The history of religious passions attests to how this divine madness often became a blind Dionysian fury wreaking havoc on

to every legal system. It is particularly difficult, however, with respect to law alleged to be divine, since this law is of the highest possible order. Unlike positivist human law, one cannot justify breaking a divine law by claiming that it conflicts with a higher system that one has a greater obligation to uphold.

7. I refer to "Halakhic Man" as understood by R. Joseph Soloveitchik in his essay of that name. (Trans. Lawrence Kaplan, Philadelphia: Jewish Publication Society, 1983). His halakhic personality is assertive, creative and strong-willed, who is "motivated by a passionate love of truth, and "recognizes no authority other than the authority of the intellect." 79.

human life and ravaging all that is holy in its path. But man is a dialectical being, moving between two antithetical poles of human existence. For contemporary philosopher, R. Joseph Soloveitchik, this constant oscillation is the source of religious depth and human creativity. It is also what redeems our religious life from insensitivity and destructiveness.[8] Similarly for us, the ground of religious sanity that offers spiritual protection from fanaticism is a dialectic of specific religious content and form, a dedication to humane life-affirming values that stands together with the formalistic commitment to halakhic obedience. To paraphrase Immanuel Kant, "Values without obligation are empty, but obedience without values is blind." Our moments of religious obligation must also include a commitment to substantive moral values. In a word, religious persons must also become responsible ethical personalities.

It should be emphasized at the outset that the insistence on "moral" or "humane" values does not equate with ethical humanism. These values are theocentric at their core: they are central to the content of both the written Torah and the oral Torah.[9] As such, they demand no less an unconditional Jewish commitment than does any *a priori* obedience to *halakhah*. The fount of these moral values is the Torah's doctrine that each person is created in God's Holy Image – *b'Tselem Elokim*. This doctrine means that a person can somehow reflect God Himself. Like *Tselem Elokim*, the ethical values that flow from it have a theological source, but their application is anthropocentric, focusing on human interaction protecting human dignity and welfare. Their *telos* is also human-centered: to develop every

8. "Catharsis," in *Tradition* 17:2 (Spring 1978), 52. Speaking in 1962, Rav Soloveitchik proved remarkably prescient. His insight regarding consequences of a shallow and unredeemed religious life have unfortunately come true in our community. Violent Jewish extremism and racism erupted in the 1970s in Israel and the United States. See also Chapter Nine for more on Jewish extremism.

9. Chapter Two explains this relationship.

person's highest and most humane qualities – a purpose, the *midrash* tells us, that is fundamental to that of *mitsvot* themselves.[10]

After the assassination of Yitzhak Rabin, numerous rabbis explained to the media that the assassin had erred because he misunderstood the technical halakhic category of *rodef* (pursuer). That was indeed the case, but it was not the primary tragedy. The main religious defect was neither that Yigal Amir was flawed in his talmudic logic, nor that his supporters were ignorant of this or that rabbinic text. Rather, the religious shortcoming was that every religious person did not instinctively recoil in horror at murder, at the destruction of one of our central religious values: the immanent presence of God found in the *Tselem Elokim* of each human being. Unfortunately, even today we have not yet cultivated in all religious Jews moral sensibilities that reject *a priori* such an act. Murder should be as emotionally and intellectually repugnant to all God-fearing Jews as the very denial of God. Indeed, because humans are created in His image, the Torah equates bloodshed with the destruction of God Himself.[11] If we allow the moral values of the Torah to be eclipsed by blind obedience, we may inadvertently build a religious *Weltanschauung* that celebrates property over persons and ritual over reason.

Such an imbalance of religious values has a precedent in Jewish history. The Talmud contends that the religious leaders in the Second Temple era valued ritual purity over human life (BT, *Yoma* 23a-b), and that Jews maintained the strict letter of *halakhah* rather than act beyond formal law (*lifnim mishurat hadin*) in order to realize the Torah's ethical values (BT, *Baba Metsi'a* 30b). This is no mere pious moralizing. Because of these axiological distortions, the sages of the Talmud taught that Jerusalem

10. *Genesis Rabbah* 44.

11. *Tosefta Yebamot* 8:4 and *Mikhilta Yitro* on "You shall not kill," (Ex. 20:13), *midrash* quoted by Rashi on Deut. 21:23 also appearing in BT *Sanhedrin* 46b.

drowned in blood from one end to the other, the Temple was destroyed and the Jewish people went into exile for 1900 years.

The Torah principle that every human being is created in the Image of God is the conceptual key to Jewish religious ethics with humanitarian values. As mentioned in Chapter Two, R. Joseph Soloveitchik considered it to be the implicit basic principle underlying all Jewish ethics.[12] A comprehensive analysis of *Tselem Elokim* is critically important to Jewish thought and understanding the Jewish ethics, but it suffices here simply to mention a few interpretations and their implications for religious morality. Maimonides identified *Tselem Elokim* with a person's conceptual capacity, i.e. his highest rational faculties.[13] Human beings are distinguished from animals because their intellect is categorically superior. By virtue of *Tselem Elokim,* humans have a notion of truth, science, law, goodness, and responsibility, and human beings can even attain a partial knowledge of the ultimate reality – God. So powerful is *Tselem Elokim* that it enables our intellect to comprehend God's voice through prophetic revelation. Prophecy is a natural category for mankind because all human beings are endowed with *Tselem Elokim.* For Rambam, the human mind was able to partially apprehend and give expression to divinity itself.

Important ethical implications flow from this interpretation. Since human thought can reflect divine truth, religious persons seeking God should listen to, respect, and study carefully all serious human intellectual enterprises that do not in turn suppress other opinions or do not violate the *Tselem Elokim* of others. Thus, political suppression of dissenting opinions diminishes the potential presence of God in the world and the possibilities for hearing God's voice on earth.[14]

12. *Shi'urim le-zekher Abba Mori, op. cit. "U-vikashtem mi-sham" op cit.*

13. Guide of the Perplexed (*Moreh Nevukhim)* I:1–2 and MT, *Basic Laws of the Torah* (*Hilkhot Yedosei Hatorah*), 4:8.

14. Rambam did not follow this line of reasoning. In his quest for truth, he was

Closer to our day, Rabbi Meir Simḥa Ha-Cohen of Dvinsk (known as, *Meshekh Ḥokhmah*)[15] locates *Tselem Elokim* in human metaphysical freedom. A person is singular in God's creation because the laws of causality do not determine his actions or his future. When *Tselem Elokim* is found in human freedom, religious persons have the moral obligation to act toward all persons in a way that maximizes that freedom. Coercion or manipulation of others for ideological, political, or personal reasons becomes morally prohibited and theologically wrong. Since human freedom is divine, political and individual liberties become sacred and inalienable rights, not accidental products of political sufferance.

Some early rabbinic sources understand *Tselem Elokim* in a physical sense and associate it with the human body.[16] On the simplest level, this implies that we are morally prohibited from not only assaulting, torturing and physically mutilating another, but also from inflicting pain or tolerating the humiliation of another person. Even embarrassment, false accusation, name calling, or damaging another's reputation is likened to bloodshed (BT, *Baba Metsi'a* 58b) and thus constitutes an assault on a person's *Tselem Elokim*. On a different level, this idea ensures that the sanctity of each person based on *Tselem Elokim* is intrinsic to, and inseparable from, that person. Because no one can leave

intolerant of theological and metaphysical error. As Abraham ben David (*Ravad*) notes on his gloss to MT, *Laws of Repentance*, 3:7, this had severe implications for some traditional and pious Jews. In the thirteenth century, Rambam assumed that his theological principles and metaphysical claims could be logically proven true. However, it is uncertain whether Rambam would have maintained his intolerance if he lived today in the modern post-Kantian universe where metaphysical claims are deemed unprovable and theological commitments are more a product of will than rational knowledge.

15. *Meshekh Ḥokhmah*, Commentary on Gen. 1:26, 27.

16. *Leviticus Rabbah* 34:3. See also A. Kariv, *Me-sod Ḥakhamim* [Heb.] (Jerusalem: Mossad Harav Kook, 1976), 121–123, and Alon Goshen Gottstein, "The Body as Image of God in Rabbinic Literature" *The Harvard Theological Review* 87 (1994), 171–195.

his body, the value accorded to each person can never be vitiated. Hence, we are morally obligated to accord dignity to every person even after his death – not merely the righteous but even the loathsome criminal guilty of a capital offense. (Deuteronomy 21:23; BT, *Sanhedrin* 46b)

Tselem Elokim is analytically tied to the imperative of imitating God (*v'halakhta b'derakhav*). The rabbis were puzzled by this *mitsvah*: "Who can walk after God? Is He not a consuming fire?" (BT, *Sotah* 14a) How can a mortal human being emulate the Perfect and Wholly Other? Maimonides understood that *imitatio dei* presupposes *Tselem Elokim*. This is hinted at by that fact that his treatment of the basic laws of the Torah that mention *Tselem Elokim* (MT, *Hilkhot Yesodei Hatorah* 4:8) precede his exposition of the laws of personality traits (*Hilkhot De'ot*), which codify *v'halakhta b'derakhav*. As noted in Chapter Two, the talmudic rabbis derived the halakhic and ethical obligations to clothe the naked, feed the poor, attend to the sick, comfort those in pain, extend mercy and compassion to those in need, and perform acts of *ḥesed* from the human power to imitate God (BT, Sotah 14a).

There is another significant way in which *Tselem Elokim* relates to Jewish moral life. The Torah commands "Do what is right and what is good in the eyes of God." (Deut. 6:18) Humans can do this only if we share His ethical judgment, if our knowledge of the right and the good can match God's understanding of these values. The presence of *Tselem Elokim* gives us this potential knowledge and permits us to conclude, as did R. Akiva, that "what is right in the eyes of man corresponds to what is good in the eyes of God."[17] The Torah tells us that because we share moral knowledge with God, we are obligated to protect the innocent and fight for what our moral sense tells us is just, as Abraham did for Sodom and Gomorrah, and to

17. *Sifri*, Deut. *Piska* 79.

conduct business with scrupulous honesty and fairness.[18] For R. Soloveitchik, *imitatio dei* means that a religious person is obligated to emulate the Creator of the universe (*Halakhic Man*, Part II). In Rabbi Soloveitchik's eyes, this creative imperative is so important that, "if a person is not a creator of new worlds he can never attain holiness." (p. 108) Under this interpretation, *Tselem Elokim* provides the key for people to build a pragmatic society that protects human interests, to erect conceptual structures that enable them to perceive truth, and most importantly, to recreate themselves via *teshuvah*. It is only repentance that can rid people of their sense of moral failure and allows them to be optimistic regarding their future. In sum, it is *Tselem Elokim* that saves us from nihilistic gloom and gives us the strength to aspire realistically to ethical achievement.

Finally, the principle of *Tselem Elokim* entails that religious Jews have a moral and spiritual connection with all mankind. Every person is created *b'Tselem* and therefore both our morality and religious life must have a universal dimension. *Tselem Elokim* is our window to humanity at large, protecting our ethics from narrow parochialism or selfish tribalism.

Each of these different interpretations of *Tselem Elokim* shares one fundamental concept: Because we are created in the Image of God, every human being is a potential source of holiness in the world. Each person possesses intrinsic value that requires each of us to protect, dignify, respect, and not abuse another – both physically and personally. Again as indicated in Chapter Two, R. Soloveitchik saw the halakhic concept of human dignity (*kavod ha-beriyot*) as merely the rabbinic formulation of the biblical concept of *Tselem Elokim*.[19] If we are prohibited from exploiting God for our own purposes, then we are forbidden to exploit His image in any way.

18. Gen. 18:17–33; *Mikhilta R. Yishmael* on Exodus 15:26.
19. *Yimei Ha-Zikharon*. (Jerusalem: World Zionist Organization), 9–11.

Importantly, the Torah concept of *Tselem Elokim* makes explicit in the clearest way the connection between ethics and holiness. Created in God's Image, people represent the most ubiquitous presence of God and transcendent values found in the material world. Because of this, violating another person through unethical action is an affront to God that undermines the divine presence. As a result, immoral behavior is a theological sin that diminishes holiness in the world, both the holiness of the unethical actor and the person who is the object of his unethical behavior. Where there is unethical action toward another, there can be no holiness.

III. "*DEREKH ERETS KADMAH LA-TORAH.*" – CIVILITY PRECEDES THE TORAH

We should be clear about what an *a priori* commitment to *Tselem Elokim* values means. When Jews confront religious texts, halakhic rulings, and voices of religious authority they should bring to the encounter a strong and healthy moral sense built on the Torah values implicit in *Tselem Elokim*. This is a difficult task, for at times the initial understanding of these texts, rulings, or voices is inconsistent with *Tselem* sensibilities. Nevertheless as R. Avraham Hacohen Kook understood, accepting any interpretation of *halakhah* that violates our moral sense leads only to religious error:

> It is forbidden for religious behavior to compromise a person's natural moral sensibility. If it does, then our *yirat shamayim* ["fear of Heaven"] is no longer pure. An indication of its purity is that our natural moral sense becomes more exalted as a consequence of religious inspiration. But if the opposite occurs, and the moral character of an individual or a group is diminished by our religious observance, then we are certainly mistaken in our path. This type of supposed "fear of heaven" is incorrect (*p'sulah*).[20]

20. *Orot Ha-kodesh*, 3:11.

In situations where our initial understanding of Jewish law conflicts with *Tselem Elokim* values, Jews need to deepen their comprehension and resolve the tension. We should ponder the texts, discuss them with others, and seek out wiser and more sensitive people to guide us in solving the problem. As long as their *Tselem Elokim* sensibility remains violated they should not rest, but must say as did the rabbinic interpretive community throughout the centuries, "The simple interpretation is not the correct interpretation," or "This *halakhah* is normative, but perhaps does not apply in the present circumstances," or "I do not understand this authority correctly." These responses are thoroughly traditional, adopted by ancient and modern rabbinic authorities, by halakhic conservatives and liberals alike.[21] In addition to the claim of *halakhah* on us, we must maintain unshakable faith in *halakhah*'s moral character. The operative faith of a morally sensitive halakhic Jew is just this: In any given situation there exists a legitimate interpretation of Jewish Law consistent with *Tselem Elokim* values. This belief obligates us to "turn over, turn over" rabbinic sources until we find that interpretation. By definition, the unethical imperative can never be normative. Even if God Himself appears to visit us at night and whisper in our ears to commit an immoral act, it is not God talking, but

21. Rabbinic tradition employed the first approach in noting that the simple literal interpretation of "an eye for an eye," (Ex. 21:24) could not be correct because of the impossibility of achieving exact justice. (BT, *Baba Kama* 83b–84a) The second response was made by Rabbi Avraham Yeshaya Karelits (*Ḥazon Ish;* 1878–1953) in his commentary on *Yorah De'ah* 13:16 when he rejected the contemporary application of the law to kill heretics. In today's changed socio-religious circumstances, he felt its implementation would be "morally corrupt and an act of violence." Considerations of fair application of principle, prevention of personal insult (*elbon*) and unfair oppression (*hona'ah*), and the effective protection of women's interests elicited the third response from Rav Ben-Zion Meir Uziel (*Piskei Uziel*, 44), when he interpreted the voice of Rambam (*Hilkhot Melakhim* 1:5) forbidding Jewish women to hold public office to mean that Rambam intended the prohibition to apply only to appointments made by the Sanhedrin and not to positions of elected office. As noted in Chapter Two, Rav Uziel employed the concept of *Tselem Elokim* to introduce these ethical considerations.

Moloch. Perhaps the lesson of the Jewish people's dark historical experience as victims of religious fanaticism and its awareness of contemporary extremism is that it is never a legitimate option to accept Kierkegaard's "teleological suspension of the ethical."

For some, this religious approach seems to run contrary to tradition and commitment. Are we indeed permitted by Jewish tradition to allow *Tselem Elokim* moral sensibilities to influence our understanding of divine *halakhah*? Do we not run the risk of substituting our own human values for God's law and allowing our subjective impulses to rule our behavior?

In response to the first question, it is not only permissible but necessary epistemologically and out of faithfulness to the Oral Torah for us to interpret God's word. It is obvious that our individual consciousness always plays a role in our understanding of religious phenomena. No text has lips, and so we are forced to understand every word we read through our critical faculties. In the end, it is human authorities who must always judge if a particular halakhic rule applies in a specific set of circumstances.

Moreover, commitment to normative rabbinic tradition prohibits us from simplistic or fundamentalist interpretation. The Torah of the Jewish people was not left in heaven. At Sinai it became a partnership of God's word and human interpretation. The Oral Torah always allowed for a varying, albeit finite, number of interpretations and legal conclusions. If this is so, then each person must make a personal autonomous choice to follow one rabbinic authority on a principled basis from among many, and therefore to be obligated by one *psak* from amongst a variety of opinions.

R. Aharon Lichtenstein has discussed the related consideration of whether the Torah recognizes ethical values independent of the corpus of halakhic imperatives, i.e. strict *din*.[22] Although there

22. "Does Jewish Tradition Recognize an Ethic Independent of Halakhah?" *op. cit.*

is a popular conception that codified *halakhah* is completely self-sufficient for the ideal religious life, Chapter Two's analysis demonstrated that this assumption is inconsistent with traditional talmudic and rabbinic thinking. The Mishna distinguishes between Torah law and *derekh erets* – what R. Lichtenstein identified as "traditions of civility," and what one prominent traditionalist rabbi defined as "all ethical matters, both those found and those not found in the Talmud; and the failure to pursue some of its elements constitutes a sin and a great transgression."[23] "Without Torah there is no *derekh erets*; without *derekh erets* there is no Torah." (*Mishna Avot* 3:17) Evidently by eliminating the consideration of ethical values, we make a correct interpretation of *halakhah* impossible. In this view the only way we can correctly derive *halakhot* is if we approach halakhic material with values that are antecedent to it.

The concept of *lifnim mishurat hadin* expresses a similar idea. It demands recognition that what is religiously correct stems from an ethical sensibility independent of *din*. Clearly, the concepts of *lifnim mishurat hadin* or *hayashar v'hatov* (the right and the good) are themselves not in the category of formal *din*. As Lichtenstein and others explain,[24] their form is too generic to be fully defined by crystallized legal directive and their content is clearly distinct from normative *halakhic* ruling. This is also the position of Naḥmanides when explaining the biblical imperatives "Thou shall be holy" (Lev. 19:2) and "Thou shall do what is right and good in God's eyes." (Deut. 6:18) Ramban maintained that there exists an entire cluster of Torah values such as holiness, the right and the good, *imitatio dei*, loving one's neighbor, and equity that are different from standard formal *mitsvot* because they are general in form and contextual in

23. R. Judah Loew ben Bezalel (Maharal, 1526–1609), *Netivot Olam*, Chapter 1.

24. Lichtenstein, *op. cit.*, 107–116. See also commentary of Rif on BT, *Baba Metsi'a 83a*.

application. They extend beyond the requirements of *halakhic* obligation *per se* and are directed toward promoting human welfare, improving interpersonal relations, and protecting individual interests fairly. They constitute the Torah's overarching goals towards which specific *halakhot* are means. Since no legal code, no matter how extensive, can cover all situations that confront us, they are necessary guides to our quest for ideal religious action. The general nature of these directives requires that we use our judgment according to the specific contexts in which we find ourselves and consistent with the moral aspirations that the Torah has delineated for us.[25]

R. Lichtenstein concisely summarizes the undeniable fact of extra-legal values in both the Torah and rabbinic tradition:

> If we equate Halakha with the *din*, if we mean that everything can be looked up, every moral dilemma resolved by reference to code or canon, the notion of the self-sufficiency of Halakha is both palpably naive and patently false.[26]

It is also instructive to consider how rabbinic tradition understood the role of positive human relations within the system of *halakhah*. According to Abaye, the purpose of the entire Torah is to promote the value of peaceful human relations. (BT, *Gittin* 59b) Maimonides (MT, Laws of *Hanukah* 4:14) also accepts peace as a central goal of *mitsvot*, citing the verse, "Her ways are ways of pleasantness and all her paths are peace." (Prov. 3:17) as the biblical proof for this. This clearly implies the prior independent value of peace. For some rabbis, many talmudic tractates end their halakhic discussions with the phrase, "talmudic scholars increase peace in the world" to teach that the function of Torah sages is to maximize peace and pleasantness,

25. See Chapter One.
26. *Op cit.*, 107.

and therefore rabbis have a responsibility to interpret *halakhah* towards those ends.[27]

IV. JEWISH MORAL EDUCATION

If we are to ensure moral integrity in the face of our ultimate theological commitments and prevent religious Jews from becoming unethical fanatics, the ethical values rooted in *Tselem Elokim* must stand at the center of Jewish life and behavior. Religious personalities must have balanced moral judgment and be able to think clearly about the role of ethical values within *halakhah*. To make murder, violence and racism unacceptable to religious Jews, healthy *Tselem Elokim* values must be used to develop them into ethical personalities.

Philosophical analyses of *Tselem Elokim* or pronouncements about the identity of Judaic values and morality will, by themselves, not achieve these objectives. Jewish educational methods and goals should be rethought and lead to reform of religious curricula. Jewish education should adopt a wider vocabulary, complementing the value of commitment to halakhic obligation with *Tselem Elokim* values. In addition to teaching the details of legal obligation and exemption (*ḥiyuv u'p'tur*) and prohibition and permission (*issur v'heter*), Jewish educators should follow the rabbis of the Talmud and talk explicitly of human dignity (*kavod ha-beriyot*), civility (*derekh erets)*, fair compromise *(p'sharah)*, respect for differing views *(maḥloket l'shem shamayim*), and the religious necessity of a sense of moral rightness and goodness that transcends legal obligation. We must also stress that the Torah commandment of, "You shall be holy" requires that we recognize the holiness of each person even more than it does the

27. According to Rabbi Shmuel Eidels (*Maharsha,* 1555–1631) commentary to the end of BT, *Yebamot*, the rabbis are obligated at times to suspend the normative application of halakhic requirements in order to achieve peace and the "ways of pleasantness."

ritual purity of objects or places. It is important to be true to the Levitical context of this *mitsvah* and interpret it in terms of charity to the poor, respecting the interests of those whose lives we touch, and loving rather than hating others.

Philosophically, the doctrine of *Tselem Elokim* constitutes a principle of God's immanence: In addition to sensing God through our study of Torah and the performance of *mitsvot*, God's presence is revealed through ethical relationships with all those who possess His image. The Talmud (BT, *Kiddushin* 30b–31a) considers the connection between human behavior and divine ontology to be even stronger: By showing respect for parents, we actually bring God into the world; by causing them pain we banish The Holy One from our midst. This suggests that one of the most effective ways to nurture religious, spiritually sensitive students is to teach them that behavior toward parents is a paradigm for all human relationships, and more generally that acting ethically toward each person with whom we meet is a religious act.

Supplementing the ethics of formal obligation with the ethics of value can be done at every stage of Jewish education and throughout its curriculum. A profound consciousness of *Tselem Elokim* with its specific Torah values of peace, love of neighbor, equity, *ḥesed*, human dignity, and *derekh erets* should saturate the study of both the Written and Oral Torah. These moral qualities reflected in the lives of the biblical ancestors should be highlighted as religious ideals when teaching *Tanakh* to young children.

During the teenage years educators should institute formal courses in Jewish ethics and teach *midrash* seriously for its moral import. The numerous aggadic and halakhic passages in the Talmud that teach *Tselem Elokim* values should be analyzed for their ethical implications with the same careful attention that we treat exclusively legal and ritualistic subjects. A simple example is instructive: Abraham interrupted his communication with God to greet strangers wandering in the desert. (Genesis 18) From that, the talmudic sages infer that, "extending hospitality to strangers has greater significance than directly encountering the *Shekhinah*." (*Shabbat* 127a) Rather than teaching this simply as a statement of the importance of the *mitsvah* of welcoming guests, its deeper religious meaning should be explored, namely how concern for the welfare of others and human relations built on moral values can be paths, similar to prayer, to deepen the spiritual dimension of our lives.

On the most advanced levels, the curriculum of Talmud students should include studying the dynamics of the halakhic process. Analyses should focus on its legal philosophy to uncover the underlying ethical values within *halakhah* and the role that moral concerns play both in the calculus of specific legal decisions and the formulation of general halakhic policy. It is also critical for Jewish students to supplement their studies of theoretical *halakhah* in the *beit midrash* by also studying halakhic decisions actually practiced by rabbis organically connected to people and communities outside the academy. All of this is a complex enterprise, not given to simplistic analysis or ready-made conclusions. While this is a complicated enterprise, we should not be daunted by complexity of trying to nurture ethical Jewish personalities.

On each of these levels interpersonal *mitsvot* can be presented as obligatory values that are understandable and oriented toward ethical values, shunning authoritarian language of *ḥok* and uncritical obedience. In areas of ethical interaction, we do well to take our cue from Maimonides and aspire to develop students who recognize the intrinsic worth of these values and who have finely honed moral judgment.[28] Surely traditional Jews should not view an ethical *mitsvah* such as the prohibition of murder in the same way they view the prohibition of wearing an admixture

28. Commentary on the Mishna, Introduction to *Avot*, ("*Shemonah Perakim*") Chapter Six.

of linen and wool (*shatnez*). Though both legally obligatory, the former *mitsvah* is more logical because it produces obvious human benefits and supports a host of other humane Torah values in a way that the latter does not. This is why Hillel, R. Akiva and Ben Azzai could each identify the fundamental organizing rule of the Torah with a moral principle and not a *ḥok*, an apparent non-rational commandment.[29] According to Maimonides, a healthy religious person recognizes this intrinsic validity of ethical commandments and feels the ethical pull of its essential integrity quite naturally. Hence a central objective of religious education should be teaching students to understand and emotionally internalize this difference, for one who is blind to this distinction has, in Rambam's language – a *nefesh ḥaserah* – a deficient soul.

Another educational point is crucial for the development of healthy moral personalities. The Bible does not hesitate to be morally critical of the failings of the generation of Israelites that left Egypt, the violent actions of Shimon and Levi in Shechem, or the sins of David – and neither should we.[30]

If we somehow justify Shimon and Levi's violence against the residents of Shechem as well as David's behavior toward Uriah and Bathsheba, we blunt our ethical sensitivity and that of our students, thereby damaging the development of their critical moral faculties. When we teach them to suspend their moral judgment and ignore the sins of Jews in the past, they will learn the lesson well. They will take ethics lightly, judge selectively – and see no moral problem with Jews today violating

29. For Hillel, it was, "What is hateful to you, do not do to your friend. (BT, Shabbat 31a); For R. Akiva, it was "Love your fellow as yourself" and for Ben Azzai it was Gen. 5:1 centered around *Tselem Elokim*. See Sifra, *Parashat Kedoshim*, 4:12 and Genesis Rabba, end Chapter 24.

30. While there are rabbinic statements denying that our ancestors sinned, these are in the minority, were made for limited purposes, and are refuted by the biblical texts themselves. They must be taught as such, in the contexts those biblical texts and of other more numerous counterbalancing rabbinic opinions.

moral boundaries and practicing insensitivity toward others. If they depart from rabbinic judgment and view the zealotry of Phineas (Pinḥas) [31] without alarm, they will experience no revulsion at the violence committed by contemporary fanatics. And when that violence occurs, our moral integrity demands that we unequivocally condemn the fanatics among us and isolate their pernicious influence from our midst.

The focus on *Tselem Elokim* values also requires us to reshape our conception of the ideal religious personality. Jewish tradition must somehow be able to hold together the seemingly contradictory traditional images of the obedient Abraham performing the binding of Isaac (the *Akedah*) found in Genesis 22 along with the image of Abraham who defiantly queried, "Shall the Judge of all the earth not act justly?" engaging God Himself to defend his sense of justice. Yet how can we be healthy and clear-thinking people if we celebrate contradictory role models for our behavior? Will not our worldview be incoherent and absurd, and our values hopelessly muddled if we accept these contrary ideals?

Hewing close to tradition, Jews should have no problem avoiding this contradiction, since Kierkegaard's assumption – that Abraham's aggressive moral behavior regarding Sodom contradicted his submission to God's immoral command at the *Akedah*[32] – is found nowhere in Jewish tradition. This mistaken claim stems from a Christian interpretation of *Akedat Yitzhak* as being a choice between religion and ethics, a preference for God's command over human moral imperatives. We need not interpret the *Akedah* this way. Indeed, no traditional Jewish source – neither Biblical commentator, nor *midrash*, nor philosopher – interpreted the Bible that way or sustains either Kierkegaard's thesis of the irresolvable conflict between religion and morality.

Even Rabbi Joseph Soloveitchik, who shared Kierkegaard's

31. Numbers 25.
32. Soren Kierkegaard, *Fear and Trembling* (London: Penguin Books, 1986).

claim that the Akedah teaches Jews total surrender, never adopts Kierkegaard's interpretation that God demands a person sacrifice morality in favor of revelation. He is faithful to the classic rabbinic worldview and follows the predominant Jewish interpretation expressed in rabbinic *midrashim* that in the *Akedah* God tested Abraham by forcing him to choose between his love for God and his love for his son. Jewish tradition understood that Abraham experienced the *Akedah* as a dilemma between piety and possession, not *mitsvah* and morality. The biblical texts of *Akedat Yitzhak* itself support this interpretation, as its language contains no hint of a conflict between morality and religious imperative. In contrast to the vocabulary in Abraham's dialogue with God regarding Sodom and Gomorrah that is saturated with moral terminology (*tsedakah, mishpat, tsadiq, rasha, shofet*), the *Akedah* contains only descriptive language. In Jewish tradition, Abraham at Mt. Moriah was a religious servant not as Kierkegaard's homicidal madman, while Abraham arguing for Sodom was a defender of the innocent, the defender of the divine values of *tsedeq* and *ḥesed*.

Rabbinic sages may have resisted Kierkegaard's interpretation because introducing considerations of the prohibition of murder into Abraham's thinking would attribute a halakhic dimension to Abraham's decision, thereby conferring on it the potential as a precedent for later halakhic behavior. There is good reason why the *Akedah* is nowhere found in halakhic literature regarding interpersonal behavior and why it plays no role whatsoever in halakhic argumentation. Judaism regards the value of the *Akedah* as exclusively homiletic. It should be used, therefore, only in situations not covered by halakhic directives. Abraham's behavior can never serve as a normative model for situations where human life is at stake, for all questions of life and death are governed by *halakhah* and its normative *Tselem Elokim* values.

Perhaps recognizing the potential for what in their eyes was a misreading of Gen. 22 that would justify violence and murder in God's name, the rabbis achieved a remarkable inversion of the text's plain meaning. Departing from absolute textual fidelity, they crafted an interpretive religious statement that is read today by religious Jews immediately after the morning liturgical recitation of the *Akedah*. As an antidote to the *Akedah*'s direct literal implications, this text stresses inculcating compassion as the divine quality worthy of human imitation:

> . . . just as Abraham our father suppressed his compassion to do Your will wholeheartedly, so may Your compassion suppress Your anger from us and may Your compassion prevail over Your other attributes. Deal with us, Lord our God, with the attributes of loving-kindness [*ḥesed*] and compassion [*raḥamim*] and in Your great goodness may Your anger be turned away from Your people. . . .[33]

Again, this prayer sees no moral dilemma in Abraham's experience. Yet the important theological point is that the prayer's plea for God's moral attribute of compassion (*ḥesed/raḥamim*) to prevail over other divine attributes implies that the moral attribute of *ḥesed* is the ideal behavior for all human beings, all of whom are made in God's Image.

Talmudic and medieval rabbinic commentary made another exegetical move in Gen. 22 that has momentous significance. Playing on the original Hebrew verb form *v'ha'aleyhu*, (lit. "cause him to go up") in v. 2 ("Take you son, your favored son, Isaac, whom you love, and go to the land of Moriah, and offer him there as a burnt offering. . . .") , a number of talmudic, medieval and modern authorities claimed that Abraham misunderstood God's demand. God's real command was not to slaughter Isaac, but merely to "take him up" to the mountain

33. *The Koren Siddur*, American Edition (Jerusalem: Koren, 2009), 34.

to jointly offer a sacrifice and then return together.[34] This interpretation moves away from the text's straight forward meaning evidently because the rabbis presupposed that God cannot and would not command Abraham to act immorally.[35] The most important implication, however, is that we can never be certain of what God means when we hear His voice. If Abraham could misinterpret God's message, then uncertainty must be built into the fabric of all God's ongoing communication with us. While the biblical prophets and rabbis of yore may have heard God clearly and legislated with certainty, in our time when "the *Shekhinah*" (God's immanent presence) is less apparent, we have no right to epistemic certainty about God's will or divine commands in our particular circumstances.[36] Indeed, as rabbinic tradition insists, the era of prophecy has long since ended and direct divine instruction is not possible today.[37]

I have argued in the traditions of Abaye, Rambam and Maharsha, who all maintained that a central purpose of *halakhah* is the realization of moral values, and in the tradition of Hillel,

34. This is the interpretation offered in BT *Ta'anit* 4a, Genesis Rabbah 55,5 and 56,8, *Pesikta Zutra* 44, the commentary of Shlomo Ben Yitzhak ("Rashi") *ad loc.*, and the modern R. Abraham Isaac Kook (Letters: Vol. B, 379).

35. This interpretation thus makes the narrative of Gen. 22 fully consistent with that of Gen. 18, where Abraham argued successfully that "the Judge of all the earth (can)not act unjustly." Kierkegaard's and other interpretations of Gen. 22 as a "teleological suspension of the ethical" cannot redeem these two biblical episodes – and God – from fundamental inconsistency.

36. In the 19th century, Kant argued for both uncertainty of hearing the divine voice and the certainty of knowing basic moral truths in his explanation of Gen. 22. ("The Conflict of the Faculties" 7:63, in *Religion and Rational Theology*, trans. and ed. Allen W. Wood and George DiGiovanni (Cambridge, UK: Cambridge U., 1996). This position is understood as "modern" stemming from the freeing of morality from theology. As indicated, however, rabbinic tradition inferred both these conclusions some 1,500 years before Kant.

37. BT, *Baba Batra* 12b. The Talmud claims that after the destruction of the Temple, prophecy was "given only to children and fools." That is, one who claims he hears a divine prophetic voice is but a fool. As indicated earlier, the talmudic rabbis (BT *Baba Metsi'a* 59b) also maintained more radically that post-Sinaitic revelation, should you hear God's actual voice telling you how to act, you should tell Heaven that It has no right to issue such commands.

Rabbi Akiva and Ben Azzai, all of whom insisted that the content of *mitsvot* could be organized around fundamental ethical Torah principles, that an essential thrust of rabbinic and halakhic tradition is the promotion of Torah morality symbolized by *Tselem Elokim*. If so, it is incumbent on Jews as morally responsible persons to believe in the ethical integrity of *mitsvot*. The practical consequence of this belief is that Jews should commit ourselves to interpretations of Jewish law that are consistent with *Tselem Elokim* values. This means following talmudic tradition that rejected the religious zealotry of Pinḥas,[38] the deception of King David,[39] and the commandment to kill innocent Amalekites and Canaanites[40] as religious ideals. When one idealizes such biblical sources and celebrates violence, (s)he departs from normative halakhic tradition that qualified the literal denotation of these imperatives, severely limited their applications, or excluded altogether the possibility of these sources becoming models for later halakhic behavior.

To attain a clear vision of religious ideals, Jews must focus clearly with both eyes. By viewing Jewish tradition with only the eye of uncritical obedience to formal law or with only the eye of ethical values distorts our vision. Of course, maintaining the dialectical commitment to formal halakhic obligation and the ethics of *Tselem Elokim* values imposes a harsh demand on a person's educational mission, as well as spiritual and ethical development.

The ethical and the spiritual life are each difficult to achieve. They are filled with pain, dilemma, questions, and uncertainty. Solutions are complex and sometimes unachievable. Yet for Jews who have a mission to lead lives of "*tsedakah u'mishpat*"

38. Chapter Eight details the rabbinic and halakhic treatment of Pinḥas' zealotry.

39. See positions of Rav in BT, *Shabbat* 56a, R. Yehuda in *Gitten* 73a, Tosefot on *Gitten* 73a, *s.v.* "*ikuhin*" and commentaries of Abravanel and Ralbag on the biblical narrative found in II Samuel 12.

40. Chapter Four examines this issue and the rabbinic response in detail.

(righteousness and justice), to be "a kingdom of priests and a holy people" and to function in history as "*l'or goyim*" ("a light for the nations"), neither immorality, nor ethical indifference, nor simplicity are spiritual options.

Chapter Four

Moralization in Jewish Law: Divine Commands, Rabbinic Reasoning and Waging a Just War

"The Holy One Blessed Be He told Moses to destroy them . . . But Moses did not do so, saying, rather: 'Should I now go and attack both those who sinned and those who did not sin?'" Midrash Tanhuma 96:3

I. THE WAR AGAINST AMALEK AND CANAAN

In a remarkable philosophic essay entitled, "Moralization and Demoralization in Jewish Ethics,"[1] Leon Roth called attention to how emending Jewish texts can denude them of their moral dimension. The clash between sacred texts and moral reasoning occurs also in classic rabbinic thought, and it is instructive to analyze the opposite dynamic at work, i.e. the moralization of biblical commands through skillful legal application and rabbinic interpretation. This essay examines perhaps the paradigm case of such an innovative interpretation to determine what presuppositions and methods informed the rabbinic tradition.

The problematics of the biblical imperatives for the Jewish people to destroy the Amalekite and Canaanite nations are well

1. *Is There a Jewish Philosophy?* (Littman: London, 1999), 128–143.

known. The Bible's brutal commands shock our moral sensibilities:

> "Remember what Amalek did to you on your journey, after you left Egypt – how, undeterred by fear of God, he surprised you on the march, when you were famished and weary, and cut down all the stragglers in the rear. Therefore, when the Lord your God grants you safety from your enemies around you, in the land that the Lord gives you as a heritage, blot out the memory of Amalek from under heaven. Do not forget! (Deut. 25:17–19)
>
> Samuel said to Saul, "I am the one the Lord sent to anoint you king over His people Israel. Therefore, listen to the Lord's command! . . . Now go attack Amalek, and proscribe all that belongs to him. Spare no one, but kill alike men and women, infants and sucklings, oxen and sheep, camels and assess! (I Samuel 15:1, 3)
>
> In the towns of the latter peoples, however, which the Lord your God gives you as a heritage, you shall not let a soul remain alive. No, you must proscribe them – the Hittites and the Amorites, the Canaanites and the Perizzites, the Hivites and the Jebusites – as the Lord your God has commanded you. (Deut. 20:16–17)
>
> When . . . the Lord your God delivers them to you and you defeat them, you must utterly doom them to destruction: grant them no terms and give them no quarter. (Deut 7:1–2)

These biblical imperatives were encoded into normative Jewish law. As the most formidable legal authority in Jewish history, Maimonides ruled in his legal code, "It is a commandment to destroy the seven [Canaanite] nations. . . . If one of them comes into your hands and you do not kill him, you have violated a negative commandment, as it says, 'No soul shall remain alive.' . . . So [also] is the commandment to destroy all trace of Amalek.[2] The

2. MT, *The Laws of Kings and their Wars* (*Hilkhot Melakhim*), 5:4–5.

imperatives to exterminate the entire Amalekite and Canaanite populations present two distinct moral difficulties:

1. Genocide – the extermination of an entire ethnic group
2. The intentional killing of civilians, including women, children and infants

Faced with a hard conflict between a canonical text and moral obligation, a religious tradition can respond along a number of different lines of logical argumentation:

1. The Kierkegaardian Argument: acknowledge the contradiction between religion and morality, and insist that God's command trumps the demands of morality.
2. The Divine Command Morality (DCM) Argument: maintain that there can be no real contradiction between morality and God's commands when we construe them literally. God sets the correct moral standard, either because moral concepts and norms are defined by divine authority, or because only God knows the ultimate reasons or relevant moral factors to make true moral judgments, which must remain inscrutable to human beings whose moral understanding is limited.
3. The Heretical Argument: acknowledge the irresolvable contradiction and conclude that the moral standard overrules the religious imperative.
4. The Casuistic Argument: adduce extenuating factors or engage in moral reasoning to justify the command despite its *prima facia* moral incorrectness.

We shall soon encounter other strategies employed by Jewish tradition, such as invoking a higher order legal/theological principle to override the commandment, postponing action on the textual command indefinitely, and allegorizing the commandment. Yet the invocation of these strategies emerges as the

---

Importantly, in the eyes of Maimonides, this commandment can be carried out only by a government and its army, not individuals.

result of rabbinic tradition's relationship toward the above four arguments.

Avi Sagi has demonstrated that the first and second arguments are absent in rabbinic tradition regarding the imperative to kill the Amalekites.[3] More generally, while the stronger analytic claim of DCM theory – that divine commands *define* morality and ethical concepts – has numerous antecedents in Christian and Moslem thought, it is absent in classic Jewish tradition. It first appears explicitly in Jewish writing only in the twentieth century.[4] Evidently traditional rabbis and Jewish philosophers concluded from Genesis 18:25 ("Shall the Judge of all the earth not act justly?") that the God who established a sacred covenant with Abraham was bound by the requirements of justice, even as humans understand them.

This is what distinguished Abraham's God from previous idolatrous conceptions. Hence, classical Jewish commentators never understood the binding of Isaac (Genesis 22) as a conflict between a divine commandment and ethical values. Rabbinic sources portray Abraham's dilemma as one between obedience and paternal love, not, *à la* Kierkegaard, as one between religion and ethics or between the divine promise of a glorious future and God's message to destroy that future by killing Isaac. That is, Jewish tradition resisted interpreting divine commands as conflicting with ethical imperatives, and conceding that theological imperatives can supersede a purportedly conflicting moral law.[5]

3. "The Punishment of Amalek in Jewish Tradition: Coping with the Moral Problem." HTR. *op. cit.*

4. See A. Sagi and D. Statman, "Dependency of Ethics on Religion in Jewish Tradition," *Between Religion and Ethics*, (Hebrew) (Ramat Gan, Israel: Bar-Ilan University, 1993), 116–144, translated as "Divine Command Morality and the Jewish Tradition" in *Journal of Religious Ethics* 23 (1995), 49–68. Sagi and Statman term the analytic connection, "strong dependence"; the epistemological connection, "weak dependence." The analytic thesis appears explicitly for the first time in the writings of R. Kalonymus Shapiro, who lived through the Holocaust.

5. See Chapter Three and R. Joseph B. Soloveitchik, "The Lonely Man of Faith," *Tradition*, 7, 2 (Summer 1965), footnote to 61–62.

II. DIVINE COMMANDS AND RABBINIC REASONS

The DCM argument holds little cogency today. After the Holocaust, the genocide in Rwanda, the terrorist attack on the World Trade Center, the massacres and beheadings by ISIS and repeated suicide bombings in Israel by fanatics committed for religious reasons, it is inconceivable that a clear-thinking moral person would accept another's claim that a religious command justifies his intentionally killing women, children and non-combatants. Of course, I can claim that *my* religious imperatives justify *my* killing innocent persons, but someone else's religious imperatives do not justify similar behavior. But I pay a heavy logical price for doing so: Such a claim puts an end to my participation in rational moral argumentation.[6]

Rabbi Norman Lamm has suggested that not even Hebrew Scriptures support DCM, since Deuteronomy itself offers ostensibly justifying reasons for killing the Amalekite nation.[7] ("He surprised you on the march, when you were famished and weary, and cut down all the stragglers in the rear.")[8] We can only speculate whether it was the close reading of this passage

6. As explained in Chapter Two, this is because the essential characteristic of moral reasons – indeed all logically adequate reasons – is their universal nature: If something constitutes a valid reason for me, it must also be a valid reason for all similar persons in similar situations. So claims of divine revelation such as, "God has commanded me to do X," are neither empirical nor open to rational determination. They are private, or at most communal, faith claims and as such one cannot rationally distinguish between false and true claims to commandedness. This explains why invoking claims of divine revelation often signifies the beginning of the breakdown of rational discourse. In reasoned discourse among believers of different faiths, therefore, ultimately all divine command claims must be relegated to the same logical category – either all are admissible as valid reasons or none are.

7. Norman Lamm, Amalek and the Seven Nations: A Case of Law vs. Morality. In *War and Peace in the Jewish Tradition*, edited by Lawrence Schiffman, Joel Wolowelsky. (New York: Yeshiva University Press, 2007).

A Kariv, *Me-sod Hakhamim* [Heb.] (Jerusalem: Mossad Harav Kook, 1976).

8. Deut. 20:18 also gives the reason for destroying the Canaanite nations: "Lest they lead you into doing all the abhorrent things that they have done for their gods and you stand guilty before the Lord your God."

or the Jewish commitment to moral discourse that prevented rabbinic tradition from entertaining DCM, but the critical point is that rabbinic tradition never considered the divine command to destroy all Amalekites to be a sufficient justifying reason.[9]

If rabbinic tradition rejected DCM, it also could not countenance the third option, The Heretical Argument. As its name implies, no religious tradition can use this argument and retain its theological coherence or moral authority. We are thus left with the casuistic argumentation (option 4), and this is precisely how Jewish tradition attempted to resolve the problem of the *mitsvah* to destroy the Amalekite people. "Attempted" because, I shall soon argue that it could not succeed in resolving the problem through this strategy.

As Sagi demonstrates, most of rabbinic tradition employed utilitarian-type moral arguments to justify the obliteration of the Amalekites: The Amalekites fought an unjust war by unjust means, hence their destruction was necessary as a deterrent against others doing the same.[10] Amalek is evil in his essence and his nation is the arch-enemy of God, the preserver of the universe's moral order; the Amalekites must therefore be destroyed to preserve morality in the cosmos.[11] Killing all Amalekites is necessary to prevent future Amalekite destruction of the Jewish people, as shown by the case of Haman, the Persian descendant of Amalek.[12] Obeying the command to destroy Amalek teaches people to obey God's commands generally, thus preventing them

9. I am grateful to Professor Louis Newman for pointing out to me that the Bible's supplying reasons for the commandment does not necessarily imply that the absence of those reasons would void the commandment. This is logically true, yet the absence of evidence for DCM in Jewish tradition indicates that the onus of proof belongs on those who advocate DCM as an acceptable Jewish theory, not those who reject it.

10. Isaac Abravanel, Commentary on Deut. 25:17.

11. Naḥmanides, Commentary on Ex. 17:16.

12. This deterministic reasoning contains another theological problem for Jewish tradition: It comes close to the heresy of denying free will to Amalekite individuals.

from making autonomous decisions that would result in violence and murder in other contexts.[13] Amalek represents commitment to physical power, warfare and violence by the sword; for the sake of justice and peace, therefore, all Amalekites must be destroyed.[14]

In attempting to supply justifications for the killing of the Amalekite nation, rabbis and Jewish commentaries presupposed that divine imperatives must rest on moral grounds, and that rabbinic tradition is committed to moral reasoning. Notwithstanding the importance of these logical points, there is no denying that all these casuistic arguments fail.

Halakhah prohibits intentionally taking an innocent life to save another person. Normative talmudic opinion indicates that one is obligated to die rather than to murder another in this situation. Murder is one of only three prohibitions that one may not transgress in order to save his own life – a type of halakhic Categorical Imperative.[15] Further still, Jewish law prefers that many people submit to death rather than acting as an indirect causal agent or being complicit in the killing of one innocent person.[16] The moral/legal principle is, "Do not set aside one [innocent] life even to save many [innocent] lives." The foundation for this anti-utilitarian ethic is the axiom that human life is created in the image of God and therefore possesses indeterminate or perhaps infinite value. The non-quantifiability of human life precludes utilitarian trade-offs of one innocent life for another and explains why consequentialist moral justifications for sacrificing

13. *Yoma* 22b. This example teaches indicates a utilitarian reason (i.e. prevention of future violence and murder) for the commandment. Under this interpretation, divine commandments may be necessary as pedagogical instruments rather than justifying moral reasons.

14. Samson Raphael Hirsch, *In the Annual Cycle* [Heb.] (B'nai Brak: *Netsaḥ*, 1966), Vol. 2, 190–193.

15. BT *Sanhedrin* 74a; Maimonides, MT, *Hilkhot Yesodei ha-Torah*, 5:1.

16. JT *Terumot* 8:10 and Maimonides, MT, Fundamental Laws of the Torah (*Hilkhot Yesodei ha-Torah*) 5:5; cf. *Tosefta*, *Terumot* 7:20.

innocents are almost never found in Jewish legal discussion.

There is one instance of utilitarian reasoning in halakhic discussion regarding sacrificing the life of an innocent non-threatening person to save another person or persons. This revolves around the tragic case described in tractate *Terumot* that poses the existential choice between handing over a specified innocent person in a city for death, or allowing the entire city to be killed.[17] One body of rabbinic opinion, which I term "the infinite value school," maintains that even to save many people, one may not hand over the innocent individual to murderers – even though he is fated to die soon in any event.[18] The other opinion – "the indeterminate value school" – rules that one is permitted to hand over the specified person in order to save the lives of others.[19] I use the terms "infinite value" and "indeterminate value" because the debate can be expressed mathematically: If the value of the life of the innocent person in question is represented by the positive value X and the value of the other lives by the positive value Y, the first school maintains that $X = X + Y$, while the second maintains that $X < X + Y$. Only $X =$ infinity satisfies the first equation.

It is crucial to recognize that this entire debate and license to hand over another is restricted to the situation *in extremis,* where the innocent is fated to die under all circumstances. It thus has little import for moral argumentation regarding killing a non-threatening Amalekite or a Canaanite non-combatant, whose survivability is not in doubt. Nor is the law of preemptively killing a "pursuer" (*rodef*) relevant. The case of *rodef* is morally different, since the pursuer presents a clear and immediate threat and is thus not innocent. "Pursuit" is also a legally distinct case,

17. See previous note.

18. Maimonides (*ibid),* and David Ben Shmuel of Lvov (*Taz,* commentary on *Shulhan Arukh, Yoreh De`ah* 157:1) Yoel Sirkes (*Baḥ, ad loc*) follow the talmudic opinion of Resh Lakish.

19. Menahem ha-Meiri (*Beit Ha-Beḥirah* on *Sanhedrin* 72b), Jacob Jeḥiel Weinberg and others follow the talmudic opinion of R. Yoḥanan. I am indebted to David Shatz for pointing out to me the "indeterminate school."

since the halakhic ruling is that one may kill the pursuer only as a last resort, while the imperative regarding Amalekites requires killing them as the first option.

Much later in history, moral philosophers exposed the incorrectness of purely utilitarian ethics by pointing out that no amount of good can justify arbitrarily killing an innocent person.[20] This is the essence of the concept of retributive justice. Intentionally killing an innocent person is not just punishment, but unjustifiable aggression. Nor can any utilitarian rationalization to ward off future evil justify the intentional mass killing of infants or harmless civilians. This is not an abstract truth for philosophers only, but a harsh lesson of recent history. The extermination of millions in the crematoria of Auschwitz was a radical evil, teaching us that no behavior could ever be sufficiently horrible to justify intentionally killing a million babies. Similarly, there can be no moral justification for the intentional mass killing of civilians for political or religious objectives. To deny this is to obliterate the distinction between just and unjust wars and to implicitly concede that terrorism is morally correct. The imperative – whether divine or human – to commit genocide against all Amalekites suffers from the same moral defect. All rationalizations for it are fallacious.

III. TALMUDIC JUSTIFICATION AND MAIMONIDES' THEOLOGY

There is good reason to assume that traditional rabbinic authorities understood full well that these arguments could never justify the genocidal commandments, for rabbinic tradition refused to rest with these utilitarian justifications. It dealt effectively with

20. See, for instance, C. Ewing, *The Morality of Punishment.* (London: K. Paul, Trench, Trubner and Co., 1929), and J.D. Mabbott, "Punishment" in *Mind*, Vol. 48, no. 190 (April 1939), 152–167.

the practical problem of acting on the imperative via the normative talmudic ruling of R. Joshua that "Sennacherib co-mingled the nations [that he vanquished]."[21] The Talmud uses this principle to conclude that after the Assyrian king's conquest, it became impossible to determine who was a member of the Canaanite nations. Logically, this should apply to the Amalekite nation as well, since it is unlikely that Sennacherib failed to apply this policy to the Amalekites he vanquished. Indeed, many medieval and modern rabbinic authorities subsume Amalek under R. Joshua's principle.[22] Hence it became impossible in principle for any Jew to fulfill the commandment to exterminate these peoples, due to lack of certain genealogical identification. This is consistent with other instances of the rabbinic strategy to render some biblical laws inoperative or barely implementable, such as the execution of the rebellious son (Deut. 21:18–21; BT, *Sanhedrin* 71a), capital punishment (*Mishnah Makkot* 1:10), and the destruction of an idolatrous city (Deut 13:13–16; BT, *Sanhedrin* 71a). There is another rabbinic tradition that all fulfillment of the command to kill the Amalekites is deferred until the messianic era.[23] The effect of these interpretations is to render the commandment inoperative, and thus avoid any immoral behavior that would result from acting in accordance with its literal meaning.

There is no reason to believe that R. Joshua invented a historical fiction, since it was the actual practice of ancient conquerors to intermingle their conquered peoples to lessen the possibility of organized rebellion. What is remarkable is the legal power that the talmudic tradition gave to this brute historical fact.

To understand the unusual nature of the talmudic ruling,

21. *Mishnah Yadayim* 4:4; *Berakhot* 28a.

22. See Elimelech (Elliot) Horowitz, "From the Generation of Moses to the Generation of the Messiah: Jews against Amalek and his descendants," [Heb.], *Zion* 64 (5759/1999), 425–454.

23. See commentary of David ben Zimra (Radbaz) on Maimonides, MT, *The Laws of Kings and their Wars* (*Hilkhot Melakhim*), 5:5.

consider the following scenario: The Israeli Army is marching through the Sinai desert led by General Yigal Yadin, who is also an accomplished archeologist. During encampment, Yadin discovers documents buried in the sand that indicate that a clan living in the area is unmistakably descended from the biblical Canaanites. Yadin takes the document to the world's leading historians and anthropologists, who unanimously conclude that the documents are authentic and accurate. In other words, all scientific opinion corroborates the claim that these specific persons are Canaanite descendants. Are religious Jews obligated to act on the basis of the overwhelming empirical data and kill these Canaanites? Probably not, for R. Joshua's talmudic principle would trump the scientific evidence and the genocidal commandment would remain inapplicable.[24] This means that the principle functions neither as a historical observation nor an empirical claim, but as a non-falsifiable legal rule. A permanent principle with legal force to override the fulfillment of a divine commandment is rare in Jewish legal tradition. It is plausible to assume that rabbinic authorities elevated this opinion to a categorical definitional principle precisely because they sensed the overwhelming moral problems with a literal implement of the commandment.

The talmudic sages (*Ḥazal*) were not philosophers, but teachers whose ultimate concern was promoting correct action in accordance with how they understood sacred Torah texts. They succeeded in foreclosing the possibility of Jews committing genocide or killing innocents because of the divine commandment, but they left untouched the theological/conceptual problem: How could God command something immoral – even theoretically? Since "The Judge of the earth must act justly," how could

24. I have found no discussion in rabbinic literature – which is famous for analyzing all theoretical options – that countenances the theoretical nullification of R. Joshua's principle.

God have ever have issued the unjust command to intentionally kill infants, minors and women or destroy an entire nation?

The theological issue was left to later authorities of more philosophic bent. It lingered until the twelfth century when Maimonides devised an elegant solution. In *The Guide of the Perplexed*, he explicitly ruled out extending the imperative to tribes other than Amalek,[25] but it is in his legal code, *Mishneh Torah,* where he made the conceptual breakthrough. Here Maimonides adopted a radical interpretation of the sacred text and the resultant interpretation of Jewish law. His first move was to boldly interpret Deuteronomy 20 contrary to its plain meaning and the accepted opinion of his time. Verses 10–15 read:

> When you approach a city to attack it, you shall offer it terms of peace. If it responds peaceably and lets you in, all the people there shall serve you in labor. If it does not surrender to you, but does battle with you, you shall lay siege to it; and when the Lord your God delivers it into your hand, you shall put all the males to the sword. However you may take as booty the women, the children, the livestock, and everything in the town – all its spoil – and enjoy the use of the spoil of your enemy. Thus you shall do to all cities that lie very far from you, towns that do not belong to the nations hereabout.

Verse 16 goes on to contrast the above "remote" wars with the objectives and rules of engagement for the war against the Canaanite nations:

> In the towns of the latter peoples, however, which the Lord your God gives you as a heritage, you shall not let a soul remain alive.

Prior to Maimonides, normative halakhic tradition understood the call for peace (v. 10) to apply only to wars against the "cities

25. III:50.

that lie far from you"[26] – i.e. the plain sense of the text. However Maimonides interpreted the requirement of calling for peace to apply to *all* wars that Jews fight – including the wars against the Canaanite and Amalekite peoples.[27] Hence for Maimonides war was never a first option or a divine preference.[28] War is always a necessary evil to be accepted only when the enemy refused peace or did not accept the fundamental laws of social order (the prohibitions against murder, stealing, sexual wildness, cruelty, idolatry, and blasphemy as not tolerating worship of God, as well as the positive injunction to live under a system of courts and laws), known as "the seven Noahide commandments" in rabbinic parlance.

Maimonides used this non-standard reading to form the basis of his next startling claim: Should any Canaanites or Amalekites accept peace and the laws of social order, one is forbidden to kill them."[29] Perplexed by this ruling that is in stark contrast to the biblical imperative, the rabbinic commentaries inferred that Maimonides must have reasoned that should a Canaanite or an Amalekite accept peace and the laws of civilization, he is no longer in the legal category of a Canaanite or an Amalekite.[30] In other words, Maimonides transformed the category from a genealogical/ethnic one to a behavioral one. It is important to note that Maimonides' non-standard reading of Deuteronomy 20 and the laws flowing from it became normative after his ruling.[31]

26. See Rashi, and Sifri *ad loc.*

27. MT, *The Laws of Kings and their Wars*, 6:1 and commentary of Abraham Botan (*Leḥem Mishneh*) *ad loc.*

28. This means that for Maimonides, there is no concept of "holy war," i.e. war as a religious ideal. This is true even of an "obligatory war" (*milḥemet mitsvah*).

29. MT, *Hilkhot Melakhim* 6:4.

30. Commentary of Josef Karo (*Kesef Mishnah*), ad loc.

31. See Naḥmanides *ad loc.*, Abraham Ben David (Ravad) *ad loc.* and Isaiah Karelits (*Ḥazon Ish*), *Bei'urim ve-Ḥiddushim al ha-Rambam*, *Hilkhot Melakhim* 5:1. See also Aviezer Ravitsky, "Prohibited Wars in Jewish Tradition." In *The Ethics of War and Peace*, edited by Terry Nardin (Princeton, NJ: Princeton U., 1998), 115–127. The contemporary Shlomo Goren claims in his compendium of *responsa*

Maimonides never stated the reason for advocating this conceptual transformation, but it is plausible that he was responding to the theological/moral problem. Maimonides was undoubtedly aware of the text of *Midrash Tanḥuma* cited above that argues against killing non-sinning Amorites on moral grounds. It concludes that since Moses refused to kill the innocent Amorites, God accepted Moses' moral argument and followed his lead.[32] Maimonides transformed this insight into codified law, creating an interpretation that enabled him to understand the divine commandment closer to the philosophical and moral requirements of justice, as well as God's commitment to adhere to just standards.

IV. A JUST WAR?

To be fully congruent with our understanding of justice, the behavioral criterion would have to be applied to *individual* Canaanites and Amalekites, not to nations or collectivities. Maimonides did not do this explicitly, but did so implicitly when he prohibited waging war against any individuals – rather than nations – in his formulation of MT, *Hilkhot Melakhim* 6:1: "One may not wage war against *any individual in the world* until one (first) offers him peace, whether in a discretionary war or in an obligatory war." (Emphasis added). He also rejected the idea of collective punishment except for idolators.[33]

---

on war, *Meshiv Milḥamah*, 153, that nearly all early authorities (*Rishonim*) maintain this Maimonidean position.

32. "Said the Holy One, Blessed Be He, I said, 'You must proscribe them' [Deut. 20:17], but you did not do so; by your life, as you said I shall do, as it is written, 'When you approach a city to attack it, you shall offer it terms of peace'" [Deut 20:10].

33. Even though Deut. 13:13–16 mandates the destruction of all inhabitants of an idolatrous city, Maimonides ruled that non-idolators of those cities must not be killed. (MT, Lawa of Idolators 4:6) In this ruling he follows the prior tradition anchored in *Midrash Tana'im* to Deut. (67 and 69, Hoffman edition) and *Mishnah Sanhedrin* 9:1, which require testimony and proof of individual guilt before execution. Maimonides did rule, however, that the wives and children of idolatrous men

Maimonides also implied that the individual criterion applies in reference to Amalek in *Guide of the Perplexed* 3:41, where, after using the biblical language of the "Amalekite nation," he undercuts collective punishment by stressing that action against Amalek is akin to due legal punishment for "a wicked man," that it must be "according to his individual wickedness" (Deut. 25:2), and that Amalek is killed by the sword because "Amalek hastened to the sword." These are all allusions to retributive justice in which punishment must be appropriate for individual behavior. If so, the commandment would seem to apply only to informed adult individuals who bear legal responsibility for their behavioral decisions, and only to those informed adults who by principle promote violence and undermine the foundations of civilized society.

Ultimately rabbinic tradition, extending the reasoning of Maimonides, explicitly asserted the criterion of individual behavior, even for Canaanites.[34] In other words, action on the commandment would constitute just punishment for threatening individuals, and the only objects of the ostensibly genocidal divine

be killed. Importantly R. Meir Abulafia (Rama) argued strenuously against this latter ruling. He insisted that no action could rightfully be taken against women and children – and for explicitly moral reasons: "Heaven forbid that God cause evil." For a fuller discussion on collective punishment and this specific legal disagreement, see Halbertal, Moshe, *Interpretative Revolutions in the Making* [Heb.] (Jerusalem: Magnes, 1997), Chapter Six.

34. Following Maimonides' interpretation of the commandment of war against the Canaanites, Naftali Zvi Yehudah Berliner (Netsiv) took this logical step and restricted the object of the Biblical mandate to kill the Canaanite nations to individual Canaanite combatants who pursued war against the Jewish people. See *Ha`ameq Davar*, Deut. 7:2. According to R. Joseph Soloveitchik, Maimonides believed that the imperative to destroy Amalek could not include innocent civilians: "In a subsequent interview, R. Soloveitchik elaborated on his view that a nation could be transformed into Amalek in a metaphysical or halakhic sense. The status of Amalek would not, according to R. Soloveitchik, create halakhic obligations concerning innocent offspring and spouses because Maimonides clearly limits actions against Amalek to unrepentant elements who have refused to make peace with Israel." Stanley Boylan, "A Halakhic Perspective on the Holocaust" in *Theological and Halakhic Reflections on the Holocaust,* B. Rosenberg and F. Heuman eds., (Hoboken: Rabbinical Council of America, 1992) 212, footnote 3.

command would be individual aggressors committed to violently destroying the moral order of society.

Rather than resort to casuistic reasoning to qualify the case or render it inoperative, Maimonides solved the problem conceptually, by redefining the commandment to make it more consistent with the demands of moral reasoning.[35] Evidently he realized that it is not a specific application of genocide that is wrong, it is the very concept itself. No amount of casuistry could succeed in bringing the commandment into line with the demands of morality or the halakhic "justice principle," i.e. "We do not punish the sons for the sins of the fathers."[36]

One might argue that the tradition's solution is exclusively legal because the halakhic system and Maimonides simply opted for this halakhic principle to supersede the literal interpretation of the biblical command. This begs the question, since the more logical approach would have been to apply the justice principle generically, but suspend it in the instance of an explicit contrary commandment that is limited to a particular situation, e.g. the genocide command toward Amalek. Without moral considerations, it is hard to explain why Jewish religious and legal traditions opted for the justice principle over the literal reading of the Amalekite command.

Maimonides' strengthens support for this supposition in his next law, where he insists that the commandment always meant what he says it means, and that Jews followed this interpretation when trying to fulfill the commandment from the time of Joshua's first war with the Canaanites onward. Whether this

35. It is important to note that Maimonides stipulates specific peace terms in the same chapter, i.e. servitude, humiliation and taxation, that appear inconsistent with contemporary just war norms.

36. Derived from 2 Chronicles 25:4, "Fathers shall not die for their children, nor shall children die for fathers, but every man shall die for his own sin." See Abraham Bornstein, *Avnei Netser, Oraḥ Ḥayyim,* 2:508.

claim is historically accurate, it was conceptually necessary for Maimonides' moral and theological theories.

One might try to resolve the problem of immoral commandments by positing a theory of moral evolution: The commandments were moral in the biblical era, but due to human moral progress we now realize them to be immoral. The evolution of moral standards over history is a thesis for which there is much empirical evidence and one that is consistent with a traditional rabbinic understanding of the way revelation functions in history.[37] In the context of Jewish philosophy and *halakhah*, there is no logical bar to Jews accepting that God gave the Torah and commandments in such a way for their values to progressively unfold. This may be why the biblically permitted or mandated institutions of polygamy, indentured servitude, and harsh punishments for heretics were practiced in early Jewish history, but have fallen into principled disuse today. Indeed, for any revelation to be comprehensible and appreciated by human beings throughout all cultures and periods of history, some type of embedded value evolution seems necessary.

Maimonides clearly accepted a theory of theological progress that entails moral progress,[38] but that thesis could not help him with the problem at hand. If the moral progress thesis claims that there is an eternal objective moral standard (e.g. not killing innocents) always known to God but understood by human beings only after the evolution of a higher moral consciousness, then the problem remains, since God would seem to have commanded something He knew to be immoral even in the biblical era. If the thesis means that God too has an evolving moral consciousness, then God's knowledge and being undergo change, which opens

37. See Nahum Rabinovitch, "The Way of Torah" *op. cit.*

38. For theological progress see, *Guide of the Perplexed* III:32. His commitment to messianic history entails moral progress. See MT, *The Laws of Kings and their Wars,* 11:4 and 12:5, and *Guide* III:11.

up a host of theological problems for Maimonides' conception of God, to which time and change do not apply.[39]

IV. A NEEDLESS COMMANDMENT?

The result is that Jewish tradition has now solved both the practical moral problem as well as the philosophic problem – in other words, totally neutralized the commandment to commit genocide. If so, what is the purpose of the commandment? In fact neither Jewish tradition nor Maimonides needed these commandments to mandate the destruction of those committed to warfare or not willing to abide by the fundamental norms of civilized society. This is known from elsewhere in Jewish law.[40] Even on a strictly heuristic level, our analysis has thus far stripped the Amalekite commandment of any value. It neither adds nor detracts from the corpus of Jewish law or ethics.

This consideration may have disturbed traditional rabbinic commentators who were committed to finding meaning in every letter of sacred texts. Some medieval thinkers and later Ḥasidic teachers translated the literal meaning of the imperative into metaphor and explained the Amalekite commandment as referring to the obliteration of each person's evil impulses.[41] According to this interpretation, the war against Amalek became every person's internal psychological and moral struggle with himself.

Perhaps the same concern vexed the famed Lithuanian talmudic tradition beginning with R. Elijah ben Shlomo Zalman, (the Ga'on of Vilna) and carried forward by the Brisker Soloveitchik rabbinic dynasty.[42] R. Moses Soloveitchik (1876–1941) asserted

39. MT, Laws of Repentance 5:5; *Guide,* I:68 and II:1.

40. See MT, *Hilkhot Melakhim* 8:10.

41. This medieval interpretation is cited (disapprovingly) by medieval talmudic authorities and rationalists. See Gershom Scholem, *Major Trends in Jewish Mysticism* (Jerusalem: Schocken, 1941), 340–41, and Sagi, HTR, *op. cit.* 334–336, for specific references.

42. For the claim that the Ga'on of Vilna maintained this line of reasoning, see

that the Amalekite nation never assimilated beyond recognition. Apparently without taking into account Maimonides' restriction in *The Guide* 3:50 of the commandment to the actual tribe of Amalek,[43] he took his cue from Maimonides' non-biological understanding of the category in the MT, where Maimonides fails to list Amalek as one of the tribes whose traces were lost.[44] Speaking during the Nazi era, R. Soloveitchik insisted that Amalek is a prototype for any person attempting to exterminate the Jewish people and that the commandment to physically destroy such persons is still binding. His son, R. Joseph Soloveitchik, applied it to Arabs trying to destroy Israel in the 1950s.[45] Instead of reducing the category to a nullity, they extended it to all individuals who exhibit this immoral behavior. Importantly, the latter's interpretation minimized the potential for individual immoral interpretation and action by restricting the operative imperative to the Jewish community as a collective.[46]

V. THE COMMANDMENT TODAY

The command to annihilate Amalek reflects the biblical insistence that radical evil exists in human experience and that people protecting the civilized order are obligated to destroy that threat without compromise. It maintains that the correct moral response

Horowitz, *op. cit.*, 428.

43. For an excellent analysis of this restriction, see Josef Stern, "Maimonides on Amalek, Self-Corrective Mechanisms, and the War against Idolatry" in *Judaism and Modernity: The Religious Philosophy of David Hartman* (Burlington, VT: Ashgate, 2004), 364–366. Maimonides also alludes to the restriction when he catalogues the commandment in *Book of the Commandments*, Positive Commandment 188.

44. MT, *The Laws of Kings and their Wars* (*Hilkhot Melakhim*), 5:4. Evidently, R. Soloveitchik separated 5:5 from 5:4, since 5:5 reads, "Similarly the command to destroy Amalek. . . ."

45. R. Joseph Soloveitchik, "*Kol Dodi Dofeq.*" In *Theological and Halakhic Reflections on the Holocaust*, B. Rosenberg and F. Heuman eds., *op. cit.*, 98. Translation by Lawrence Kaplan.

46. See Chapter Four, footnote 34 for the elaboration of R. Joseph Soloveitchik's view.

to radical evil posed by individuals is itself harshly radical – that short of a fundamental moral transformation by the individual persons committed to such evil, one should offer neither quarter nor forgiveness. The moral imperative demands the rejection of any agreement toward co-existence, for ultimately coexistence is impossible. If not conquered totally, absolute evil ultimately destroys the moral and social foundations of human civilization.

Of course, any literal implementation of the imperative to destroy without limit individuals considered to be evil incarnate, strikes fear in the hearts of morally sober persons. These biblical texts with their sub-human depictions of Amalek and the Canaanites were not lost to religious authorities and zealots throughout history: During the Crusades, Pope Urban II considered Muslim conquerors of Jerusalem to be Amalek. In medieval times Jews considered Christians to be Amalekites, and in modern times anti-Zionist Jews considered Zionists to be Amalekites, while radical Jewish nationalists have identified as Amalek Arabs, the Palestinians, Jewish leftists, and Israeli officials advocating ceding biblical land to Palestinians.[47] Nor is it an accident that Baruch Goldstein's murderous rampage in Hebron took place on the holiday of Purim, when Jews read the imperative to kill Amalek.[48] In the 1970s, the political extremist Meir Kahane advocated expelling all Arabs from Israel based on the Deuteronomic prohibition calling for intolerance toward Canaanites. More recently a book by rabbis was published justifying killing gentile civilians in war[49] and in December 2010

47. Elimelech (Elliot) Horowitz, "From the Generation of Moses to the Generation of the Messiah: Jews against Amalek and his Descendents," [Heb.]. *Zion* 64 (5759/1999), 425–454.

48. See Sprinzak, *op. cit.,* 263. For a list of national religious rabbis identifying Arabs and Palestinians as Amalek, see Lubitch. Ronen. "The Extermination of Amalek and the Arab Enemy: Between Biblical Commentators and Contemporary Rabbis [Heb.]. *Shanon* 22 (1977), 43–78.

49. Yitzhak and Elitsur Shapira, Yosef. *Torat Hamelekh* [Heb.] (Israel, 2010), particularly 17–18, 185, 205–206. Unofficial English translation at http://torathamelech.blogspot.com/.

some nationalist Israeli rabbis issued a public letter arguing that it was forbidden to sell or rent land to Arabs in Israel. Both these documents are based on the premise that the contemporary gentiles to which they refer are subsumed under the biblical Canaanite prohibition.[50]

This is not mere rhetoric, but license for religiously motivated persons to kill. Undoubtedly this violent potential is what led talmudic authorities, medieval thinkers and contemporary rabbis to try to protect the moral integrity of Jews by barring them from acting on the simple meaning of the divine commandments to exterminate the Amalekite and the Canaanite nations – or any innocent person no matter what his genealogy.

50. For a legal and moral refutation of this ruling, see Rabbi Shlomo Riskin, "Selling Land in Israel to Gentiles" *Meorot* 2011, found at https://library.yctorah.org/files/2016/07/Riskin-Selling-land-in-Israel.pdf.

Chapter Five

On Liberty – and the *Halakhah*

The Blessed One, Holy Be He, held a mountain over their heads, and said, "If you accept Torah, it is well. If not, this shall be your burial place. R. Aba B. Jacob observed, "This constitutes a protest against the Torah." Said Raba, "They accepted [Torah] in the days of Ahaseurus."(BT, Shabbat 88a)

I. MODERN POLITICAL LIBERTY & HALAKHIC OBLIGATION

I speak as a religious Jew, bound to the Torah of Israel, the traditions of Israel and the People of Israel, who takes the value of personal liberty as a given. There lies the challenge. After thriving in the freedom of democratic society, is there someone among us who does not deeply value the right to choose, to express his own beliefs, to decide his own life-style, his politics, or his place of residence? Now we are all committed "libertarians" – political conservatives as well as liberals. All of us accept the fundamental principle of liberty, differing only over the extent to which it should be applied.

Liberty represents the political dimension of the larger concept of autonomy. Philosophically, autonomy means that people have the ability to determine their actions based upon principles they give themselves. Since the influence of Immanuel Kant, however, that metaphysical capability has been understood as a moral imperative: To act autonomously is the highest responsibility that we have as moral agents. In short, acting from our own principles is what makes moral behavior possible.[1]

In a more popular sense, autonomy means the necessity of choosing for ourselves, of rejecting decisions imposed on us by external authority. Autonomy and choice are the hallmarks of modern experience, for what was largely a person's fixed destiny in the past – such as social and economic status, geography, religious identity and life style – has become largely a matter of choice today. That is, the process of modernization entails a transformation from fate to personal decision.[2] All modern thinkers who defend traditional religion struggle to find a legitimate place for individual freedom and autonomy within their systems. This is also true for modern Orthodox theology, whose thinkers consider choice to be an inescapable datum of our experience. For them it has *a priori* justification and its value is not subject to acceptance or rejection by *halakhah*.[3]

Yet the commitment to autonomy when expressed as political liberty is at *prima facie* odds with Judaism's central categories of

1. For an Orthodox treatment of *mitsvot* sympathetic to the principle of moral autonomy, see Walter Wurzburger, *Ethics of Responsibility* (Philadelphia, 1994).

2. Peter Berger, *The Heretical Imperative* (Garden City, Long Island: Doubleday, 1979), Chapter 1. As Berger points out, the modern situation of the individual having to choose the essential characteristics of his life is a mixed blessing. It can bring with it a host of cognitive maladies, chief amongst them being alienation. See also, Putnam, Robert, *Bowling Alone* (New York, 2001). For good or for bad, the lack of axiomatic belief and the demand for personal choice is the very situation in which the modern individual finds himself. Rene Descartes is considered to be the first modern philosopher. His thought is distinct from his predecessors because he did not take as a given any religious tradition or substantive worldview. Standing alone with only the awareness of his own consciousness, he recreated God, material objects and the universe *ex nihilo* from a voluntary cognitive act. Nearly all modern philosophy has assumed this solitary, individualistic starting point.

3. David Singer offers the thesis that the writings of the American thinkers David Hartman, Irving Greenberg and Michael Wyschograd constitute a "new Orthodox theology." *Modern Judaism* (February, 1989), 35–53. As will be explained, even the more traditional R. Joseph Soloveitchik accepted the necessity of freely choosing Torah and commandments.

divine authority and commitment to *mitsvot*. Simply put, according to traditional theology, God has commanded and Jews must obey. The Torah is an obligation-based system, rather than a rights-based political culture. Further still, since Sinai "the Torah no longer resides in heaven."[4] Thus traditional Judaism invested human institutions (e.g. rabbinic authorities and courts) and techniques (e.g. halakhic directives, excommunication, sanctions and fines) with the authority to coerce Jews to obey and to punish them for disobedience. If these instruments are viewed as implementations of God's will as realized in the *halakhah*, where lies the basis for individual political freedom? And on a national level, is there room for liberty in a religious Jewish polity?

If the authentic implementation of *halakhah* ultimately denies the legitimacy of political freedom, no amount of dialectical analysis will make Orthodoxy compatible with Western political thought. On an existential level, no amount of economic affluence or participation in the mainstream of modern society will allow a halakhic Jew to feel at ease. Orthodox Jews living in the modern democracies of American and Israel will be condemned to lead a fractured life, torn between committing to the religious principle to obey political expressions of Torah authority and their deeply rooted freedom-consciousness.

This conflict is being played out regularly in Israel, where the use of political authority to enforce religious law is a real option. Modern religious Israelis and their political parties repeatedly agonize over how much they will support religious legislation that imposes Orthodox standards upon the Israeli populace. Such legislation would deny the rights of individuals to violate the Sabbath in public, to marry and divorce according to their preferences, and to extend full equality under the law to all other citizens. In the actual confrontation between human rights and

4. Deut. 30:12 and BT *Baba Mesi'a* 59b.

coercive religious legislation, where can a modern religious Jew stand?[5]

The problem is much deeper than the psychological discomfort of some religious Jews. It casts ominous clouds over the religious and political future of all Jews as a national and ethnic collective. Barring some messianic intervention that changes the socio-political conditions of Jews today, it is certain that any philosophy or political arrangement that denies individual freedom will be rejected by the overwhelming majority of the Jewish people. In other words, any conception of *halakhah* that fails to make room for personal liberty means that most of the Jewish People will never return to Jewish tradition and believing in the authority of Judaism and *halakhah*. In Israel, such a conception means that when consistent, religious Israelis have no halakhic alternative to pursuing a politic that limits fundamental civil liberties through religious legislation. Thus Israel's political arena will be the scene of an unending *kulturkampf,* with religious Jews battling against the free democratic structure of the State.

II. LIBERTY & MODERN JEWISH IDENTITY

To understand the halakhic attitude to political freedom, we must first clarify the general concept of liberty. In his celebrated

5. Examples of this conflict crop up periodically in Israel. In 1989 Israel's religious parties steadfastly resisted the passage of a Knesset bill entitled, "Basic Law: Human Rights." Orthodox politicians opposed the bill since its provision for freedom of religion guaranteed Israelis the right not to practice Sabbath observance in public and to choose heterodox interpretations of Judaism. The long-standing Orthodox opposition to a constitution for the State of Israel is grounded in the same type of thinking. Legislation regarding Sabbath and *kashrut* restrictions continue to generate controversy, most recently the 2019 supermarket bill allowing supermarkets to be open on the Sabbath. Many Israelis believe that legislation permitting civil marriage and divorce will be raised soon. Of course, one should ask whether religious opposition to such legislations is based primarily on the desire to preserve familiar social patterns (the "status quo"), on political opportunism, or on impartial inquiry into Jewish law.

essay, Isaiah Berlin explicates two different notions of political liberty appearing in Western thought.[6] The first, negative liberty, stresses the right of a person to act without interference from others. It is personal independence, the right to act however one likes in certain areas of his life. Deliberate interference by others within these areas constitutes a lack of political freedom, implying oppression and coercion. John Stuart Mill put it best: "The only freedom which deserves the name is that of pursuing our own good in our own way."[7]

British political philosophers (Hobbes, Mill, and Locke) all agreed on this concept of freedom, even though they disagreed over the extent to which a state should protect these rights. They knew that unlimited political freedom produces social chaos, a primitive "state of nature" that destroys justice, security and even freedom itself. Berlin put it well: "Complete freedom for the wolves means death for the lambs." Yet all these thinkers agreed that there is a certain domain of action that ought to be impervious to both legal and social control. The values that we cherish so dearly such as freedom of religion, of speech, the rights to property, privacy, and political expression, all emerged from this British school of thought to become the bedrock of American society and the foundation of Western democracies.

Moreover, the passionate defense of liberty always runs along the same lines. Without liberty humans cannot fully develop their natural faculties. Our religious, intellectual and moral character are all frustrated when we are overly constrained by others. Indeed, once a person surrenders totally to an outside authority, he is so degraded that he loses his essence, his "personhood," becoming more akin to a member of the animal world.

Thus the lack of freedom is not only oppressive, it is humanly

6. Isaiah Berlin, "Two Concepts of Liberty. In *Four Essays on Liberty* (New York: Oxford U., 1969), 118–172.

7. Ibid, Introduction.

self-defeating. While these thinkers may debate what constitutes the human essence that pervasive authority destroys and what is the minimum requirement of liberty, they all agree that freedom from absolute political authority and external interference is a fundamental value. The freedom to decide one's own actions is as necessary to human health and creativity as the air a person breathes. Coercing an adult person for the sake of his own religious, rational or moral interests is never justified.

The second concept of freedom, "positive liberty," is not a "freedom *from*" outside authority but a "freedom *to*" be and do. It is the freedom to be one's own master, to act from reasons which are one's own, rather than from external causes. Simply put, it is the impulse to be a rational, morally responsible subject, not merely an object.[8] Each person, of course, is a complex personality with multiple dimensions often in conflict. Some philosophers saw the true challenge of life to be the realization of one's ideal or "higher" self, and the liberation from his lower nature. The higher self is usually identified with some form of reason or rational will while the interfering or baser human dimensions are identified with man's irrational impulses, his uncontrolled desires, or his undisciplined character. A person swept along by every gust of desire is no better than a brutish animal. It is the disciplined person, acting out of rationally accepted principles, who realizes his humanity, his true self to the fullest. According to positive liberty, freedom is a function of *what* one chooses and believes, while according to negative liberty, freedom is determined by *how* his action is determined.

Superficially, negative and positive liberty seem to be two sides of the same coin: They appear to express the same concept with a mere change in qualitative mode. How different is acting without interference from others (negative liberty) from acting out of one's true being (positive liberty)?

8. Ibid. op. cit., 131.

"Enormous" is the simple answer. In fact, as Berlin notes, Western thinkers developed the two concepts in divergent and ultimately antithetical directions. The British empirical philosophers seized negative liberty and developed it as actual behavior within a field without obstacles, while the political rationalists (Plato, Rousseau, Kant, and Hegel) focused on positive liberty expressed more as a metaphysical notion of self-mastery. The latter were more concerned with freedom from spiritual slavery than with breaking the bonds of pervasive political authority. More important than freeing oneself from others was the task of being free from himself.

It is here that positive liberty can conflict with the concept of negative liberty. According to the doctrine of positive liberty, realizing your empirical will or your actual preferences does not make you free. Freedom emerges, rather, from some idealized metaphysical will of what you *would* choose or how you *would* act if you were fully realized, perfectly rational or in accord with a particular philosophy's supreme human attribute (e.g., obedience, productivity, or social conscience). This leads to the paradox of the possibility of one person "forcing another person to be free."[9] For if I am (or think I am) more rational than you, I can in the name of positive liberty force you against your expressed will to act on my perceived rational choice. It is not my power to force you that astonishes here; it is my moral justification for coercing you. Indeed, it is not coercion at all, but mere assistance in your own self-realization. According to positive liberty, my control "extends" your moral choice and freedom.

There is no need to explain here how dangerous the political application of such a conception can be. It is the basis for an Orwellian "Newspeak" universe, where the worst forms of repression and totalitarianism are justified in the name of freedom. Enough manipulation of the definition of a person's essence can

9. J.J. Rousseau, *Social Contract* (London: Penguin, 1968), Book I, Ch. 7.

transform freedom into whatever the manipulator wishes to do to you. Even well-meaning paternalism ultimately produces a coercive and repressive political structure.[10] In the end, it is no accident that in Plato's ideal republic an entire class of people was required to act as policemen, forcing the philosopher-king's choices upon the irrational majority. This is what led Kant to declare that, "paternalism is also a form of despotism."

Which concept of liberty is most consistent with Jewish thought? Certainly the positive, metaphysical concept of freedom with its notion of man conquering himself, resonates throughout Rabbinic literature. The dual notions of the good and evil impulses, *yetser ha-tov* and *yetser ha-ra,* in perpetual conflict, provide the Jewish philosophical background for this conception. Who is the truly strong and autonomous person? He who conquers his passions.[11] Who is really free? He who sheds the bonds of nature and impulse, losing himself in the rational pursuit of Torah.[12]

Maimonides formulates the most prominent basis in halakhic literature for analyzing the concept of positive liberty. After asserting that a bill of divorcement (*get*) is defective when it is obtained through coercion by a heathen court, but valid if the coercion is at the order of a *bet din,* Rambam explains the apparent inconsistency:

> And why is this *get* not null and void seeing that it is the product of duress, whether exerted by the heathens or by the Israelites?

10. Berlin, *op. cit.* 131–134. See also the same author's, *Freedom and Its Betrayal: Six Enemies of Human Liberty* (Princeton, NJ: Princeton U., 2002), where Berlin demonstrates how great positive libertarians (e.g. Rousseau, Hegel, and Fichte) concluded with totalitarian coercive political structures. Twentieth-century totalitarian systems-both Communism and Nazism have roots in this doctrine. Both political systems proceeded to deny the intrinsic value of the individual, ultimately slaughtering him in the name of a substantive political ideal.

11. Paraphrase of Mishna *Avot* 4:1.

12. Paraphrase of Mishna *Avot* 6:2.

> Because duress applies only to him who is compelled and pressed to do something that the Torah does not obligate him to do, for example, one who is lashed until he consents to sell something or give it away as a gift. On the other hand, he whose evil inclination induces him to violate a commandment or commit a transgression, and who is lashed until he does what he is obligated to do, or refrains from what he is forbidden to do, cannot be regarded as a victim of duress; rather he has brought duress upon himself by submitting to his evil intention. Therefore this man who refuses to divorce his wife, inasmuch as he desires to be of the Israelites, he wills to abide by all the commandments and to keep away from transgressions – it is only his evil inclination that has overwhelmed him. Once he is lashed until his inclination is weakened and he says, "I consent," it is the same as if he had given the *get* voluntarily.[13]

This passage contains ambiguities that are mirrored by textual variations. One interpretation supported by the above version implies that Rambam is making one unified argument that articulates the Jewish concept of positive liberty with all its classical elements: A Jew has an essence, or "higher will" (to obey commandments), as well as a lower alien dimension (evil inclination) that impels him to transgress commandments. When the evil inclination "overwhelms" his true self, the court may administer corporal punishment or other sanctions until the husband relents. The issuance of the *get* is valid because the husband gives it voluntarily, as a result of his ideal metaphysical will, even though he appears to be coerced and his consent is extracted under duress. The *halakhah* of *get,* it appears, is oblivious to the Jew's empirical will and actual preferences; it concerns itself only with a predetermined metaphysical will as defined by halakhic obligation. Evidently the Jewish people's original collective acceptance of the Torah's obligations when the nation stood at

13. MT, Laws of Divorce 2:20 (Yemenite manuscript version).

Sinai millennia ago eclipses all subsequent individual volition to obey or disobey. Hence the action of the court is "therapeutic," not punitive or coercive. The court is merely administering a kind of benevolent, albeit painful treatment to assist the husband in discovering his true self.

Note that Rambam's formulation is not restricted to the one case of divorce. He is positing a general principle of ideal will: Individual Jews are necessarily guided by an objective will to be Jewish. This, by definition, entails the voluntary acceptance of the Torah as a normative system, as well as the desire to abide by each particular commandment.

Once this view is accepted, there is little room for the right of Jews to act without interference from Torah authority and its human agencies, i.e., to exercise negative liberty. Rabbinic authorities, courts or state institutions acting as agents of rabbinic authority will always be justified in ignoring the actual wishes of Jews and employing coercive measures to induce halakhic obedience. In principle, the freedoms of speech, travel, assembly, privacy, and political expression all collapse under the weight of halakhic directives. In other words, when we claim that every Jew today has accepted the Torah at Sinai and stands obligated to obey its halakhic canons, the concept of negative liberty seems to have no place in halakhic political theory. Accordingly, individual Jews would have no inalienable right to basic political freedoms in a Torah society.

And should it be otherwise? If Plato, Rousseau, Hegel, and Marx all were willing to sacrifice liberty to promote the highest values of their systems, should *halakhah* be any less committed to establishing its ideals and enforcing obedience to *mitsvot?* For a traditional Jew, the rule of Torah should supersede all other values. Perhaps political freedom, tolerance, and individual rights are merely respectable Western values that are simply a product of non-belief and a lack of religious commitment. Negative liberty may be a *desideratum* only for a community that lacks substantive value commitments or for individuals mired in theological apathy. In other words, negative liberty may actually be a "freedom of indifference."

An interesting problem arises from this reading of Maimonides. May rabbinic courts coerce one who has converted out of Judaism? In the eyes of *halakhah*, the convert is a sinning Jew and is still obligated by *mitsvot,* i.e., his ideal will still wishes to follow *halakhah*, even though his empirical will indicates he does not "desire to be of the Israelites, to abide by all the commandments and keep away from transgression." If we are concerned with his metaphysical will only, it follows that the court may still "coerce" the issuance of the *get.* Yet to ignore the fact that the convert has opted out of Judaism flies in the face of the real situation with which Jewish law is dealing. Indeed, according to one opinion such a person cannot be legally lashed. His source? The very same law with a slight textual variation:

> We have found in the Maharit Zahalon who has questioned this (and maintains) that we do not coerce a convert to divorce even though he is one about whom the law rules (for other reasons) that he is to be coerced, and he bases his opinion on that which Maimonides has written: "And why is this *get* not null and void seeing that it is given under duress? Therefore this man who refuses to divorce his wife,
>
> in as much as he desires to be of the Israelites and he desires to abide by all the commandments, and to keep away from transgression, it is only his inclination that has overwhelmed him. Once he is lashed until his inclination is weakened and he says, "I consent," it is the same as if he has given the *get* voluntarily."
>
> According to this a convert who has transgressed every commandment indifferently and angers his Creator through serious transgression (and is coerced), is thereby consenting under duress; he is just like someone forced to give a present. And even after he is lashed and has divorced, his soul will not rest and he will be full of anger toward those who brought him to do this. Even though

> he performed a *mitsvah*, the soul of every evildoer is evil, "For the wicked boasts of his heart's desire." And so, he is completely forced to do this; therefore, how do we coerce even if the law decreed that for other reasons he should be coerced to divorce?[14]

The above text, the one that was before *Or Same'aḥ* and *Maharit Zahalon,* contains the additional conjunction "and": ". . . in as much as he desires to be of the Israelites *and* he desires *(ve-rotseh)* to abide by all the commandments . . ." This implies that Maimonides is concerned not exclusively with an ideal will, but also with a Jew's actual will to obey *mitsvot* and the evidence for realistically presuming that empirical desire.

Under this interpretation, Rambam is making two connected arguments: First he asserts the principle of the ideal will: A Jew acts in accordance with his will when he performs the commandments. But how does Maimonides know this? Evidently it flows not from the immutable historical revelation at Sinai, but from a second, more empirical assumption: Each Jew actually "wants to be of the Israelites." This consent to communal membership provides the warrant for claiming that the Jew really desires to abide by all the commandments, a desire deeper than any temporary inclination to disobey. Thus the application of lashes is justified only because by opting for membership in the Jewish people, the individual has told the Jewish community that he really wants to fulfill the *mitsvot*.

This thesis also need not be restricted to the sole category of divorce. It establishes the general principle of empirical will: one's actual consent, or presumption of consent, to obey *mitsvot* is necessary to justify coercive legal action. Thus *Maharit* maintains that in the case of the convert who demonstrates that he does not want to be a member of the Jewish people, the presumption

14. R. Meir Simcha HaCohen (*Or Same'aḥ*, 1843–1926), Commentary on MT, Laws of Divorce 2:20.

that he wants to perform *mitsvot* dissolves and with it disappears any rationale for coercion. Although disagreeing with *Maharit* in the case of the convert, *Or Sameaḥ* also requires some realistic warrant for the assumption that a Jew actually wants to obey *mitsvot,* maintaining that when we know in advance that lashing or other sanctions will not induce some actual expression of acceptance of *mitsvot,* coercion has no halakhic justification whatsoever.[15]

Of course both interpretations support "coercion" – but, importantly, for very different reasons. In the first reading, only the ideal will is relevant. That objective will always express a preference to be a part of the Jewish people and this membership connotes acceptance of Torah obligations. Here the very concept of Jewish identity means being a party to the covenantal agreement at Sinai; therefore wanting "to be of the Israelites" conceptually entails acceptance of *mitsvot.* An "unobligated Jew" is a contradiction, as misconceived as a "married bachelor" – and almost as difficult to find.

According to *Maharit*'s reading of Rambam, the will to be Jewish is contingent, yet it serves as a sufficient basis for presuming that a Jew has an empirical desire to obey *mitsvot. Maharit* could assert this because throughout our history Jewish self-perception had always testified to that linkage. Before the Emancipation,

15. *Ibid,* and MT, Laws of Rebels 4:3. Ironically, today's widespread problem of the *agunah,* when a recalcitrant husband refuses to issue a *get,* is a clear case where coercive and punitive legislation needs to be vigorously enacted. The justification for such legal intrusion, however, lies in eliminating the victimization of the "chained" wife and protecting her right to lead a productive life, not in preventing the husband from violating *mitsvot.* The distinction between victimless and victimizing sins and the principle of forceful intervention only in the latter category is rooted firmly in *halakhah.* See *Mishna Sanhedrin* 8:7 and the ensuing talmudic discussion 73a–74a. This discussion, as well as the majority of rabbinic commentary on this text, make clear that the primary halakhic consideration for intervention is the protection of the potential victim, rather than the severity of the transgression or the maintenance of the spiritual state of the transgressor. Moreover, the text indicates that prudential limits to intervening in instances of sinful behavior, i.e., "coercion" of proper religious behavior, apply to both negative and positive *mitsvot.*

there was a broad general consensus amongst Jews that obligation to Torah law constituted their identity. Every medieval Jew saw himself as a commanded person, even if he failed to be systematically observant. Only through conversion could he escape the "yoke of the commandments." The case of the convert is illuminating precisely because it was the rare exception to the cultural norm. It shows how far a Jew had to travel to shed his identity of "commandedness."

However, today in our post-Emancipation Jewish communities of Israel and the Diaspora, what was unthinkable for Maimonides and unknown for *Maharit* – namely, the unobligated Jew – has become the sociological norm. In the words of one rabbinic authority, "in our day the observant (Jews) are called separatists and it is the sinners who go the way of the land."[16]

Thus in the Jewish people today there is no consensus regarding what it means to be a Jew. Moreover, a lack of observance pervades Jewish life. Now there are wholly secular, nationalistic, and ethnic formulations of Jewish identity for which acceptance of the Torah and traditional *mitsvot* are largely irrelevant.[17] These formulations may be heretical and even conducive to long-term assimilation, yet it is undeniable that today most Jews define their own Jewish identity independent of theological belief and halakhic commitment. These Jews do not seek assimilation. On the contrary, they often exhibit unflagging dedication to the Jewish people at great personal sacrifice. As R. Abraham Isaac HaKohen Kook observed of the nonobservant majority of the Jews of his day, "they go astray, nevertheless many of them are loyal to their nation and are proud to be called Jews, even though

16. Hoffman, R. David Zvi. *Melamed LeHo'il* I. no. 29.

17. This is most blatant in Israel, where a new Israeli-Jewish identity is continuing to emerge that is largely uncommitted to commandments and *halakhah*. See Camille Fuchs and Shmuel Rosner, *#IsraeliJudaism: Portrait of a Cultural Revolution* (Jerusalem: Jewish People Policy Institute, 2019).

they know not why."[18] That is, they "wish to be of the Israelites," but do not wish to be obligated by the commandments – at least not the *mitsvot* as defined by halakhic tradition.

This radical shift in Jewish self-identification has posed a challenge for all post-Emancipation rabbinic leaders and *poseqim*. Unwilling to dismiss it as a mere chimera or product of heresy, even the most right-wing religious authorities have given halakhic status to the fact that modern Jews act and think of themselves in non-traditional categories. This consideration has been materially relevant to reformulating the answers to a variety of halakhic questions regarding punishment for Sabbath desecration, eligibility for a *minyan*, conversion to Judaism and the contemporary definition of an apostate, to name but a few. Consider the opinion of R. Jacob Ettlinger in 1874 regarding heretics and Sabbath violators:

> But I do not know how to consider Jewish sinners in our time, unless to apply to them the rule of "one who says it is permitted," which means that they are only close to being sinners. For because of our sins the sore has spread greatly, to such an extent that for most of them the desecration of the Sabbath has become a permissible act. There are those among them who offer Sabbath prayers and sanctify the day and then violate the Sabbath.[19]

Or the position of Rabbi David Zvi Hoffmann at the turn of the 20th century:

> In our time one is not called a public desecrator of the Sabbath, because most people are such. Were the majority of Israel innocent, and a few audaciously violated the law, they would thereby deny the Torah, boldly commit an abomination, and separate

18. *Collected Letters*, no. 332.
19. *She'elot u-Teshuvot, Binyan Zion ha-Ḥadashot*, [Heb.] no. 23.

> themselves from Israel as a whole. But since most Jews have breached the fence, their failing turns to their advantage. The individual thinks that it is not such a major offense, and one need not commit it only in private.[20]

Even Rabbi Moshe Feinstein, one of the most fervent Orthodox rabbis in rejecting any heterodox ideology or institution, acknowledged that a mere general intention to join the non-observant Jewish community without any commitment to Sabbath observance was not a necessary impediment to valid conversion with its attendant Jewish identity.[21]

Most important is the position taken by Rabbi Abraham Isaiah Karelitz (*Ḥazon Ish*, 1878–1953) one of the great fathers of twentieth-century ultra-Orthodoxy. Noting the pervasive lack of faith in modern times, he formulates a new halakhic approach to Jews who are non-observant in fact and in principle:

> It seems to me that the law of throwing (the heretic) into a pit (to be left to die) applies only to those periods when the Blessed Lord's Providence is apparent, such as when miracles took place, or the Heavenly Voice functioned, or the righteous men of the generation lived under a generalized Divine Guidance visible to all. At such times, those who commit heresy are acting with deliberate perversity, allowing their evil impulse to lead them into passion and lawlessness. It was at periods such as these that the destruction of the wicked was a salutary measure to save humanity, for all know that were the generation to be led astray, world catastrophes, such as plagues, wars, and famines would result. But when Divine Providence is concealed, when the masses have lost their faith, throwing (heretics) into a pit is no longer an act against lawlessness. On the contrary, it is an act which would simply widen the breach; for they would consider it an

20. *Melamed Leho'il I,* [Heb.] no. 29.
21. *Iggrot Moshe, Yoreh De'ah,* [Heb.] no. 160 (1950).

> act of moral corruption and violence, God forbid. And since our entire purpose is to remedy the situation, the law does not apply to a period when no remedy would result. Rather, we must bring them back through the bonds of love and enlighten them to the best of our abilities."[22]

Not only does the law to kill the heretic not apply today, but the commandment to admonish lapsed Jews cannot be implemented since today we do not know how to reproach effectively. In fact, because we cannot offer effective reproach the entire halakhic category of the heretic becomes inoperative.[23] Both *Ḥazon Ish* and Rav Kook consider nonobservant Jews today to be pawns of the intellectual forces of the day:

> Yes, my dear friend, I understand well the sadness of your heart. But if you should concur with the majority of scholars that it is seemly at this time to utterly reject those children who have swerved from the parts of Torah and faith because of the tumultuous current of the age, I must explicitly and emphatically declare that this is not the method that God desires. Just as the [*Ba'ale*] *Tosafot* in [BT] Sanhedrin (26b) maintain that it is logical not to invalidate one suspected of sexual immorality from giving testimony because it is considered an *ones* [one who is coerced] – since his instincts overwhelmed him-and the [*Ba'ale*] *Tosafot* in [BT] *Gittin* (41b) maintain that since a maidservant enticed him to immorality he is considered as having acted against his will, in a similar fashion (is to be judged) the "evil maidservant" of the current age . . . who entices many of our youngsters with all of her wiles to commit adultery with her. They act completely against their will and far be it from us to judge a transgression

22. Commentary on *Yoreh De'ah,* 13:16.

23. See BT *Arakhin* 16b and *Ḥazon Ish* commentary on MT, Laws of Moral Dispositions 6:3. Norman Lamm, "Loving and Hating Jews as Halakhic Categories," *Tradition* 24:2 (Winter 1989).

> which one is forced to commit (*ones*) in the same manner as we judge a premeditated, willful transgression.[24]

Ḥazon Ish and Rav Kook struggled painfully with the obvious fact that most of the Jewish people in modern times lacked a principled commitment to Torah and *mitsvot*. Rather than reject the nonobservant by invoking biblical and talmudic categories mandating reproach, *ḥerem*, or corporal punishment, they believed that changed sociological and intellectual conditions demanded a new understanding of halakhic categories and a pragmatic course of action.

But what of the classic approach of coercion? It appears that when these modern rabbinic authorities are understood in conjunction with each other, the halakhic imperative to coerce the sinner also disappears. *Maharit* establishes the principle of empirical will: coercion is justified only when we can reasonably assume the Jew accepts the obligation of *mitsvot*. But *Ḥazon Ish* and Rav Kook now assert that the Torah considers contemporary nonobservant Jews, being "coerced" by modern culture, to be in a category of individuals who lack this sense of obligation. For technical reasons they escape the reproach and punishment accorded to heretics as they have not willfully rejected *halakhah*. Yet as coerced parties they do not willfully express, nor can we presume that they would express, any acceptance of *mitsvot*. In the absence of such acceptance, coercion provides no halakhic solution.

III. COERCION AND PERSUASION

If the previous analysis is correct, we see that there are two models within *halakhah* for dealing with Jews who consistently violate Jewish law, even those whose life-style bespeaks a lack

24. Abraham Isaac Kook, *Iggerot ha-Re'iya*, Volume I [Heb.], no. 138.

of commitment to *mitsvot*. Biblical and talmudic literature often emphasize correction through coercion, since prior assent to *halakhah* is assumed. Late rabbinic literature delineates the halakhic option of a non-coercive approach, applicable prior to assent, which focuses on education and moral suasion and tolerates behavior that conflicts with *halakhah*. Once the legitimacy of both approaches is established, the central question facing halakhically committed Jews is one of *techne,* of means: Which approach will be the most effective instrument for bringing Jews to a greater appreciation of Torah and its commandments? In the words of *Ḥazon Ish,* which halakhic policy is likely to "remedy the situation," and which will "widen the breach?"

On the pragmatic level experience indicates that the non-coercive approach yields the best religious results. No one familiar with today's Israeli society can deny that coercive religious legislation – even the specter of such legislation – has caused deep alienation from and disrespect for Torah and its political spokesmen.[25] Non-religious Jews in Israel harbor a well-founded suspicion that the Rabbinate is continuously seeking to expand its coercive political power, and that the objective of its politics is to manipulate non-religious Jews for its own ideological benefit, rather than treating them with the respect due all human beings. It is ironic that at a time in Israeli society when fewer citizens hold philosophies that in principle reject the theological and ethical ideas of Torah, nearly all non-religious persons evince a disgust for the coercive policies of religious political leaders. Quite simply, Israelis are more anti-clerical than anti-religious.[26] This is doubly tragic, for with the withering of socialist Zionist ideology many Israelis yearn for a value structure that Torah has to offer. Yet they find religion repugnant because the image of religious leadership is one whose face sneers at non-religious Jews

25. Camille Fuchs and Shmuel Rosner, *op. cit*, Chapter 8.
26. *Ibid*, Chapters 1 and 2.

and whose hands clutch at the throats of their civil liberties. In the prophetic words of *Ḥazon Ish,* the policy of pushing restrictive religious legislation is viewed as an "act of moral corruption and violence."

Nevertheless, Judaism values action – performing the *mitsvot* – not only attitude and relationship. If a Jew cannot perform *mitsvot* out of conviction and love of God, is not his obedience caused by threat of legal punishment preferable to his free disobedience? Indeed, the talmudic rabbis claim repeatedly that "a person should always immerse himself in Torah and commandments even if his motive is impure; for from acting from impure motive, he will come to act with pure motive."[27] If this dictum is a principle of empirical prediction rather than dogmatic axiom, Israeli experience contradicts it, for it has produced the opposite results. Coercive legislation has induced only animosity and the denigration of Torah, not a voluntary attraction to *mitsvot.* Even on a strictly behavioral level, the coercive policy has failed. All the restrictive Sabbath legislation has not made even one Israeli a Sabbath observer according to halakhic standards – (s)he is just someone who does not ride buses on Friday evening, someone who watches home videos instead of frequenting the theater.[28]

27. BT, Pesaḥim 50b, in the name of Rav.

28. Even if religious legislation were to somehow be miraculously effective and succeed in preventing Israelis from violating the *halakhah*, their observance would have dubious religious value. Given the present hostility to religious legislation, it is safe to assume that Israelis would intend not to fulfill any *mitsvah* via action demanded by such legislation. In a situation where the intent is not to fulfill religious obligations, Rabbi Menahem ha-Meiri maintains "there is no doubt that one does not fulfill (the *mitsvah),* for no person can fulfill his obligations through coerced action." (*Bet ha-Beḥirah, Pesahim* 114b) Even when we do not assume negative intent, if the sins of someone who disobeys *halakhah* under "cultural duress" are mitigated, then the converse is also true. Obedience stemming from external coercion (political or otherwise) lacks authentic religious meaning. Norman Lamm alludes to this ("Loving and Hating Jews as Halakhic Categories," *op. cit.*): ". . . there is no spiritual merit in faith and obedience in the presence of revelation or, derivatively, in circumstances when the Zeitgeist moves an individual to belief and observance. In both cases the environment exercises a form of duress on the

Examining each talmudic context of this dictum, we see that it is intended as prudent advice for a person to continue to voluntarily participate in *mitsvot*, even when he lacks immediate religious motivation. There is no hint whatsoever in the sources of any outside authority that would constrict personal freedom or choice.[29] This is not surprising as *halakhah* usually adopts prudent and reasonable means to realize its end values. If the Torah's goals are idealistic, its methods to achieve them are pragmatic. To quote Rav Kook, "Know that good sense is a fundamental value in our law. We are therefore, obligated always to achieve the central purpose of good sense."[30]

The talmudic sages were keen students of human behavior. They knew that a person can, by the power of his own will, condition himself to experience new-found love, joy, and religious meaning in any halakhically required act even when he is in the throes of spiritual malaise. *Ḥazal* had the "good sense" to know, however, that when any person or authority imposes laws on another, denying him free choice in the name of a doctrine to which he does not himself subscribe, no constructive religious motivation or character would result.

Understood as council to continue voluntary assumption of *mitsvot* however lacking in proper motivation, the dictum of "out of acting from impure motive, one will come to act with pure motive" contemporary Israeli experience does not falsify

individual. The maximum opportunity for freedom of choice, and therefore credit or blame, occurs when circumstances are neutral and equidistant from both extremes.

29. The context of Rav's statement is a discussion of the merit of the custom refraining from work after *minḥah* on the eve of *Shabbat* or *Yom Tov*, followed in only some communities. The fact that this is a custom and not enforceable law, that there is no mention of punishment and only heavenly reward, indicates that the claim is prudential moral advice to individuals. It is also instructive that Rambam codifies this dictum in MT, Laws of Torah Study (3:5) and in the Laws of Repentance (10:5) – two areas of religious observance that are more personal than public and for which a voluntary attitude is critical to their performance.

30. *Collected Letters*, no. 20.

the rabbinic claim. It points, rather, to the lack of wisdom of authoritarian religious politics.

IV. TORAH TODAY

Clearly, classical Judaism posits a metaphysical and moral ideal of human experience. It maintains that a human realizes its highest being when relating to the Divine Will and obeying His commandments. Philosophically, the Torah is committed to this conception of positive, substantive liberty. Yet in practice, the option exists to pursue a policy of tolerance: one that poses no coercive interference to Jews following their own will, so long as that individual liberty does not diminish the rights and religious opportunity of others. In other words, it is a policy that allows for political freedom and fundamental human rights. Paradoxically, this policy also holds out the most hope of encouraging positive religious attitudes, given the historical and intellectual conditions of the Jewish people today.

Adopting such a "libertarian" policy that allows for personal political liberty does not necessarily imply value relativism or lack of commitment to the ideal of the commandments being obligatory for the Jewish people. Nor does it lessen the religious obligation for all Jews to be responsible for one another, including the promotion of halakhic observance. The policy shifts the thrust of religious politics from an authoritarian approach to one stressing education, tolerance, and identification with the whole of the Jewish people. The political approach utilizing coercive law appears to be a "quick-fix," but that is nothing more than an illusion. In purely practical terms, attempting to deny a Jew the liberty to violate religious law is not an option in the Diaspora and does not work in Israel, as we have seen. The quick-fix is a fantasy, nurtured by a longing to retreat to the ghetto of the pre-Emancipation past that is much too narrow to house the majority of the Jewish people today. As fantasy, it is a flight from any serious religious responsibility towards the lives of Jews today, either individually or collectively.

Religious Jews can continue to be resolute in their conviction that halakhic behavior represents an ideal. When one confuses legal tolerance with pluralistic value equivalence he strays from both *halakhah* and traditional Jewish thought. Because of the belief in the validity of *mitsvot,* religious Jews both in the Diaspora and in Israel have a responsibility to be active in promoting religious and educational opportunities in which every Jew can study, assess, and personally decide on his acceptance of Torah. Rather than a posture of social isolation, this educational approach implies a difficult and long-term program of "openness" toward all Jews. It means developing honest relationships with heterodox and secular Jews, sharing experiences where all treat each other with full dignity and where voluntary religious appreciation is nurtured. It also requires utilizing personal, institutional, and even state resources towards these ends.[31]

Without a serious commitment to a program of voluntary religious opportunity and Jewish education, any Jewish society where civil liberties and human rights are legally guaranteed can easily yield a "freedom of indifference," and evolve into a society where pockets of religious commitment are lost in the dominant cultural quest for pleasure. It is clear however, that Israeli Jewish society is not moving in that direction, nor do the majority of Israelis aspire to do so.[32]

31. This does not require the total separation of synagogue and state, creating an Israeli "naked public square." Allocating Israeli state funds for voluntary religious experiences and education should be supported by religious Jews. Nor does it exclude the establishment of public religious standards in a community or institution when those standards are voluntarily accepted by its residents or members. It does, however, exclude state funds used to coerce individual Israelis to observe tradition and halakhah, and giving one rabbinical institution such as today's Chief Rabbinate a monopoly on official religious authority, since most Israelis do not accept that authority. On openness to different types of Jews, see also Chapter Seven.

32. Fuchs and Rosner, *op. cit*, Introduction, Chapters 1 and 2, and Afterword.

V. TOLERANCE AND COVENANT

The pragmatic argument for adopting a policy of political freedom in a Jewish society is compelling. Its attractiveness for religious Jews lies in its ability to synthesize Judaism's conception of religious action as the ideal of human experience (positive liberty) with a commitment to the modern democratic values of tolerance, autonomy and human dignity (negative liberty).

The previous argument that makes room for liberty – and its concomitant of tolerance – is casuistic, the classic method of argumentation of law in general and *halakhah* in specific. How effective this argument can be in securing a permanent acceptance of personal liberty within Jewish law remains to be seen. By definition, casuistic arguments apply to specific cases and are embedded in particular empirical assumptions. Hence their conclusions are inevitably limited in scope and contingent on circumstances. On this basis, liberty seems to be an unstable value not only within the Western political tradition,[33] but also in *halakhah*. Liberty within the halakhic system is further imperiled because the argument depends on the lamentable historical conditions, i.e. the absence of national consensus, agnosticism, and widespread rejection of the authority of the Torah and its commandments. Thus the casuistic argument helps us only "to muddle through." Liberty flows from religious failure, rather than from a spiritual or political ideal. In short, "because of our sins" we are allowed to be free.

Whether or not the casuistic argument can serve as a secure foundation for liberty in Jewish society, we cannot deny that it is spiritually unsatisfying and philosophically inadequate. Liberty should be an inspiring value that emerges from principle, not a concession to circumstance. Is there such a principle within

33. Bernard Williams, "Toleration: An Impossible Virtue" in *Toleration: An Elusive Virtue,* edited by David Heyd (Princeton NJ: Princeton U., 1996).

traditional Jewish culture that can illuminate political freedom as such a value? In the previous chapters, I have explored *Tselem Elokim* as a foundational concept for the ethics of human respect and dignity. In this concept there are fertile seeds for a conceptual breakthrough, one that transforms freedom into a principled ideal within Jewish thought and law. While R. Meir Simcha HaCohen identified *Tselem Elokim* with human freedom,[34] this does not go far enough, for we have seen that traditional rabbis as well as Enlightenment rationalists and romantics all understand freedom as positive liberty that can easily lead to totalitarian politics. Further development is required for the concept of *Tselem Elokim* to lay the foundations of negative liberty.

Human beings created *b'Tselem Elokim* are the crowning glory of God's creation. The contemporary rabbinic thinker R. Nahum Rabinovitch has observed that *Tselem Elokim* has two constituent components.[35] First, human beings are differentiated from beasts because God gave them the unique metaphysical gift of free choice. Second, God's ideal for creation is for each person to employ this gift by freely choosing the good. Both are necessary and neither is sufficient for the divine plan to be complete. Unbounded free will can opt for evil and return creation to its primordial darkness and chaos. Involuntary human behavior undermines God's plan for the universe by transforming human action into determined behavior akin to that of lower animal species. Since the absence of freedom robs a person of his unique humanity, preserving individual freedom (i.e. negative liberty) and promoting choice for the good (positive liberty) are both requisites for realizing *Tselem Elokim*.

Isaiah Berlin never tired of telling us that freedom and order must exist in tension with each other. Neither condition can be realized absolutely. It is only in the messianic era that both values

34. *Meshekh Ḥokhmah*, Gen. 1:27. See also Chapter Three.
35. *Darkhah Shel Torah*, op. cit.

will concurrently blossom into full expression. In our unredeemed world, therefore, we need to adopt a dialectical political policy. On religious grounds this policy should seek to maximize *Tselem Elokim* by restricting individual liberty only when allowing individual choice would undermine the liberty, dignity and equality of another. The rationale for limiting liberty is functional and social, not any religious ideal. In principle, restricting personal freedom and coercing behavior for any ideological or halakhic end robs such behavior of its spiritual character, and as such it is devoid of religious value.

Mishnah Sanhedrin 4:5 teaches that human diversity testifies to the greatness of God: "The Holy One, Blessed be He, created all persons through the [one] imprint of Adam, yet no person is identical to any other." As the *Mishnah* indicates, from *Tselem Elokim* flows the uniqueness of each human person. Differences in human opinion and behavior should therefore be celebrated as religious values. Though this *mishnah* text is old, the recognition of diversity – and the tolerance required for it to flourish – is a modern religious insight. Previously, religious cultures prized uniformity, but the bold claim of this *mishnah* is that the empirical pluralism of modernity is a religious value that reflects God's glory, not religious failure. The human right and freedom to be different illuminates God's miraculous infinite creative power and each human being's sacred uniqueness. Hence, flattening out differences and coercing toward uniformity are spiritual sins that are tantamount to rebelling against God's plan for creation.

It is precisely here that Judaism must differ from other philosophies espousing objective values and substantive positive liberty. For Plato, philosophical truth and the rational ordering of society were ends in themselves. For Marx, productive labor represented the highest human value. Because of their absolute commitments to these values, any means to optimize them were justified. In the political systems of these thinkers, individual human beings were regarded only as instruments toward realizing these goals. Indeed, it is hard to find even a hint of considerations of individuality in these philosophies. Ultimately, a person's real hopes, desires, choices, and values – his empirical will – were robbed of any worth, and his identity was reduced to a dispensable part of a well-running rational organization. Accorded no intrinsic value of "personhood" or "humanness," the individual was crushed under the weight of a rational totalitarian politic.

Because Judaism posits that every person is created in the Image of God, it insists on the unique spiritual integrity of each human being and can never lose sight of his immeasurable value. Judaism's ideals are intrinsically spiritual: the love of God and man's honest testimony to the Divine Presence. The religious goals of Judaism, therefore, cannot be merely external behavior in conformity with religious law. *Halakhah* and *mitsvot* are only means – perhaps indispensable means – of a system designed to realize these goals for every person.

Here the contradictory nature of the coercive approach is apparent. Today, when no prior voluntary assent to Torah and *mitsvot* exists, imposing halakhic standards entails forcing a person against his will. In as much as free will is necessary for one's religious and spiritual development, "imposing" the love of God on a person in contemporary circumstances is a sterile, self-contradictory policy. On a collective level also, the Jewish people is charged with being a holy people whose behavior and values testify to God's sovereignty. But if religious observance is merely a result of political decision, human legislation and police enforcement, our observance testifies only to the fear of governmental punishment and speaks nothing of divine acknowledgement. Such observance corrupts the halakhic meaning of witness (*edut*). In classic rabbinic parlance, it is *edut sheqer* – false testimony.

The above is fundamental to those who understand the Torah's concept of human beings created in the Image of God as insuring the dignity and worth of every individual. The divine character of every human being demands that each person be considered an end-in-himself. He may never be used merely as a means within some larger system, and must never be dominated completely by any form of coercive political or legal authority.

God created neither robots nor slaves to acknowledge Him. He acted out of divine *ḥesed* (lovingkindness), endowing each person with free will, reason, and a spiritual character. At Sinai, God offered the Torah to the Jewish people and they voluntarily accepted with complete understanding and freedom.[36] The proper religious approach for Jews today is one that fulfills the commandment of *imitatio dei,* emulating that divine standard: one that preserves the dignity and liberty of each person, touching his spiritual character while simultaneously bringing him to Sinai so (s)he can also freely accept the Torah.

It is true that the conceptualization of *Tselem Elokim* that celebrates freedom, tolerance and human diversity as religious ideals constitutes a break with the past. Previously, attempts to pressure toward both religious observance and communal uniformity were normative values in Jewish life. Yet, this conceptual change need not be viewed negatively. The evolution of authentic moral ideals can be understood as part of God's plan for Jewish history and the flowering of ultimate Torah values. We have gone as a people from sacrifices to prayer, from polygamy to monogamy, and from monarchy to democracy as part of the positive evolution of Jewish values. Unlike the Western philosophic proponents of positive liberty who moved from freedom to coercion in their political vision, the dynamic of Jewish thought must

36. See Soloveitchik, Joseph. "The Lonely Man of Faith," *Tradition* 7:2 (Summer 1965) 29: "The very validity of the covenant at Sinai rests upon the halakhic principle of free negotiation between Moses and the Jewish people to submit to the Divine Will." (Second footnote) As he explains, the midrashic statement found in BT, *Shabbat* 88a ("He held the mountain over their heads") fails to have any literal application to the initial acceptance of *mitsvot* or halakhic-juridic import. The presupposition of the talmudic discussion is that had the acceptance of Torah been coerced, its obligatory nature would be invalid.

move from coercion to freedom. The talmudic ideal dramatized in BT, *Shabbat* 88a points to a necessary logical relation, and resolves the freedom/obligation paradox that has long bedeviled political thinkers: The validity of legal obligation grows out of voluntary acceptance, not the reverse. Only with prior free acceptance of Torah do religious *mitsvot* and the system of halakhic responsibility make moral sense.

As the talmudic passage indicates, movement from an authority-based understanding of observance to the voluntary acceptance of *mitsvot* is also an evolution toward the Jewish people's fuller acceptance of Torah and effective testimony to God. Out of the power of *Tselem Elokim* a new world awaits us – one with broad horizons and exciting challenges that nurture hope for a future heading closer to the messianic dream. It is a society where the Jewish people express God's Image fully, where they bear witness to the gift of freedom and acknowledge Torah out of the noblest human spirit reflecting God.

Of course there is no absolute certainty that Jews in both Israel and the Diaspora will emerge from a politically free society to voluntarily return to religious values. This lack of *a priori* certainty is the price we must pay for treating each other as dignified human beings, as moral creatures who quest after spiritual achievement. Yet Jews have good reason to believe that modern Jews will ultimately resist the allure of radical secularism. Just as in biblical times when Jews voluntarily accepted God's Torah, the Jewish people today can choose similarly when it is brought to Sinai with love and understanding. The Torah promises this, for God offers each new generation of the Jewish people the opportunity to renew the covenant:

> Neither with you only do I make this covenant and this oath; but with him that stands here with us this day before the Lord our God, and also with him that is not here this day.[37] (Deut. 29:13)

37. The biblical and talmudic (BT, *Shevuot* 29a) models of the Jewish people

Religious Jews today believe in the God of Israel and the truth of His Torah. Are we to believe any less in the eternal spiritual capacity of the Jewish people to accept, with integrity freedom and conviction, partnership with the Divine?

---

obligating themselves to Torah via an oath also presuppose voluntary consent, since a coerced oath has no halakhic value. Moreover, while Jewish law allows me to obligate myself through the medium of an oath, I cannot impose obligations upon others – either contemporaries or my descendants through that medium. Thus it is unclear how the voluntary actions of our biblical ancestors can generate a binding covenant upon Jews today. This implies that the fundamental acceptance of Torah obligations must be voluntarily renewed by each generation. As Rabbi Soloveitchik notes, only when such acceptance is freely expressed are coercive measures toward implementation halakhically justified.

Chapter Six

Receiving but not Donating Organs: Ethical and Jewish Considerations

"Keep and do them [the laws], for that will be proof of your wisdom and discernment to other peoples, who on hearing all these laws will say, 'Surely that great nation is a wise and discerning people.'" (Deut. 4:6)

The definition of death belongs to the provinces of rabbis, medical authorities and legislators. As indicated in Chapter Two, whether clinically certified brain death or permanent cardiac cessation constitutes death has momentous implications: Should we permit transplanting vital organs from a brain-dead person to a needy recipient to save the recipient's life, or should we forbid it as murder of the donor? In this essay, I take no position on this question and leave it to the appropriate rabbinic, medical and legal authorities.

My purpose here is to evaluate the moral status of the position of some rabbis who forbid a Jew from donating his or her vital organs for transplantation if (s)he becomes brain dead, because in rejecting brain death as a sufficient criterion for halakhic death they understand organ removal to be an act of murder, while at the same time they allow Jews to receive vital organs from another person certified as brain dead. For purposes of brevity, I refer to this position as "RBND" – receive but not donate – and will limit my analysis to heart donations and receptions, since according to those rejecting brain death, heart transplants always entail killing or shortening the life of the donor.

RBND is a complex claim consisting of two separate ethical judgments: (1) It is wrong for a brain-dead person to donate his heart for transplantation, even to save another person, and, (2) it is not wrong to receive a heart from a brain-dead person. It is possible that each of these moral statements is tenable by itself; it is also possible that independently each is morally untenable. Conceptually, each of these claims might be proven valid on substantive grounds, but I am concerned here with the logical coherence and moral validity of both claims taken as one position, and will analyze the position in light of ethical reasoning and the logic governing correct moral discourse.

In this analysis I will try to demonstrate three theses: First, RBND violates proper ethical reasoning by contradicting essential principles of moral discourse. If so, RBND is morally unjustifiable on logical grounds. Another way of saying this is that RBND is morally incoherent in light of the accepted meaning of moral concepts because it contains a basic inconsistency and cannot be defended as morally correct. Second, commitment to ethical standards is essential for proper Jewish religious behavior, as talmudic and later rabbinic authorities have taught. That is, Jewish integrity – particularly behavior derived from Jewish values, *halakhah* and rabbinic texts – demands that proper Jewish action not violate morality or any objective moral law.[1] As a consequence, neither rabbinic authorities, nor Jewish leaders, nor those deciding Jewish policy are free to ignore the fundamental

1. This is the central thesis that is argued extensively by Aharon Lichtenstein in his influential essay, "Does Jewish Tradition Recognize An Ethic Independent of Halakha," *op. cit.* Lichtenstein's conclusion is critical: ". . . traditional Judaism demands of the Jew both adherence to Halakha and commitment to an ethical moment that though different from Halakha is nevertheless of a piece with it and in its own way fully imperative." 119.

requirements of morality. Finally, I argue that were RBND to be a widely practiced Jewish policy, it would cause great harm in both the loss of human life and in disrespect for religious Jews, the Torah and the God of Israel.

I. YOU CAN'T THINK WHATEVER YOU WANT ABOUT MORAL QUESTIONS

As we observed in Chapter Two, we all use moral terms such as "responsibility," "ought," "right" and "wrong" and also make arguments that attempt to establish the correctness of our ethical judgments. Some moral claims seem self-evident, while others are more ambiguous and require a good deal of thought before we are convinced they are correct.

Unlike empirical scientific assertions, moral judgments are notoriously difficult to prove and they give rise to wide disagreement. This is because moral reasoning – even good moral reasoning – contains a host of components that include objective facts, subjective preferences and counterfactual considerations.[2] Nevertheless, there are limits to what is ethically valid and not every position can lay claim to moral legitimacy. For example, if someone insists that "everyone ought to be kind to me even when such kindness is inconvenient, but I have no obligation to act with kindness toward other people," ethically right-thinking people would not acknowledge this as a legitimate moral position. Even if we could not explain why this is wrong, we would accurately see it as the unfair pursuit of self-interest that only masquerades as principle, and as such, we would correctly judge it to be unethical. Despite the difficulty of proving many moral claims, not every position is worthy of the name "moral" or is a

2. Good ethical reasoning includes all of the following elements: empirical facts, logic, subjective choices and moral imagination. See R.M. Hare, *Freedom and Reason,* op. cit., 94. More on these elements later.

legitimate ethic, even if it is passionately held. Not all descriptive *mores* qualify as prescriptive *morals*.

Modern philosophers have analyzed moral language, concepts and arguments. They do this not to establish esoteric truths that only philosophers recognize, but to understand how moral reasoning works, to define the bounds of what is ethically possible, to determine which moral reasoning is valid and which is not, and which moral disagreements are resolvable and which not. These philosophical inquiries also clarify what we mean when we use ethical words like "right," "obligation," and "ought," how we should use them and how we can accurately evaluate whether a given moral argument is valid or invalid. In other words, much of moral philosophy attempts to make explicit the principles and logic that are latent in our minds when we make good moral claims and arguments.

Many feel instinctively that RBND is morally wrong, and more than 100 Orthodox rabbis declared this position to be "morally untenable."[3] (I am one of the signatories of this declaration.) The statement, however, offered no explanation of *why* RBND is ethically wrong. Unfortunately, without indicating where the error lies, such a declaration carries little weight with those rabbis who advocate RBND and cuts little or no ice with Jews who consider themselves bound by their halakhic rulings. I would like to use the insights gained from moral philosophy to analyze RBND and understand why it is morally unjustifiable.

When I refer to ethics and morality here, I am not speaking about the popular opinions, inclinations or preferences that all of us hold and that we sometimes couch in judgments containing

3. "To adopt a restrictive position regarding donating organs and a permissive position regarding receiving organs is morally untenable. Such an approach is also highly damaging to the State of Israel, both internally and in regards to its relationship with the larger world, and to the Jewish People as a whole. This approach must thus be unequivocally rejected by Jews at the individual and the communal level," found at http://organdonationstatement.blogspot.com, accessed on February 5, 2020.

words like "ought" and "good." I mean, rather, value judgments that imply general principles, stand the test of sound logic and point to something beyond autobiographical information of the person making the moral claim.

There are two fundamental logical characteristics of ethical judgments and sound moral reasoning: prescriptivity and generalizability (sometimes called "universalizability"). It is these two properties that give ethical judgments the force to make moral claims on others and that distinguish ethical judgments from mere subjective expressions of preference and interest. When we try to decide what is moral in a specific situation, we look for an action that we can commit ourselves to ("prescriptivity"), and that we are prepared to accept as a principle for others to abide by also in similar circumstances ("generalizability"). Saying that something is morally right (or wrong) *for me* implies that it is not unique to me, but is right (or wrong) *for all other people like me in a similar situation*. Morality is about principles and principles are, by definition, general. If I am unwilling to generalize my judgment to others, then logically I am only expressing a private preference or desire, not a moral principle or value.[4]

This is true of all logical thinking. Scientific statements of fact and causality also are descriptive and imply generality. This descriptivity is what allows us to use logic to establish empirical and causal truths because logic relies on reasons and causes, and part of the very meaning of reasons and causes is that they are general.[5] Yet there is a logical difference between scientific

4. Hare. *op. cit.* 89–90.

5. For instance, the claim "This is a red object" implies "Everything that is like this object with respect to its color is red" and the causal statement "The car stopped because it ran out of gas" entails the claim that "Every similar car that runs out of gas stops." If we deny these implications we deny the very meaning of "red" and "because" and eliminate the possibility of these statements describing the world around us. Whereas empirical claims have a general implication about similar things, moral judgments carry a general implication about similar people. On this point, see Max Black, *Critical Thinking*. (New York: Prentice Hall, 1952), 324; Marcus George Singer, *Generalization in Ethics* (New York: Atheneum, 1971), 36–46.

empirical statements and prescriptive moral statements. While empirical claims imply generality about similar things, moral judgments carry a general implication about similar people: "You ought not to lie" implies that everyone like you in relevant respects (including me) is also prohibited from lying. If someone denies this entailment, he is misunderstanding and/or misusing "ought" as a moral term.

It is this generalizable property that gives morality its fair, non-biased character, and precludes favoring my own interests over those of other people who are in similar situations. It is also what allows us to try to argue about, prove or disprove moral judgments with other people, in a way that we cannot for personal preferences. I can argue with someone and adduce reasons for why it is right for him to pay taxes or wrong for her lie to others in a specific situation, but I cannot argue logically about whether he or she should prefer chocolate ice cream to vanilla ice cream.

As we saw in Chapter Two, another way of stating this is "What is morally right (or wrong) for one person must be right (wrong) for anyone in similar circumstances."[6] This is the basis of all moral logic and what led R. Akiva to assert that its variant in Leviticus 19:18, "Love your fellow as yourself," is the fundamental principle of the Torah. (A more logically precise formulation is, "It is right to do to others what you believe is right for them to do to you.") The logical implication of generalizability is also what led Hillel to formulate the principle negatively as, "What is hateful to you, do not do unto your neighbor," i.e. what you think others ought not to do to you, you ought not to do to others.[7] Hillel's principle leads us to a critical test for moral integrity: If I accept a rule as a moral principle, then I must

6. Singer, op. cit., 15.

7. For Akiva's principle, see *Sifra, Kedoshim* 4:12 and Genesis Rabbah, end Chapter 24; for Hillel's principle, see BT *Shabbat* 31a.

be willing to accept the negative consequences of other people adopting the same rule and acting on it toward me. Accepting the consequences of our values and actions is the price we pay for moral integrity and for following our principles. And if I am unwilling to do so, then my rule is not a moral principle at all, just a statement expressing my personal interest.

We can now see why it is so easy to reject the position cited earlier of someone claiming that "everyone ought to be kind to me even when it is inconvenient for him, but I have no obligation to act that way toward others." If Reuben adopts a principle that requires other people to act in a way that benefits him but won't allow others to act on that same principle, or if Reuben claims that others should adopt behavior that disadvantages them while insisting that he has no similar obligation to sacrifice his own interests, then Reuben's moral reasoning is illogical. And if Reuben acts on that claim, his actions are unethical. Reuben may be a hypocrite or an opportunist, but he is not someone with ethical integrity acting on moral principle. This is illustrated many times in both Jewish and general literature.[8] Anyone who thinks clearly about ethics arrives at this fundamental principle of generalization in some form.[9]

8. Examples abound from a variety of cultures and systems. Here are a few: "Love your neighbor as yourself." (Lev. 19:18 and Matthew 22:39); Kant's first formulation of the Categorical Imperative, "Act only on principles you could will as a universal law." "Justice is blind," and of course the colloquial, "What is good for the goose is good for the gander." The famous biblical dialogue between King David and Nathan (II Samuel 12:1–7) dramatically illustrates this principle. David condemns a rich man who takes a sheep from a poor man, and then understands that if it is a principle, the moral condemnation must apply equally to him when Nathan announces, "You are the man!"

9. See Chapter Two and Hare, *op. cit.*, Part I. Hare offers the following example (pp. 90–92): Let's assume Alan is in debt to Bob, and at the same time Bob is in debt to Charles. In their country, the law allows creditors to recover their money by imprisoning their debtors. Since Bob is interested in recovering his money, he would like to have Alan imprisoned. Is it *morally right* for Bob to do this to Alan? Bob can agree to the claim, "Let me put Alan into prison," but for Bob to correctly argue that *it is morally right* to do so, he must be willing to generalize the principle and allow other people in his situation to act the same way. This means that Bob must

II. JEWISH REASONING ABOUT ORGAN DONATIONS AND TRANSPLANTS

The ruling of Rabbi Shlomo Zalman Auerbach regarding organ transplants in Israel is fully consistent with this moral logic. He ruled that it was forbidden for a brain-dead person to donate his vital organs in Israel, and he ruled also that a person in Israel is forbidden be a recipient of vital organs – for the identical reasons. R. Auerbach rejected brain death as a sufficient condition for halakhic death and considered a brain-dead person to be possibly dead or possibly in the process of dying (*safeq met/goses safeq*).[10] As a result, he believed that removing the heart of a brain-dead person constituted possible or indirect murder (*shefikhat damim* – literally "bloodshed").[11] He thus forbade someone from donating his heart because in doing so he would become an accomplice to the surgeons' crime of possible murder by removing his heart. Moreover, R. Auerbach correctly understood that these halakhic (and moral) obligations are not personal: they apply equally to everyone. Hence R. Auerbach also ruled that it was forbidden for a person to be a recipient of a heart transplant, for in doing so he would be an indirect cause of the transplant doctors murdering the donor. For R. Auerbach,

agree that Charles can put him into prison, since Bob's debt to Charles is similar to Alan's debt to Bob. If Bob is not willing to let Charles put him into prison, then Bob cannot correctly maintain that he ought to put Alan into prison as an ethical principle. This simple moral argument works because the moral "ought" is both prescriptive and general.

10. *Minhat Shlomo*, responsum dated 17 *Adar*, 5753 (1993) and correspondence between R. Feivel Cohen and R. Auerbach dated 22 *Tevet* (1992) in *Nishmat Avraham,* section 5, found at http://www.medethics.org.il/articles/NA2/NishmatAbraham.yd.339.asp, accessed on February 5, 2020, and letter by Robert H. Schulman in *Tradition,* 29:2 (Winter 1995) 102 quoting R. Auerbach's judgment on the status of a brain-dead person.

11. While *halakhah* does not consider *shfihat damim* (indirect or passive killing of another) to be identical as direct murder (*reḥitsah*), it is an extremely grievous sin that is "akin to murder" and to be avoided in nearly all circumstances.

even putting one's name on a recipient list constituted being a significant cause of the transplant and was therefore forbidden.[12]

It is important to note the two empirical symmetries between (1) organ reception and organ donation and (2) the organ recipient and the organ donor. Every reception of a (non-artificial) heart requires a donation, and every recipient requires a donor. In addition, there is a strong causal link: Every act of removing a heart for transplant is performed for a specific recipient, someone identified before the surgery occurs who agrees to receive the specific heart and who waits for the heart to be implanted as soon as it is removed from the specific donor.

This fact immediately gives rise to an ethical symmetry according to moral logic: if it is wrong for me to be a heart donor because it leads to my murder by others, it must also be wrong for to me to be a recipient because receiving the donor's heart similarly involves my causing the murder of the donor. The moral reason is general and must apply to everyone in similar circumstances, i.e. both when I am the potential donor and another person is the recipient and when the other is the donor and I am the potential recipient. As a result, claiming that it is wrong for me to donate but not wrong for me to receive fails the generalization test of the principle, "I ought not to donate my heart." R. Auerbach's halakhic decision ruled out the morally untenable position of me having a privileged status over others by receiving someone else's heart when the other person could not receive my heart because I refuse to be a donor.

If I want to be ethically consistent and save my life by receiving a heart transplant, I have to be willing to acknowledge the moral permissibility of heart extractions and donations. Logically, I can claim that a brain-dead person is still alive and removing

12. *Minhat Shlomo*, responsum dated 17 *Adar*, 5753 (1993). R. Auerbach limited this ruling to Israel, where it can be assumed that the majority of doctors and donors are Jews. I discuss the moral issues of this limitation later.

his heart constitutes possible murder and as a result refuse to participate in transplants. I am also free to claim that brain death constitutes death and then admit the moral permissibility of both donating and receiving. What I may not do is pull the string from both ends: Claim that my donating my heart is morally wrong because it constitutes illicit bloodshed, and simultaneously claim that it is morally right for me to be an active agent and facilitate shedding the donor's blood so that I can benefit as a recipient. If those who forbid heart transplants as possible murder want to act with moral integrity, it would be correct for them to take a sacred oath to never agree to be a heart recipient and to never encourage any loved one to save his/her life by accepting a heart from a donor.[13]

Rabbi Auerbach correctly forbade someone from being a recipient in Israel even though he knew that due to the great number of Israeli patients waiting for heart transplants, Israeli doctors *will actually* remove the heart of the donor and perform the transplant whether or not I (or any other person) refused to be the recipient in a given case.[14] Again, this is consistent with good moral logic, because the scope of moral logic's generalization rule includes the hypothetical situation of everyone adopting my principle, *even though we know that, in fact, everyone will not adopt the principle and some will surely violate it.*[15] For instance, I cannot validly argue that I am morally free not to pay my taxes because even when I do not pay, others surely will pay and thus sustain the tax system. It is unjust for me not to pay taxes and benefit from the tax system, because if everyone *would*

13. It would also be morally consistent for them to condemn all transplant doctors as immoral shedders of blood and all hospitals that perform heart transplants, in America and in Israel, to be institutions that commit bloodshed – and institute all the appropriate social opprobrium that is normally imposed on people who willfully commit murder.

14. *Nishmat Avraham*, section 5, found at http://www.medethics.org.il/articles/NA2/NishmatAbraham.yd.339.asp.

15. Hare 93–94, 107, 172–17.

act like me, the tax system *would* collapse and the benefits I want to receive from tax revenues *would not* be available.

The counterfactual generalization is an essential element in correct moral reasoning, and it is irrelevant to moral logic that *in fact everyone will not do as I do*. My rejection of the counterfactual situation where everyone follows my principle is logically sufficient to establish the principle as wrong. It is the hypothetical case of generalization that is relevant to the moral argument, not the factual non-generalization of the principle. In our case of organ donation/reception, it is morally irrelevant that doctors will remove the heart for another since we know that not everyone will refuse to be a recipient (as I may do) and hence the donor will be murdered anyway. And as we shall see, even if the donor is killed in any event for another recipient, when I agree to be the recipient of this particular heart, I am a material cause in the process of killing that specific donor. Again, this logic is part of R. Auerbach's reasoning regarding vital organ donation/reception in Israel.

The strongest way to apply the logical requirement of considering counterfactual situations is by reversing the identity of the parties involved: Would I still hold a principle that works to my advantage while disadvantaging others if I were the one suffering the disadvantage? Would I discriminate against a class of people if I were a member of that class? Would I, on principle, deny to other people the option of life-saving heart transplants if I (or my child) were the one in need of the heart? If so, I am morally consistent, and acting on this principle might be ethical. However, if not, and I permit receiving while forbidding being a donor, the principle has failed the generalization requirement. I cannot validly claim it as a moral principle, and when I act on this rule my behavior is unethical.

This explains why "moral imagination," empathy and real-life interaction with other people is a critical aid to good moral reasoning. Human experience helps us to identify deeply with the feelings of others and hold their interests as important as are our own, i.e. to empathize with them and be fair when their interests and ours conflict. This underlies the biblical principle, "Love your fellow as yourself," and Hillel's principle "What is hateful to you, do not do to others." Both demand that we think of ourselves as the other person and decide on our actions *as if we were the other person*, acting toward that other the way we *would* act (or in Hillel's case, *would* refrain from acting) toward ourselves. Good ethical reasoning demands that I try to see and feel myself as the other person, and the fact that I am really not the other fellow and he is really not me is not germane to the moral argument.[16]

Reversibility also helps ensure that we maintain the equality of all persons under moral consideration, their interests, and, in particular, the equal value of their lives. This is fundamental to Jewish ethics. Both reversibility and equality are expressed by the axiomatic talmudic principle, "Who can say that your blood is redder than his? Perhaps his blood is redder than yours,"[17] which governs Jewish ethics regarding sacrificing one life for another.

However Rabbi Auerbach and some others did permit a Jew in the Diaspora to be a heart recipient from a brain-dead donor while they forbade him from being a donor.[18] Rabbi Auerbach's reasoning is based on the specific halakhic parameters of the prohibition against a Jew inducing gentile doctors to commit bloodshed (*lifnei iver*) compared to inducing a Jew to commit

16. Moral imagination and reversibility are also the essential import of the rabbinic maxims "Do not judge another until you stand in his place," and "Let your fellow's *honor* be as dear to you as your own," and "Let your fellow's *money* be as dear to you as your own." (*Mishna Avot* 2:5,15,16) These adages demand that we imagine ourselves as the other. As we saw, these characteristics are also prominent in the stinging rhetorical question asked in *Ketuvot* 23a: "If these were your daughters would you have spoken of them so lightly?"

17. BT *Sanhedrin* 74a.

18. Shlomo Zalman Auerbach, *Minḥat Shlomo*, II, Section 86, letter of 17 *Adar* 5753 (1993).

that crime.[19] If the former prohibition is not as strong as the latter, then the great counterbalancing good of saving the recipient's life tips the scales toward permission to be a recipient.

The question before us is not whether RBND is correct *qua halakhah*, but whether it is ethical.[20] This RBND reasoning appears to be logically inconsistent and hence morally invalid in two ways. As we saw, Rabbi Auerbach was aware that Israeli doctors *will* perform the transplant (and hence possibly commit murder) even when a specific person refuses to be a recipient. Yet he correctly considered this to be irrelevant to the permissibility of being a recipient. His concern was focused on the individual illicit act of extracting the heart for the specific recipient and the causal role that the recipient would play in that crime. He thus ruled it was forbidden for that person to be a recipient. Again, this is consistent with the counterfactual generalization: If everyone *would* follow his rule (and refused to be a recipient), the donor's blood *would not* be shed.

The proposed argument RBND does not proceed similarly regarding Diaspora transplants. There the governing consideration appears to be the *factual* situation that the doctors *will* remove the heart anyway for another waiting recipient, a fact that serves

19. It does not appear that R. Auerbach's argument rests in principle on whether or not the organ donor is a Jew. As far as I have been able to tell, he mentions only once in passing that the majority of patients in the Diaspora are gentiles, and never specifies that this is an essential requirement. His argument turns on the operating doctors being gentile, since the critical issue for him is *lifnei iver*. An important point in R. Auerbach's halakhic argument is the assumption that the majority of doctors in the Diaspora are gentiles and hence one may assume in any given transplant procedure in the Diaspora that the sinning doctors are gentiles. If his ruling is followed consistently, however, *de facto* the donor pool would be restricted to gentiles.

20. Unlike ethical principles, legal judgments need not conform to the generalizability criterion to be valid law, since they apply (implicitly) to specific jurisdictions only. For example "It is illegal for two people of the same sex to marry" is location-specific – true in some jurisdictions and not in others – and therefore not generalizable. The moral claim, "One ought not to marry someone of the same sex" as a valid moral judgment would apply universally. See Hare 36.

as a permitting factor.[21] This violates moral logic's requirement to consider the counterfactual consequences of generalizing his principle, i.e., "If everyone would refuse to be a recipient, the donor would not be murdered," and it is this violation that renders this reasoning morally fallacious. The converse also illustrates this: "If everyone would refuse to be a donor (like me), I could not be a recipient." In conclusion, if it is wrong for me to be a donor, it is wrong for me to be a recipient.

The second logical fallacy is related to the first. The defense of RBND is often phrased as, "why shouldn't the potential recipient be saved by the transplant after the heart has been removed by others, even if the extraction was done unethically? It is not always wrong to benefit from unjust gains."[22] This, however, is an inaccurate description of what actually takes place. The RBND argument fails because it ignores the critical fact that each heart extraction is recipient-specific: The doctor removes the heart only after the particular recipient consents to receive it and for the explicit purpose of implanting it into that one recipient. Hence the causal connection between the recipient and

21. Jerusalem Talmud, *Terumot* 8:10 depicts a morally analogous situation in which the only way many people of a town can save their own lives is to deliver a specific person to killers and therefore facilitate his death. Many rabbinic authorities like Maimonides (MT, Fundamental Laws of Torah 5:5), David Ben Shmuel of Lwow (Taz, commentary on *Shulhan Arukh, Yoreh De`ah* 157:1), and Yoel Sirkes (Baḥ, *ad loc*) forbid being an accomplice in anyway of the death of any innocent person, even though he will die anyway and sacrificing him will save many other lives. The fact that the individual will die anyway is legally (and morally) irrelevant for them. There are dissenting rabbinic opinions (e.g. Menahem ha-Meiri, commentary on *Sanhedrin* 72b) that permit facilitating the death of the innocent to save many lives in this instance. However, if one relies on those opinions to justify being a recipient, consistency would demand that those opinions should be used also to justify being a donor. Either way RBND remains inconsistent.

22. This constitutes part of the justification of RBND in the cited 2010 RCA report on definition of death and organ transplantation: "All agreed that even if an organ was removed *b'issur* [illicitly], it still may be used. Thus there is no merit in arguments that various *talmidei ḥakhamim* have supported organ donation since we find them permitting receiving such organs." (47) Note the explicit rejection of moral logic.

the heart extraction is explicit and definite. The removal of the heart is done *for the specific recipient upon his willingness to receive it* and hence the recipient is an essential participant in the extraction process. The claim that the recipient is not a material cause of removing the heart is contrary to the facts.[23] Because of this strong causal connection, if the removal of the heart entails possible murder, the recipient is an indirect agent of that murder.

In Rabbi Auerbach's analysis, the conclusions differ regarding the cases in Israel and the Diaspora, despite the fact that the relevant empirical facts and the transplant procedures are identical in Israel and the Diaspora. It is difficult to see how the differing religious identities of the operating doctors are morally relevant, since the ethical prohibitions against murder and bloodshed are identical for both Jews and gentiles.[24] Specifically, the religious identities of the doctors performing the transplant are irrelevant to the ethics of receiving and donating. If in Israel the recipient

23. This is unlike transplanting an organ drawn from an organ bank, which is not recipient-specific. An organ bank organ is removed before a recipient is identified, after which it is held in the bank until a single recipient out of numerous possible recipients is selected. Hence the actual recipient is not a material cause of the act of removing that specific organ.

24. This is true in both philosophical and Jewish ethics. In rabbinic ethics, the prohibition against bloodshed is found in Gen. 9:6, and applies to all human beings without discrimination. Similarly, the prohibition against bloodshed is grounded in Noahide law that applies to all human beings (see Maimonides, MT, *The Laws of Kings and their Wars,* 9:1). This is reiterated for Jews in Sinaitic revelation described in Ex. 20:13. The fact that the punishment for a Jew committing homicide against a gentile may not be identical to the punishment for homicide against a fellow Jew for technical reasons, this indicates nothing about the severity of the prohibition in Jewish law. On this point see *Mekhilta* on Exodus 21:14: "Issi b. Akiva states: Prior to the giving of the Torah, we were enjoined with respect to bloodshed [via Noahide prohibition against homicide]. After the giving of the Torah, instead of [this obligation] becoming more rigorous, [is it conceivable] that it became less so?" The Talmud (BT *Hullin* 33a, *Sanhedrin* 59a) demands that this is not merely a general attitude but a definitive legal principle to be applied in specific situations, asking rhetorically: "Is there anything which is permitted to the Jew but prohibited to a gentile?" In Jewish law, Jews have a greater obligation than gentiles to avoid murder and to preserve human life, but RBND augurs for the very opposite: As a recipient, Jew may participate in the bloodshed of the donor, yet may not be a donor to contribute to saving another's life.

is a causal agent and hence an accomplice in the murder of the donor, the recipient bears the same liability in the Diaspora.[25] Once again the argument permitting heart receptions in the Diaspora when agreeing that it entails possibly murdering the donor fails the generalization test that is necessary for all valid moral principles.

It is obvious why Rabbi Auerbach (and others who rule like him) seize on legal distinctions to allow organ reception even while they forbid heart donations. They do so because they have the noble goal of saving the potential recipient's life. However, both rational ethics and classic Jewish moral principles insist that it is unethical to purchase one's life with the death of someone else – even indirectly. Because no person's blood is redder than another's, such action is morally unjustifiable.[26] And if we assume that it is permissible to sacrifice the life of a moribund brain-dead person to save the life of another who could be restored to health via a transplant, then this must be the case both when I am the recipient and when I am the donor. In other words, if it is permissible for me to receive a heart under those circumstances, it must be permissible for me to be a donor under those circumstances.

Of course, the RBND argument would be logically consistent were one to claim that that "Jewish blood was redder than gentile blood" and therefore one may be an active accomplice in killing a gentile to save a Jewish life. However, Rabbi Auerbach

25. The failure to properly generalize principles is common and frequently not caused by malice, but by limited moral imagination and the inability to empathize equally with all persons, whether Jew or gentile.

26. This is the ruling in the paradigmatic talmudic case (BT Sanhedrin 74a) where one life is set against another, which is morally analogous to our transplant scenario: If gunman A tells me to kill B or he will kill me, I cannot justify my killing B with the utilitarian argument that one person will die in any event and my life should have priority. It is *my* agency in the killing that is strictly forbidden and *I* may not kill him even to save my life. Importantly for our transplant case in which it is the doctors who actually commit the crime not the recipient, according to halakhah, I am similarly prohibited from enlisting others to kill B for me. (See Maimonides, MT, *Laws of Murder* 2:2–3).

never claims this. Quite the contrary: He states explicitly that it is forbidden to shed the blood of gentiles. The racial hypothesis may be formally (i.e. logically) consistent in itself, but it is objectionable on substantive moral grounds and should be forcefully rejected. Jews have suffered more than any other people from racial doctrines and know well the heinous ethical horrors resulting from such racial discrimination.[27]

As we saw in Chapter Two, the equality of human life and the values of fairness and impartiality are fundamental to our moral thinking. This is why if we assume that heart transplants constitute possible murder, *there is no legal technicality or casuistic distinction that can succeed in justifying permitting a person to receive an organ while he refuses on principle to donate.* If I am alive as a potential donor when I am brain-dead and this is the reason I refuse others to remove my heart, then another brain-dead person is equally alive when I need his heart, and it is unethical for me to play a role in his death by participating in the removal of his heart. Such action violates the reversibility and moral consistency tests, asserting that transplants are wrong when I am a donor and another is the recipient, but right when I am a recipient and another is the donor. RBND extends an unfair privileged position to me over others when I am a recipient, one which it does not extend to them when I am a donor. As such, RBND reasoning is ethically illogical and unprincipled, and if someone acts upon it, his actions are immoral.

27. No normative talmudic or halakhic source supports this position. Even *M. Horiyot* (3:7), which depicts the triage situation where many are in peril and only some can be saved and which forces a choice between saving either a man or woman, allows the preference to save one person over the other only when such action does not entail *active and direct intervention* that raises the chances of the non-saved dying. It is the tragic conditions of the status quo that cause the death, not any active behavior of the choosing third party. This distinction between active intervention to save a person and passive non-action that allows a person to die is critical to both Jewish law and rational ethics.

III. IMMORAL CONDUCT AND DESECRATION OF GOD'S NAME

I have argued that RBND is contrary to correct moral reasoning and hence ethically unjustifiable. Whether or not the fallacies of RBND reasoning are sufficient to discredit it as valid *halakhah* is for halakhic authorities to decide. The debate between natural law theorists and legal positivists regarding whether there can be an immoral *halakhah* is complex and need not be repeated here. Certainly there is much evidence in the Torah, the Talmud, and post-talmudic rabbinic opinion indicating that *halakhah* must be consistent with justice and morality and cannot violate what is morally right. This position insists that if a particular halakhic opinion contravenes moral norms, it is *ipso facto* non-normative. Here we do well to note again the words of R. Abraham Ha-Kohen Kook:

> It is forbidden for religious behavior to compromise a person's natural moral sensibility. If it does, then our *yirat shamayim* ["fear of Heaven"] is no longer pure. An indication of its purity is that our natural moral sense becomes more exalted as a consequence of religious inspiration. But if the opposite occurs, and the moral character of an individual or a group is diminished by our religious observance, then we are certainly mistaken in our path. This type of supposed "fear of heaven" is incorrect (*p'sulah*).[28]

Nevertheless, others argue that Jewish law is based solely on internal halakhic logic and therefore it remains unaffected by moral requirements. For the sake of this discussion, let us assume this is true and that *halakhah* can be at variance with moral ideals. In many instances, the Torah and Jewish law do

28. Abraham Isaac Kook. *Orot Ha-kodesh*. Chapter Two also presents many classic Jewish sources as evidence for the halakhic non-normativity of immoral claims.

not legislate perfect behavior, only permitted action.[29] R. Joseph Soloveitchik frequently expressed this by saying that "*halakhah* establishes a floor (i.e. the minimum acceptable behavior), not a ceiling (i.e. the ideal)." But RBND poses an even greater problem, as it attempts to permit not what is merely imperfect, but what is morally wrong. If this is so, the important question regarding organ donations is whether RBND as *halakhah* is the proper religious course for Jews to follow, rather than another halakhic opinion that is more consistent with moral principles (e.g. either refusing both to donate and receive organs or agreeing both to donate and receive).

As explained in the earlier chapters, the Talmud acknowledges that correct Jewish behavior sometimes must transcend formal *halakhah*. This is the concept of *lifnim m'shurat ha-din* – going beyond what the formal law allows. Talmudic authorities considered acting beyond the law to be an absolute necessity for the Jewish people and that because the leaders of Second Temple Jewish society were guided narrowly by law and were oblivious to ethical values,[30] Jerusalem was drowned in blood from one end to the other and the Jewish people were sold into slavery. We also saw that the great medieval rabbinic authorities insisted on the religious need for Jews to hew closely to ethical standards. Naḥmanides advocated acting beyond formal *halakhah* and urged Jews to sometimes separate themselves from what is halakhically permitted. Without this extra-legal commitment, one cannot lead a holy life and might become "a loathsome person within the bounds of the Torah."[31] Maimonides, too,

29. For example, Rabbi Shlomo Yitzhak (Rashi) conceded that the Torah law permitting a woman war captive (Deut. 21:12–13) is not the ethical ideal but represents a concession to the soldiers' "evil inclination."

30. BT, *Baba Metsi'a* 30b. See also the comments of R. Naftali Zvi Yehuda Berlin (Netsiv) on this tragedy in his *Ha-Emeq Davar*, introduction to Book of Genesis. There he asserted that "God could not tolerate the 'righteous' people during the Second Temple era who complied with the law but were intolerant of others."

31. See Naḥmanides commentaries on Lev. 19:2 and Deut 6:17.

recognized the need to act beyond the requirements of formal *halakhah,* claiming that without a commitment to fundamental ethical standards, Jewish behavior would degenerate into pagan immorality and desecrate God's name.[32]

And certainly the Palestinian Talmud (*Baba Metsi'a* 2:5; 8c) makes this point most forcefully in recording the remarkable story of Shimon ben Shetaḥ that we analyzed in Chapter Two. This rabbinic sage demanded that his students return the lost jewel of the pagan, even though Jewish law allowed him to keep it. He recognized the necessity of acting according to ethical values beyond what the strict *halakhah* demands.

Not only is actual immoral behavior condemned by the talmudic Sages, but they even insisted that the *mere appearance* of unethical behavior by religious Jews was a great sin that profanes God's Name:

> What constitutes profanation of God's Name (*ḥillul ha-Shem*)? Rav said: If, for example I take meat from the butcher and do not pay him immediately. . . .
>
> If someone studies Bible and Mishnah, and attends on the disciples of the wise, is honest in business and speaks pleasantly to persons, what do people then say concerning him? "Happy is the father who taught him Torah, happy is the teacher who taught him Torah; woe unto people who have not studied the Torah; for this man has studied the Torah look how fine his ways are, how righteous his deeds!"
>
> But if someone studies Scripture and Mishnah, attends on the disciples of the wise, but is dishonest and discourteous in his relations with people, what do people say about him? "Woe unto him who studied the Torah; woe unto his father who taught him Torah; woe unto his teacher who taught him Torah!" This man studied the Torah: Look, how corrupt are his deeds, how ugly his ways. (BT, *Yoma* 86a)

32. MT, Fundamental Laws of the Torah 5:11, and Laws of Servants 9:8.

All these talmudic and rabbinic texts argue strongly that Jews need to refrain from acting contrary to ethical values because such behavior is wrong intrinsically. The stakes are very high in both Jewish moral integrity and religious purpose. Jewish behavior inevitably leads Jews and gentiles alike to judge the God of Israel and His Torah: When Jews behave ethically, the Name of God is sanctified and blessed. When Jewish behavior is immoral – or even perceived as immoral by others – the Name of God and the Torah of Israel are profaned.

The double Jewish commitment to *halakhah* and ethics is commanded by the biblical imperative that requires Jews to behave according to the demands of *halakhah* as well as ethical standards: "You shall do what is right and good in the eyes of the Lord." (Deut. 6:18) This is not simply a reiteration of halakhic obligations, but a divine command for Jews to act beyond the limits of the law.[33]

IV. "A WISE AND DISCERNING PEOPLE?" THE CONSEQUENCES OF ADOPTING RBND

I have tried to demonstrate that RBND violates the canons of moral logic and is unethical *per se*. In addition to its intrinsically immoral character, prudent Jews must consider the probable unacceptable consequences a policy of RBND would bring.

Were RBND to become policy in Israel, transplants of all vital organs except kidneys would cease. According to the National Israeli Center for Organ Transplants of the Israeli Health Ministry (ADI), between 2009 and 2019, there were 2,588 vital organ transplants from non-living donors performed in Israel.[34] According to the logic of RBND, any non-trivial medical procedure

33. This is how Naḥmanides understood this *mitsvah*. See his commentary on this verse as well as on Exodus 15:26.

34. https://www.health.gov.il/Subjects/Organ_transplant/transplant/Documents/Hashtala_ old_EN.pdf, accessed on February 5, 2020.

on a brain-dead person is forbidden, since according to *halakhah* moving a moribund person hastens the death process, which also constitutes illicit bloodshed. Thus according to RBND, it is not only hearts and lungs that are forbidden to be removed from brain-dead persons, removing any organ whatsoever is forbidden. It is important to note that importing transplant organs into Israel is not an option since the European Network of Organ Sharing does not share its organs with Israel precisely because Israel does not have enough donated organs to contribute for transplantation elsewhere. Israel is known as "a parasitic country" regarding organ sharing since Israelis seek but cannot supply organs, and as a result no foreign organs have been donated to Israel since 2011. This odious reputation is the direct result of an almost *de facto* national RBND policy. Implementing RBND as a formal policy would severely worsen this problem.

Due to the critical shortage of vital organs available for transplantation in Israel, in 2008 more than 900 Israelis waited unsuccessfully for vital organ transplants from non-live donors. In 2009 more than 1,060 waited, and in 2010 more than 1,100 waited to no avail. The majority of these patients died for lack of the needed organ. In 2018, only 70 successful life-saving heart and lung transplants were performed and in 2019 there were 73 such transplants. As indicated, between 2009 and 2019 there were 2,588 transplants of organs in Israel from non-live donors, and a policy of RBND would eliminate the possibility of most of these transplant procedures. This would result in more than 200 Israelis dying each year from the lack of available donated organs.[35]

These deaths are a price that Israelis, the Israeli medical establishment, the Israeli government and the Chief Rabbinate are not willing to pay.[36] The moral and social pressure to save

35. *Ibid.*

36. The Chief Rabbinate accepted the permissibility of donating and receiving

these lives is enormous, and numerous Israeli organizations now broadly publicize the need for life-saving organs as well as the social value and virtue of donating organs.[37] If RBND becomes the operative halakhic standard, it will be ignored and disdained by most Israelis, further estranging *halakhah* from Israeli life. Nor can one criticize those who reject RBND in Israel: How many of us would refuse a life-saving transplant for our son or our daughter? No one who has had a loved one saved by an organ transplant fails to see the ethical good of this medical option. Indeed, the very fact that so few of us are prepared to refuse receiving a heart when our lives or the lives of our sons and daughters are at stake demonstrates that refusal to donate is unethical.

In the Diaspora, RBND's logic does not preclude Jews in theory from receiving vital organs from other Jews. Should RBND become Jewish policy, however, the *de facto* reality would emerge that Jews would receive organs from gentiles only. In today's culture of near instantaneous and pervasive communications, it is impossible today to hide any controversial opinion from the public. As a result, it is certain that RBND will become widely known as a Jewish racial policy. Not only do hundreds of Orthodox rabbis, millions of laymen, the entire medical community and professional ethicists see RBND as morally untenable, nearly all people with a commitment to fairness and equality do. The public will see Jews – more specifically religious Jews – as willing to take organs from gentiles but unwilling to donate their organs toward saving gentile lives. RBND will lead to widespread beliefs that Jews are unethical opportunists who value Jewish life more than a non-Jewish life and who are willing to be accomplices in murdering gentiles (by their own reasoning) in order to save

organs in 1986. In fairness to RBND advocates using R. Auerbach's logic, it is important to state that they are willing to pay this heavy price in Israel.

37. e.g., Halachic Organ Donor Society (HODS), Israeli Ministry of Health, and National Israeli Center for Transplantation (ADI).

their own lives. It is inevitable that the reputation of *halakhah* and religious Jews will be blackened. At best, Jewish law and religious Jews will be seen as foolish; at worst they will be judged to be immoral hypocrites. It is hard to imagine a greater badge of shame for Jews and Judaism than this perception by gentiles and Jews alike.

In addition to the public repugnance and potential discrimination against those adopting RBND, this perception will surely produce a *ḥilul ha-Shem* – the public desecration of God's Name – and a desecration of the Torah and the Jewish people. Thus we arrive at a tragic paradox: Jewish law requires Jews to sacrifice their own lives rather than to participate in the murder of another. Such sacrifice constitutes "the sanctification of God's Name." Yet adopting RBND will lead not to the public sanctification of God's Name, but the very opposite, its desecration.

Eight hundred years ago Maimonides saw the terrible effects of Jews interpreting Torah irrationally and immorally. His words are both prophetic and alarming when we apply them to the idea of Jews following RBND today: "Those who interpret Torah in an obviously irrational way cause others to say, 'surely this is a foolish and despicable people,' instead of the Torah's ideal of causing others to judge Jews as 'wise and discerning people.'" [38]

In contrast to this deplorable situation, human wisdom, moral integrity and prudent policy all dictate that RBND be rejected. If so, many precious lives will be saved, the integrity of Torah safeguarded and people will again be able to echo the Torah ideal espoused in BT, *Yoma*: "How pleasant are the ways of people who study Torah and how sweet are their actions."

38. Introduction to Mishna, Chapter *Ḥelek*, pt. 2. Maimonides' statement is a play on the original Hebrew of Deut. 4:5–6. As indicated, instead of the Bible's, *am ḥakham v'navon* ("a wise and discerning people"), Maimonides used *am sakhal v'naval* – "a foolish and despicable people." See Chapter Two.

V. POSTSCRIPT: A FLIGHT FROM REASON?

The opinion forbidding organ donation while permitting their reception violates fundamental morality and ethical reason. It also points to a larger dangerous trend in religious life today. Because the near unanimous consensus of medical authorities is that brain death is clinical death from which there is no return and therefore is the appropriate definition of death, RBND represents a rejection of both moral and scientific reason. In effect, RBND presents us with a Torah and *halakhah* that are divorced from rational judgment.

As we saw in Chapter Three, Maimonides understood the Divine Image (*Tselem Elokim*) with which God endowed all persons to be the human capacity for scientific and philosophical reason.[39] For him, the rejection of reason was a denial of the Image of God and he urged all people to realize their highest human potential by exercising their rational faculties. A more modern rabbinic authority, R. Meir Simcḥa Ha-Kohen of Dvinsk, believed that the Divine Image is found in people's innate moral sensibilities.[40] For both these rabbis, denying reason causes human beings to separate themselves from God, holiness and their uniquely human character.

Tragically, immoral behavior committed in the name of religion is commonplace today. Many religious people around the world have freed their ideas from reason and their behavior from moral restraints, and as we shall see in the succeeding chapters the inevitable result is violence and extremism. During the COVID pandemic of 2020 and 2021, some religious Jews refused to acknowledge scientific evidence and advice based on proven cause and effect conclusions – with tragic and deadly consequences. Jews should resist the temptation to follow this path.

39. *Guide of the Perplexed*, I:1 and III:54.
40. *Meshekh Ḥokhmah*, commentary on Genesis 1:26.

Near the end of the Holocaust and in another context, R. Joseph Soloveitchik pointed out the terrible historical consequences of rejecting reason, and warned against adopting this trend in the future:

> The individual who frees himself from the rational principle and who casts off the yoke of objective thought will in the end turn destructive and lay waste to the entire created order . . . Therefore religion should ally itself with the forces of clear logical cognition uniquely exemplified by the scientific method.[41]

Jews today would do well to follow his advice.

41. *Halakhic Man. op. cit.* note 4, 141.

Chapter Seven

The Open Torah of Maimonides

> *"The issue of negative blessings is no small matter. In many ways, these blessings represent three areas that distinguish Open Orthodoxy – our attitude toward the gentile, the most vulnerable and women. For many people, articulating them in the negative sends a wrong message – that we don't care about them."*[1] *(Rabbi Avraham Weiss)*

In the last few years, a new term has emerged in America: "Open Orthodoxy." It refers to Orthodox Jews who have been touched by modern values and who strive to relate to all of God's children with sensitivity, ethical integrity and religious meaning.

The ideas of Open Orthodoxy have stimulated intense debate regarding whether they are part of authentic Jewish tradition and Orthodox thinking: Is the vision of Open Orthodoxy a new phenomenon that has broken away from a legitimate Orthodox understanding of Torah, *mitsvot* and *halakhah*? Some claim this is so, yet Maimonides, the greatest religious thinker and master

1. "*Shelo Asani Ishah*: An Orthodox Rabbi Reflects on Integrity, Continuity and Inclusivity." In *Conversations*, Autumn, 2013. (New York: Institute for Jewish Ideas and Ideals, 2013), 156. The Three blessings are: "Blessed are You, Lord our God, King of the Universe, who has not made me a heathen," "Blessed are You, Lord our God, King of the Universe, who has not made me a slave," and "Blessed are You, Lord our God, King of the Universe, who has not made me a woman," all of which are recited daily by traditional Jews in the morning liturgy.

of *halakhah* in all Jewish history, espoused a conception of Torah and religious life that mirrors some of the same values of Open Orthodoxy. Rambam believed that living God's Torah correctly demands that Jews relate to every human being with dignity, compassion and *ḥesed*. Rambam's spiritual universe includes all people – Jews and gentiles, men and women, the free and those trapped in servitude.

I. MAIMONIDES AND SLAVERY

Rambam's inspirational spiritual message on this point is found not in his philosophic opus, *Guide of the Perplexed*, but in his halakhic code, *Mishneh Torah* (MT). It appears in The Laws of Servants *(Hilkhot Avadim)* Chapter Nine, section 8. I consider it the most beautiful passage in that magisterial work:

> It is permissible to work a gentile servant harshly. Even though this is the law, the attribute of piety (*midat ḥasidut*) and the ways of wisdom (*darkhei ḥokhmah*) dictate that a person be compassionate and pursue justice, not make his slaves carry a heavy yoke, nor cause them distress. He should allow them to partake of all the food and drink he serves. This was the practice of the sages of the first generations to give their slaves from every dish of which they themselves would partake. And they would provide food for their animals and slaves before partaking of their own meals. And so, it is written (Psalms 123:2): "As the eyes of slaves to their master's hand, and like the eyes of a maid-servant to her mistress' hand, so are our eyes to God."
>
> Thus we should not embarrass a servant by our deeds or with words, for the Torah gave them over for service, not for humiliation. Nor should one shout or vent anger upon them. Rather, one should speak to them gently and listen to their claims. This is explicitly stated with regard to the good paths of Job for which he was praised (Job 31:13–15): "Have I ever shunned justice for my slave and maid-servant when they quarreled with me. . . . Did

> not He who made me in the belly make him? Was it not the One who prepared us in the womb?"
>
> "Cruelty and arrogance are found only among idol-worshipping gentiles. By contrast, the descendants of Abraham our patriarch, the Jews, whom the Holy One, blessed be He, influenced via the goodness of the Torah and commanded to observe "righteous laws and rules," they are compassionate to all.
>
> "Similarly, with regard to the attributes of the Holy One, blessed be He, which He commanded us to emulate, it is written (Psalms 145:9): "His compassion is upon all of His works." And whoever shows compassion to others will in turn be showered with compassion, as it is written (Deut. 13:18): "He will show you compassion, and be compassionate to you and multiply you."

This placement of this passage in MT is not arbitrary. Maimonides scholars have noted that Rambam systematically places the most important message of each book of the MT in the book's final passage.[2] These messages are each book's philosophic summation, its spiritual lodestar, and it is each of these last sweeping teachings that Rambam wants the reader to remember when he closes each book of the halakhic code. This passage from *Hilkhot Avadim* is an instance of this technique, appearing as the very last section of the Book of Acquisition (*Sefer Qinyan*).

The passage is a guide for the Jew attempting to nurture a sensitive religious personality and lead a spiritual life. It makes three basic points that are essential to Torah values and religious philosophy, and I would like to analyze closely the entire passage for its power, nuance and message. As is well known, the Torah significantly ameliorated the ancient institution of slavery and

2. See Isadore Twersky, *Introduction to the Code of Maimonides (Mishneh Torah)* (New Haven, CT: Yale U, 1980), 371–373 and Kellner, Menachem and Gillis, David. *Maimonides the Universalist: The Ethical Horizons of the Mishneh Torah*. (London: Littman Library of Jewish Civilization, 2020). For other examples of significant perorations in MT, see final passages of Book of Knowledge (*Sefer Mada*), Book of Seasons *(Sefer Zemanim)* and Book of Judges (*Sefer Shoftim)*.

decreed that a Jewish master must free his slaves after six years of service (Ex. 21:2). It also limited the duration and type of work that a Jewish master may order a slave to perform.[3] Both limitations serve to preserve the slave's intrinsic dignity. Through these legal and moral restrictions, the Torah transformed the ancient institution to make it more similar to a system of indentured servitude rather than to the institution of slavery in antiquity in which the master owned the slave's body and the slave had no rights.

Yet the Torah is explicit that these humanizing limitations apply with reference to a Jewish servant (*eved ivri)* and not a gentile slave (*eved kana'ani*) serving a Jewish master. The same passages that limit the permitted duration and workload of the Jewish servant, explicitly remove these limitations from gentile servitude. This is codified *halakhah* over which there is no debate. A Jewish master does not free his gentile slaves in the seventh year and he is legally free to work them as harshly (*b'farekh*) as he wishes.

II. HALAKHIC FLOORS AND ETHICAL CEILINGS

Rather than restrict himself to the strict legal definition of gentile slavery as one would think in this halakhic work, Maimonides opens this passage by overriding the halakhic standard and asserting forcefully, "Even though this is the law, the attribute of piety and the way of wisdom dictate that a person be merciful and pursue justice, not make his slaves carry a heavy yoke, nor cause them distress." Here Rambam declares that there are two levels of behavioral norms for the religious Jew: the strict *halakhah* (*din*) in contrast to the ethical demands of piety (*ḥasidut)* and wisdom (*ḥokhmah*) – stressing that the latter are no less

3. Lev 25:44 forbids working an *eved ivri* harshly (*b'farekh*). Rabbinic tradition defined harsh labor in specific terms in Sifra, *Behar*, Ch. 6, *halakhot* 2–3. Rambam repeated this delineation in *Hilkhot Avadim* 1:6–7.

imperative for Torah Jews. Crucially, Rambam insists that it is the meta-halakhic ethical value that defines the religious ideal.

According to Rambam the strict *halakhah* governing the practice of gentile slavery falls below the acceptable minimal standard for a pious Jew. How serious is the failing when a Jew follows the strict parameters of *din* exclusively and neglects super-legal kindness (*midat ḥasidut*),[4] practical wisdom (*darkhei ḥokhmah*) and basic fairness (*tsedeq*) when relating to other people? Rambam's language is extreme, shocking the reader who is used to Maimonides' otherwise moderate and balanced style throughout MT: "Cruelty [i.e. the absence of *ḥesed*] and arrogance are found only among idol-worshippers." No matter how "halakhic," acting without *ḥesed* toward others, removes a Jew from the community of the pious and places him in the community of immoral idolators. Nor is this mere hyperbolic rhetoric: Rambam ruled that a Jew who is cruel, hates others or who lacks compassion toward another person, is suspect and that his Jewish lineage should be investigated.[5]

Rambam's insistence on the insufficiency of strict halakhic obedience for Jewish behavior is the normative rabbinic view, shared by others from the Talmud through the Middle Ages. For *Ḥazal*, it was exclusive compliance of narrow halakhic standards that led to the destruction of the Second Temple;[6] as we saw in Chapter Two, according to the first century talmudic sage, Shimon ben Shetaḥ, myopic concern for the letter of the *halakhah* yields barbaric behavior,[7] and for Naḥmanides in medieval times,

4. *Ḥesed* is frequently associated conceptually and in actual cases with *lifnim m'shurat hadin*, i.e. acting beyond the strict requirement of *halakhah*. See Eugene Korn, "*Legal Floors and Moral Ceilings: A Jewish Understanding of Law and Ethics.*" *The Edah Journal* 2:2, Tammuz 5762 at https://library.yctorah.org/files/2016/09/Legal-Floors-and-Moral-Ceilings-A-Jewish-Understanding-Of-Law-and-Ethics.pdf. Accessed on February 18, 2020.

5. MT, Laws of Forbidden Relations 19:17.

6. BT, *Baba Metsi'a* 30b.

7. JT, *Baba Metsi'a* 2:5; 8c.

narrow minded pan-legalism produces a Jew who is "a loathsome person within the domain of Torah."[8] While it is commonplace to hear some religious Jews today defining Torah as a pan-halakhic system and claiming that *halakhah* defines all Jewish values, clearly Rambam disagrees – and vehemently so. For him, there are essential religious values outside of strict *halakhah*, and when a Jew ignores these values he fails miserably to live a correct Torah life.

Furthermore, Rambam uses the phrase "righteous laws and rules" (*ḥukim u'mishpatim tsadiqim*) from Deuteronomy 4:8: "What great nation has laws and rules (*ḥukim u'mishpatim tsadiqim*) as perfect as all this Teaching that I set before you this day?" As Maimonides emphasizes in *Guide of the Perplexed*, this verse refers to the universal moral behavior of Israel that even the nations of the world will understand, not particularist *halakhah* meant only for Israel.

III. MAIMONIDES ON HUMANITY

The second major thesis in Rambam's passage is that Jews are members of universal humanity. For Maimonides there is no genetic or ontological difference between Jews and gentiles. He insists that all humans are identical in their essence. Jews and gentiles *are* different, but it is only the influence of Torah teachings and values that separates Jews from gentiles, not any innate or genetic property: "By contrast [to gentiles], the descendants of Abraham our patriarch, [and his descendants, who are] Israel, whom the Holy One, blessed be He, influenced via the goodness of the Torah and commanded to observe righteous statutes and judgments, are merciful to all."

Rambam participated vigorously in the philosophical debate that began in the Middle Ages and that continues in some Jewish

8. Commentary on Lev. 19:2.

circles today:[9] Is there a common humanity, or are Jews fundamentally different from gentiles? Rambam is unambiguous and consistent, writing repeatedly throughout his many works that Jews and gentiles share the same defining human characteristics and are part of the same humanity.[10] For Rambam, what differentiates Jews from gentiles is "software" acquired by learning Torah, not any inherited genetic or spiritual "hardware."[11] As quoted above, Rambam poignantly cites Job to drive home this point: "Did not He who made me in the belly make him? Was it not the One who prepared us in the womb?" Maimonides' citation of Job reflects Rambam's conceptual elegance and reinforces this point: In rabbinic tradition there is no consensus regarding whether Job is Jew or gentile, a historical personality or merely a literary *personna*. Job is everyman, the prototypical universal figure of humanity.[12] For both Job and Rambam, we are all children of the same universal God of Heaven and Earth who creates Jews and gentiles the same way in the same womb.

9. The most famous advocates of the idea that Jews are ontologically different from gentiles are Yehuda Halevi, who maintained that even after gentiles convert to Judaism, they remain spiritually inferior to Jews, and the authors of the Zohar and the Tanya, who maintained that gentiles possess only an "animal soul" (*nefesh behamit*) while Jews also possess an additional "divine soul" (*nefesh Elokit*). Shockingly, it is common today to hear even *roshei yeshiva* in rationalist Lithuanian *yeshivot* espouse this mystical non-rational claim.

10. See MT, Laws of Shmitah and Jubilee, 13:13, Laws of Kings 8:11. Maimonides, *Guide of the Perplexed*, 1:1, and *Letter to Ovadiah the Proselyte*. In Shilat, Ya'akov, *Iggerot ha-Rambam* (Jerusalem: Ma'aliyot, 1988) Vol. 1, 231–241. Also "Eight Chapters" in *The Ethical Writings of Maimonides,* edited by Raymond L. Weiss, (NY: Dover 1983). For a fuller treatment of this thesis, see Menachem Kellner, *Maimonides on Judaism and the Jewish People* (Albany NY: SUNY Press, 1991), particularly Chs. 4–6, 10, and Kellner and Gillis, op. cit., Ch. 12.

11. This accurate metaphor of software/hardware was coined by Prof. Daniel Lasker.

12. The talmudic rabbis (B.T. *Baba Batra* 15a/b) disagree whether Job is Jewish or gentile, fact or fiction. According to Maimonides, Job may be only a literary personality (*Guide of the Perplexed* III: 22) or a gentile –"Epistle to Yemen," in *Epistles of Maimonides: Crisis and Leadership*, translated by Abraham Halkin (Jerusalem: Jewish Publication Society, 1985), 110–112. I thank Menachem Kellner for pointing out these references to me.

The insistence that there are no intrinsic differences between Jews and gentiles is all to the glory and importance of the Torah. Were Jews ontologically different from gentiles, Jews would not need Torah to preserve their uniqueness and ensure their spiritual survival.[13] According to Rambam, Jewish identity is neither an ethnic nor a racial category. Jews are a spiritual and moral community shaped by the values of Torah. Again, some traditionalists today believe that Jews comprise a different species, that they have different DNA (be it physical or "spiritual") and that this essential difference justifies religious Jews closing themselves off to the rest of humanity – both gentiles as well as heterodox Jews. For religious, philosophic and communal reasons, Rambam could never have pursued this policy.

At times some Jews went to great lengths to "correct" Rambam's belief in Jews sharing humanity and a common human destiny with gentiles. Scholars know that there are varying manuscripts of MT. One instance of a textual variation that carries significant implications is the very last *halakhah* of MT (*The Laws of Kings and their Wars*, 12:5), the soaring crescendo of the entire work. Most of our printed texts read:

> In that time, there will be no hunger, nor war, nor jealousy, nor competition. Goodness will be greatly influential, and all good things will be as plentiful as dust. The entire world will be concerned only with the knowledge of God. Therefore in Israel there will be great sages who will know hidden matters and will achieve knowledge of their Creator as much as is within human ability, as it is said, "Knowledge of God will fill the earth just as water covers the sea (bed)." [Isaiah 11:9]

13. Rambam's insistence on no fundamental difference between Jews and gentiles is also sadly confirmed by how easily modern Jews assimilate into gentile culture and lose their Jewish identity in open pluralistic societies. Were the difference ontological, it would be immutable and ineradicable, and hence complete assimilation of an individual Jew to non-Jewish identity would be impossible.

However, all logical and bibliographical evidence indicates that this is a doctored version of Rambam's words. This version's ending limitation, that only Israel will have great sages who reach the apex of human wisdom about God, is manifestly inconsistent with the stunning universal vision ("The *entire world* will be concerned only with the knowledge of God.") that Rambam paints earlier in the passage. Hence it should be no surprise that all early reliable manuscripts indicate that Rambam never used the word "Israel" here.[14] Instead he wrote:

> Therefore there will be great sages who will know hidden matters and will achieve knowledge of their Creator as much as is within human ability, as it is said, "Knowledge of God will fill the earth just as water covers the sea (bed)."

Evidently a particularist Jew inserted the word "Israel," convinced that Maimonides could not have believed in a common humanity or universal spiritual destiny.[15] Yet Rambam did believe precisely that, as our passage in Laws of Servants indicates.

IV. *HESED* AND *RAHAMIM*

Rambam closes with the third important thesis. Here he teaches that that the defining and most crucial personality trait of a Torah Jew is *raḥamim* – empathetic compassion. If there is one essential characteristic of the faithful Jew, it is to be motivated by *raḥamim* that expresses itself in acts of *ḥesed* toward all people. As we saw in Chapter Two, *ḥesed / raḥamim* is one of the essential values of ethics. While having social, communal and moral implications, these virtues are nevertheless fundamentally religious and theological. For Rambam, the ultimate objective

14. See Yemenite manuscript and Yosef Kapiḥ edition of MT.

15. See Menachem Kellner, "*Farteitcht un Farbessert* – On Correcting Maimonides," *Meorot* 6:2 at http://www.yctorah.org/content/view/330/10. Accessed on February 18, 2020.

of the religious life is to come close to God, and we achieve this by cultivating a personality of kindness and empathy that opens us up to sensitive relations with all human beings. ("He has compassion on all his creatures.") The God-intoxicated Jew is a *raḥamim* personality who acts with unbounded *ḥesed* toward all God's creatures.

Because Rambam was a masterful pedagogue who knew his audience well, he was undoubtedly aware of how difficult it is for most people to act from the virtues of compassion and empathy alone. Most of the time people need the promise of tangible reward to motivate him/her to act properly, and so Rambam adds at the end of the passage, "And all who show compassion toward others, are in turn showered with compassion," in order to give each person the practical incentive to show lovingkindness and compassion to all other people.

If the purpose of commandments and halakhic duties is to draw Jews nearer to the Creator, then the test of successful halakhic obedience must be judged by the extent to which we are open to and compassionate toward all others – Jew and gentile, man and woman, superior and subordinate, free person or servant.[16] For Rambam, lack of compassion in a Torah Jew is impossible – a contradiction in terms[17] and the signal theological indication of a person's distance from his nurturing Creator.

In Rambam's eyes, closing oneself off to God's world and His creatures is simply not an option for the religious Jew. When we display empathy and openness, we approach the Divine, fulfill the ideal of *imitatio Dei* ("we are commanded to imitate all the attributes of the Holy One, Blessed Be He") and help bring God's

16. Chapter Two identifies the expansion of full considerations of *raḥamim* and justice (*tsedeq*) to women, heterodox Jews, gentiles and people with same sex orientations as one of the primary challenges for future Jewish ethics.

17. Maimonides was certainly not naïve, and he surely encountered Jews who did not act with compassion. In this passage he formulates this painful failure as impossible for pedagogical emphasis, in effect admonishing reader, "If you do not act with compassion toward all, you do not deserve to be called a Jew."

immanent presence to earth. This is the character of the ideal religious life, and as such it is an end in itself.[18]

V. FIDELITY TO TRADITION

The 20th philosopher Leo Strauss maintained that "genuine fidelity to a tradition is not the same as literalist traditionalism, and is in fact, incompatible with it. It consists of preserving not simply the tradition but the continuity of tradition."[19]

Eight hundred years before Strauss, Maimonides understood this concept of fidelity to tradition. Maimonides was both a great leader and authority in rabbinic history, but Rambam was also a monumentally controversial figure. His universalism and openness to all human wisdom, his insistence that strict *halakhah* does not define Torah nor exhaust Jewish religious obligations, and his belief that philosophical inquiry was necessary to understand religious truth all generated great conflict in the Jewish community. Because he rejected "literalist traditionalism," some of his books were banned and later burned by Jews. Rambam knew deeply that correctly understanding Torah and religious life demands rethinking common religious assumptions of the day, and sometimes entails changes in attitude and practice – while resolutely holding fast to the fundamental values of Torah and *halakhah* that he expressed in MT, the Laws of Servants 9:8.

As did Rambam, to make Torah life-affirming and meaningful in our world today, Jews must bring acute moral sensibilities to the issues of our time. Unlike the eras of our ancestors, many

18. Rambam also expresses this religious principle as an ultimate theological truth of in the culmination of his philosophic work in III:54 of *Guide of the Perplexed*. There he insists that the sign of intellectual perfection is the acquisition of *ḥesed*, defined III:53 as "*haflagah*" (overflow), i.e. autonomous free expression of the ideal human being. Interestingly, *ḥesed* here is in direct contrast to *gevurah* (heroism) as limitation or constraint imposed upon a person by heteronomous authority, law or communal convention.

19. *Spinoza's Critique of Religion.* (NY: Schocken, 1965), 24.

God intoxicated and Torah-oriented Jewish women today thirst for dignity and equality in Jewish communal life and practice. Heterodox Jews do not aim to assimilate out of our people, nor is their motive rebellion against God and His Torah. And modern Jews regularly interact with gentiles who are not enemies of our people and whose religions cannot be properly understood as idolatry. These new realities demand that faithful Jews open up new horizons in Torah – horizons that include women's voices, the entire people of Israel (*Kelal Yisrael*) and all human beings. They entail rethinking some of our liturgy and practices, while we continue to hold fast to the deepest values of Jewish practice and ethics.

After the storms that Rambam created calmed, he became the spiritual inspiration for generations of Jews who cherish Torah, who are faithful to *halakhah* and who work to bring God into the world. His wisdom, commitment to ethical values and universal concern for humanity continues to inspire all types of Jews to lead lives dedicated to the deepest values of Torah and what Jewish tradition asks of them: "To act justly, to love mercy and to walk humbly with your God." (Micah 6:8)

Chapter Eight

Religious Violence, Sacred Texts and Theological Values

"Without believing in God, I would never have had the power to do this"

I. RELIGION AND VIOLENCE

More than ever before, the sacred has proven radically ambivalent, both sanctifying and profaning God's Name on earth.[1] The confession in this chapter's subtitle could well have been whispered by Mother Theresa about her saintly work with the poor in India or shouted by Mohamed Atta as he flew his plane into the World Trade Center on September 11, 2001 with the Koran at his side. In fact, it was part of the testimony of Yigal Amir in the 1996 trial for his assassination of the Israeli Prime Minister Yitzhak Rabin in 1995.[2]

In Chapter Three I noted that there has been a global renaissance of faith and religious passion in America, the Middle East

1. In Jewish tradition, gratuitous violence against human beings – even sinners and criminals, who are also created in God's Image – is a form of blasphemy against God Himself. See Chapter Three.

2. Report: The State Investigation Commission in the Matter of the Murder of the Late Prime Minister Yitzhak Rabin, 89. Cited in Ehud Sprinzak, *Brother Against Brother* (Free Press: New York, 1999), 276.

and Africa, disproving Karl Marx's prediction that religion was destined to disappear in modern times. This modern religious fervor has brought both curse and blessing. The pace of religious violence[3] has palpably quickened recently and the past thirty years has seen a dramatic increase in conflicts around the world in which religion is a salient factor. We have witnessed an exponential increase in murder, terror and violence committed by religious extremists on local levels – all done in God's name. Although believers of some religions today resort more to violence today than do believers of other faiths, religious violence is not limited to a particular faith: it has stained, and continues to stain, religious Muslim, Christian, Jewish, Hindu and even normally pacifist Buddhist communities.[4]

The phenomenon of people who strive to make the world holy and resorting to violence is not new. As we saw earlier, fanaticism and violence are rooted inherently in the posture of faith and in recognizing God's absolute authority. If God is infinite and His will perfect while our knowledge is finite and fallible, then divine authority is categorical, and the obedience we owe to God is unlimited. In principle God's will eclipses all human reason and judgments. So the nature of our relationship with God requires a believer to surrender himself to God's Will and Word, and disregard all practical and accepted moral norms. This unlimited commitment is, quite literally, fanaticism.

A religious fanatic is not necessarily illogical. He can be understood as the consistent religious servant, willing to subordinate his personal interests and ethical obligations to his understanding

3. Here and throughout the chapter, my references to violence are to acts that are morally unjustified, i.e. done for reasons other than self-defense, and which is directed against people who pose no realistic empirical threat at the time of the attack or the imminent future. *Religious* violence as violence committed in the belief that God, sacred texts, religious law or religious authorities command or approve of that violence and where that belief is a significant motive for committing the violent act.

4. See Mark Juergensmeyer, *Terror in the Mind of God* (Berkeley, CA: University of Cal., 2000), chapters 2–6.

of what God dictates. Hence fanatical extremism is potentially present in all communities of believers.

Of course it was Kierkegaard who famously portrayed this problem of religious life.[5] He argued that when God commanded Abraham to sacrifice Isaac, Abraham became trapped in inescapable contradiction: According to Kierkegaard's understanding, in order to be loyal to God, Abraham had to become a murderer. He chose to "teleologically suspend the ethical," and resign himself to God. For his choice of faith over morality, Abraham earned the eternal blessing of becoming a father of a great people (Genesis 22:16). To Kierkegaard, the heroic Abraham became a religious role model precisely *because* he was a fanatic, refusing to allow logic, self-interest or morality to interfere with his obedience to God. In choosing the immoral, the violent and the absurd, he became the model of religious perfection, the *homo religiosus par excellence.*

Is the Bible not clear, then, on the requirements of religious devotion and imperative for faith to supersede morality? Genesis 22 poses a theological-ethical problem not only for Kierkegaard, but also for believing Jews, Christians and Muslims, and all who accept "the binding" as a sacred text. For Jews in particular, this is a critical issue. *Akedat Yitzhak* is a Jewish story that traditional rabbinic theology considers part of the divinely authored and inerrant Torah. Moreover, Jewish tradition has given this drama high prominence, making it an integral part of the daily morning liturgy and legislating that it be read aloud to the community on the solemn holiday of *Rosh Hashanah* (New Year).

For Jews too, Abraham is praiseworthy for his zealousness in fulfilling God's will. It is precisely *because* Abraham voiced no critical judgment and displayed no hesitation in obeying the unintelligible command to take Isaac's life that Jews consider him as the paradigm of God's faithful servant. Yet while the text and

5. Soren Kierkegaard, *Fear and Trembling. op. cit.*

its exalted place within Jewish tradition contain the potential for a violent ethic and the rejection of moral constraints, normative Jewish tradition rejected Kierkegaard's reading and its potential to idealize unethical behavior. Rabbinic tradition refused to use the story as a precedent or basis for any normative (legal) conclusions regarding human relations,[6] and Kierkegaard's interpretation of it as a conflict between divine commandment and moral agency is not reflected in rabbinic teachings.[7] Nevertheless, the essential theological problem and its potential for moral horror remain for all of us.

Modern religious violence is nearly always embedded in political, historical and psychological conditions, like poverty, inequality, greed, shame, disempowerment, and subjugation. These conditions give rise to grievances, belligerent emotions and hostile motives in individuals perpetrating religious violence. But as the shocking confession of Amir indicates, religion and religious ideas are not merely minor epiphenomena in the decision to commit violence. Most religious fanatics kill out of religious motive,

6. Gen. 22 was used as a precedent during the Crusades, when Jewish parents slaughtered their children in advance of the Crusaders, who Jews assumed would either forcibly convert or kill the children. See Shalom Spiegel, *The Last Trial: On the Legends and Love of the Command to Abraham to Offer Isaac as a Sacrifice: The Akedah.* (New York: Jewish Theological Seminary, 1950). The use of this Genesis text was inspirational, not legal, and is highly questionable from the point of view of Jewish law. As such, it is the subject of much rabbinic and historical discussion. See Haym Soloveitchik, "Religious Law and Change: The Medieval Ashkenazic Example" *AJS Review* 12 (1987), 205–221.

7. Gen. 22 was one of the most popular springboards for rabbinic imagination and hermeneutical interpretation expressing the classic Jewish religious worldview. Nevertheless, the predominant motif in the hundreds of rabbinic *midrashim* on Gen 22 is that God tested Abraham by forcing him to choose between his love for God and his love for his son. I have found only one such *midrash* that alludes to Kierkegaard's understanding of Abraham as a murder – and that appellation is put in the mouths of the enemies of rabbis, not the rabbis themselves. See Green, Ronald M. *Religion and Moral Reason.* (New York: Oxford University Press, 1988) 77–102, particularly 86. Green confirms that Kierkegaard's thesis of the conflict of morality and faith is nowhere found in traditional Jewish interpretations of Gen. 22. Only in the 20th century do Jewish interpretations of the *Akedah* appear that are consistent with Kierkegaard's reading.

and their violence cannot be explained adequately by exclusively social, political, nationalistic or psychological conditions.

Religious extremists draw on their understanding of God, sacred texts, religious traditions and values, as well as the encouragement of their religious communities and authorities to provide them with both the conviction and the justifications to carry out their acts.[8] Thus religious violence will never be fully understood or remediated by technical, social or political stratagems that ignore the roles that theology and religious texts play in fomenting that violence. To ignore theological factors, as many have done, is to adopt a secular bias.[9] In order to confront religious violence effectively, we need to reshape our understanding of our sacred texts, our theological values and even God.

Religious violence takes many forms, such as institutional injustice, racial discrimination, and persecution of heretics, infidels and undesirables. Yet here I am interested primarily in the physical violence perpetrated by individual religious extremists. How can we identify the reasoning and values that nurture fanaticism, as well as the religious traditions and texts that extremists use to justify immoral violence against others? More importantly, are there theological and religious responses to the seemingly

8. See Oliver McTernan, *Violence in God's Name.* (Maryknoll, NY: Orbis, 2003), 45–76. And Jonathan Sacks, *Not in God's Name: Confronting Religious Violence.* (New York: Schocken Books, 2015). On the role played by religious concepts and authority, see full statement of Amir cited later.

9. Ibid 20–44 and *American Academy of Arts and Science Report*, Martin Marty and Scott Appleby, eds. There is also an opposite secular bias at work in "the new atheists," who maintain that religious beliefs necessarily lead to violence and that such beliefs are the root of violence by religious actors. They disregard nearly all political, social and non-religious ideological factors in religious violence and naively they seem to think that proving religious belief irrational will suffice to eradicate it. The greater increasing prominence of religion in contemporary politics and cultures demonstrates otherwise. See also Sam Harris, *The End of Faith: Religion Terror and the Future of Reason* (New York: Norton, 2004); Richard Dawkins, *The God Delusion* (Boston: Houghton Mifflin, 2006); Daniel Dennett, *Breaking the Spell: Religion as a Natural Phenomenon* (New York: Penguin, 2006); and Christopher Hitchens, *God is not Great: How Religion Poisons Everything.* (New York: Hachette Book Group, 2007).

permanent cancer of religious fanaticism? Can God be saved from becoming the agent of desecration, death and destruction? Even if fanaticism cannot be entirely eradicated, what religious teachings and values can effectively limit this horrific phenomenon?

Religious zealots who perpetrate violence are not deranged persons acting impetuously under the force of emotional compulsion. On the contrary, they are usually educated and accomplished persons who carefully plan their violence and who are swayed by some type of religious reasoning.

Amir was a competent law and computer science student at Bar Ilan University, and his decision to assassinate Prime Minister Rabin was influenced by arguments relating to the talmudic categories of "pursuer" (*rodef)* and a "denouncer" (*moser*).[10] Atta was an educated architect and technician, who carefully planned for his attack on the World Trade Center in the belief that it was his duty to establish Allah's kingdom on earth. The American Protestant clergymen Michael Bray and Paul Hill defended burning abortion clinics and murdering their staffs by recourse to similar arguments to establish God's law on earth, claiming their violence was defensive and prevented infanticide. Bray even cited Dietrich Bonhoeffer's attempt to assassinate Hitler as a justifying precedent for his act of violence in pursuit of a higher good.[11] Baruch Goldstein murdered 29 Arabs at prayer in Hebron in 1995, but he was a careful doctor who had previously healed sick Jews and Arabs alike. Because his homicidal rampage was so inconsistent with his earlier behavior, people initially assumed that he had "snapped," but the evidence indicates that he was influenced by radical ideologies of unbridled nationalism and arguments for sanctifying God's name.[12]

10. Sprinzak, 5.
11. McTernan, 29–30.
12. Sprinzak, 239–242.

All this religious violence was animated by the conviction that God demands true believers to change the world, violently and murderously if necessary, to bring it into harmony with God's rule and design. Once again, God's will and the theological argument to obey it without limit trumped morality and ethical restraint.

The September 2001 terrorist attack on the World Trade Center generated vigorous debate about the nature of Islam. Immediately after the attack, George W. Bush publicly announced that "Islam is a religion of peace." Soon after that, Pat Robertson demurred, stating that Islam preached violence: "If you get right down to it, Osama bin Laden is probably truer to Mohammed than some of the others." On his television program, the 700 Club, Robertson further announced, "I take issue with our esteemed president in regard to his stand in saying Islam is a peaceful religion. It's just not. And the Koran makes it very clear: 'If you see an infidel, you are to kill him.'"[13] Jerry Falwell, Franklin Graham and a host of others agreed with Robertson about the "essential violent nature of Islam."

Bush was wrong – but so were the others. Both sides committed a conceptual and historical error. Indeed Islam has incendiary sacred texts that advocate violence, yet the Koran also contains passages that council peace and tolerance. Which is essential and which marginal? Both Jewish Scriptures and the New Testament also contain intolerant and violent, as well as tolerant and pacifistic texts.

Though these religions venerate their sacred scriptures, none of these contradictory sacred scriptures define a static "essence" of its religion. Rather, *it is how the living religious community*

13. An apparent reference to the Koran 9:5 and 9:14: ". . . fight and slay the pagans wherever ye find them, and seize them, beleaguer them, and lie in wait for them in every stratagem. . . . Fight them, and God will punish them by your hands."

interprets, prioritizes and lives the meanings of its sacred texts that defines its religion.

Thus there is no "essential unchanging nature" of our faiths or texts – only the actions, thoughts and testimonies that our living communities manifest at a given time in history. Throughout the Middle Ages, Christian teachings and communities demonstrated intolerance and frequent violence toward Jews, yet today normative Christianity is largely tolerant and non-violent. Conversely, Islam often demonstrated greater tolerance (although never equality) toward Jews and Christians in the 11th through 13th centuries, but today anti-Semitic and anti-Western violence and hatred reigns in much of the religious Muslim (and particularly Arab) world. Judaism has been non-violent over the last 1,900 years and the classic talmudic authorities succeeded in transmuting all military virtues into social and spiritual ones,[14] yet today a number of religious Jews have taken to violence and tribal-like hatred against Arabs, gentiles and other Jews.

The sacred texts of these faiths have not changed throughout the eras, but the interpretations, priorities and valences that religious authorities and their followers have given them have. No text, however sacred, speaks for itself; all depends on our human understanding and explanation. History has proven – for bad and for good – the talmudic principle that "before revelation, the Torah was in Heaven, but after Sinai, the Torah is no longer in heaven."[15] That is, everything depends upon the interpretations of human beings. This applies not only to the Torah, but to the sacred texts and of all faiths and the experiences of the faithful in all communities.

14. Mishna *Avot,* 4:1, and Judah Halevi, *The Kuzari* (New York: Schocken, 1987), 1:109–115.

15. BT, *Baba Metsi'a* 59b. In this talmudic passage, the rabbis audaciously told God to stay out of a dispute over the correct ruling of a biblical law. They justified this independence from divine authority by creatively interpreting Deut. 30:12: "It [the Torah] is not in heaven."

I reiterate that some religions today – radical Islam and its jihadis in particular – manifest more violence than do some others. Contemporary violent religious extremism is undeniable. Indeed, the existence of religiously motivated violence is a very real problem, and it cannot be reduced to illusion by logical arguments. Yet the critical point here is that no religion is "essentially" and hence, necessarily, violent because of its sacred texts. The meaning of those texts is far less important than how a religious tradition uses them. Most crucially, it is how those texts are taught, interpreted and used at a given point in history that determines the religion's violent or non-violent character, its extremist or moderate tendencies. If so, every religion can be redeemed from violent behavior through teaching ethical interpretations of its sacred literature. Tragically, the converse is also true.

The existence of dangerous sacred texts is the "dark side" of text-based religions. The real challenge is how we understand, appropriate and live these texts: Do our communities follow their literal authority and raise their prescribed violence to a religious ideal? Do believers and authorities disregard the moral character of God and plunge the world back to its primordial chaos? Or do we confront the problem and refashion and teach different normative understandings of God and His revelation, understandings that are consistent with a human social order suffused with moral consciousness?

Nearly all religious extremism employs common theological elements. They include (1) certain knowledge of what God "wants," (2) reliance on religious authority or sacred texts, (3) dehumanizing the enemy, (4) prioritizing religious ideals over ethical norms, (5) restoring the honor of God/avenging the shame of God, and (6) absolutizing non-rational belief in the justness of its cause and rejecting compromise.

How did rabbinic tradition respond to this challenge? What strategies did classic rabbinic authorities employ to "de-toxify" some of the most dangerous texts in the Torah? What values governed those interpretative moves? These sacred texts are dangerous conceptually because they appear to advocate violence on the command or authority of God. This is not limited to theory, for historically they have been used as justifications for Jewish (as well as non-Jewish) violence. Lastly, I will offer some assessment of the extent that these hermeneutics and their governing values can help prevent the phenomenon of individual religious violence.

II. VIOLENT JEWISH SCRIPTURES AND THEIR INTERPRETATIONS

As we saw in Chapter Three, the *Akedah* can be used as a seminal source for rejection of morality in the name of religion. Yet Jewish commentators avoid using the sacred text that way by interpreting it contrary to Kierkegaard and seeing Abraham's test as a choice between piety and possession, not between *mitsvah* and morality. Moreover, the Bible and rabbinic tradition ensured that no one repeat Abraham's decision to kill an innocent person on the grounds of alleging to hear a divine voice by making human sacrifice the paradigm of idolatry. While sacrificing the innocent Isaac began as an apparent act of fidelity to God's word, it was transformed into the paradigm of idolatry and enshrined as normative Jewish law: "You must not do the same for the Lord your God, because every abhorrent thing that the Lord hates they have done for their gods. They even burn their sons and daughters in the fire to their gods." (Deut. 12:31)

Finally, rabbinic tradition refused to draw any halakhic or behavioral conclusions from Abraham's test. It used the narrative exclusively for homiletical purposes, going so far as to invert the text's plain meaning to ensure that compassion, not strict obedience, remain central to religious life and the imitation of God.

We also saw in Chapter Four that the Talmud interpreted the divine commandments in Deuteronomy and I Samuel to exterminate the Canaanite and Amalekite nations in a way that rendered those *mitsvot* inoperative in post-biblical times. Maimonides went so far as to reinterpret the commandment so that even in biblical times God required offering peace to the enemy before going to war and permitted only killing the belligerents in war.

There is one more biblical passage that encourages and rewards violent religious fanaticism. Chapter 25 of Numbers describes and evaluates the actions of Pinḥas (Phineas) the religious zealot. Sadly, his zealotry has been used as a theologically justifying precedent for Christian and Jewish violence in the past and present.[16] How did the talmudic rabbis, who ascribed divine authority to this passage and thus were not free to reject or override its validity, deal with this toxic text?

Numbers 25 appears to extend divine approval to individuals taking justice into their own hands to violently kill those they consider enemies of God. The narrative of the murderous Pinḥas portrays him as a religious model who was rewarded with peace and priesthood:

> The Lord said to Moses: "Take all the ringleaders and have them publicly impaled before the Lord, so that the Lord's wrath may turn away from Israel." So, Moses said to the judges of Israel: "Each of you slay those of his men that have attached themselves to the *Baal Pe'or*." Just then one of the Israelites came and brought a Midianite woman over to his companions, in the sight of Moses and of the whole of the Israelite community who were weeping at the door of the Tent of Meeting. When Phinehas, son of Eleazar

16. Former Presbyterian minister, Paul Hill, shot and killed an abortion doctor in Florida in 1992. Hill justified his behavior as "a Phineas action." Charles Selengut, *Sacred Fury* (Walnut Creek, CA: AltraMira, 2003), 37–38. Josephus traces the violent Jewish groups, the Zealots and the *Sikari'im* ("ones with daggers") during the Jewish-Roman wars to the model of Pinḥas (McTernan, 54). Amir also saw himself in the tradition of Pinḥas (Sprinzak, 281) as do ultra-Orthodox Jews today who engage in non-lethal violence against secular and Zionist Jews (Sprinzak, 102).

> son of Aaron the priest, saw this, he left the assembly, and taking a spear in his hand, he followed the Israelite into the chamber and stabbed both of them, the Israelite and the woman, through the belly. Then the plague against the Israelites was checked. . . .
>
> The Lord spoke to Moses, saying: "Phinehas, son of Eleazar son of Aaron the priest, has turned My wrath from the Israelites by displaying among them his passion for Me, so that I did not wipe out the Israelite nation in My passion. Say, therefore, 'I grant him My pact of friendship. It shall be for him and his descendants after him a pact of priesthood for all time, because he took impassioned action for his G-d, thus making expiation for the Israelites.'" (Numbers 25: 4–15)

On a literal level the Bible grants unqualified approval to Pinḥas' zealotry, but rabbinic tradition assessed his violence differently. According to the talmudic authorities, Pinḥas' zealous attack contradicted normative law; hence they regarded him as a murderer. Only the public divine revelation ("The Lord spoke to Moses . . .") proved that in this exceptional case alone, zealotry was permitted:

> It was taught: This was not met with the approval of the Sages. . . . Rabbi Yehudah bar Pazi said: "They sought to excommunicate him had not the Holy Spirit alighted upon him and said 'And he and his seed after him will possess a covenant of eternal priesthood . . .'"[17]

Without this divine intervention, Pinḥas would have been convicted of murder and correctly executed. The rabbis creatively established the general rule that religious zealotry is permissible only when there is no legal court to prosecute those who flaunt the law (based on Numb. 25:6, "Moses and the whole Israelite

17. JT, *Sanhedrin* 9:7. According to Rabba bar Hana and Rav Hisda in BT, *Sanhedrin* 82a, Pinḥas was an unlawful pursuer of human life.

community were weeping at the entrance of the Tent of Meeting"), and only as a spontaneous unpremeditated act committed at the time of the offense ("Pinḥas saw this . . . and stabbed both of them . . ."). As a further deterrent to imitating this behavior, rabbinic law denied legal protection to zealots, and ruled that the zealot's intended victim has every right to kill the zealot without bearing any legal liability. Lastly, zealotry – even in these limited circumstances – may not be taught to anyone who inquires about its legitimacy.

These are bold hermeneutical steps, ones that undermine the text's literal meaning and its positive valuation of zealotry. *Ḥazal* were morally sober and understood that zealotry can never be a normative religious or political model, whether it is motivated by "doing God's will" or any other ideal. Its legitimacy is countenanced only *in extremis*, when the rule of law is absent, and is limited to *post facto* toleration. One rabbinic authority claimed that Pinḥas was given the priesthood not as a reward but to confine him to the Temple precincts in order to shield society from his violent nature. Another saw the "blessing of peace" as a cure for his disease of zealotry.[18] Because of the biblical text, Jewish tradition could not condemn Pinḥas himself, but it condemns everyone who would plan to emulate him.

III. VIOLENCE AND THEOLOGICAL VALUES

Though bound by their commitment to Hebrew Scriptures, traditional Jewish thinkers interpreted these violent texts contrary to their literal meanings because their understanding of God and religious worldviews were governed by particular theological values. Through the lens of these values, they explained the texts in ways that deny the legitimacy of religious violence.

Stripping the enemy of his human face is a psychological

18. *Ha-Emeq Davar*, ad loc.

requirement for violent religious arguments to take hold, and is usually a first step down the path to bloodshed. Dehumanization and demonization preceded all the fanatical acts cited above, whether the victims were ancient biblical characters, Prime Minister Rabin, contemporary American citizens or Palestinian Arabs.[19]

As noted, Amalek is the prototype of demonization. Without systematically dehumanizing the Amalekite nation it would have been impossible to contemplate its legitimate extermination. It was precisely the acknowledgement of the possible moral integrity of Amalek (should they be willing to live in peace), and the recovery of the potential humanity of Amalekite and Canaanite nations – or more precisely the un-dehumanization of those nations – that informed the rabbinic hermeneutics of the commandment to annihilate all vestiges of these peoples. By rendering the genocide commandment non-operational, the talmudic authorities asserted that any attack on innocent persons no matter what their racial, tribal or genetic backgrounds is theologically and legally untenable.[20]

The foundation of this theological orientation is the doctrine that all people, even those manifesting evil, are created *b'Tselem Elokim*, in God's Holy Image. This metaphysical quality bestows intrinsic value on every person, and prohibits attacking any person who does not pose an imminent physical threat. If a person is willing to live in peace with others, his humanity must be respected and his person not violated. By accepting Maimonides'

19. Nor is this a new phenomenon. It was also used in a different way by the Christians in the First Crusade against the Saracens. They justified their barbaric slaughter by considering the enemy "not real people" and "perennial temptations who were obstacles to real life." Richard L. Crocker, "Early Crusader Songs." In H.E.J. Cowdrey, *The Genesis of the Crusades in Holy War* (Ohio State U., 1976), 96–97.

20. This reasoning can be extended to a *de jure* rejection of violence or punishment against heretics, homosexuals, Sabbath violators and others who commit ritualistic biblical offenses. This has already been done *de facto* in Jewish history and some rabbinic legal argumentation. See Chapter Five.

hermeneutical reconceptualization of Amalek, normative Jewish tradition implicitly adopted the principle that no human being may be legitimately shorn of his humanity; even when he is legitimately killed out of self-defense.[21] While defensible, that act remains a theological tragedy over which there is no rejoicing in Heaven or on earth.[22] Ultimately, any human death or violation of the human body desecrates the Divine.[23]

The *Midrash Tanḥuma* 96:3 quoted in the beginning of Chapter Four in which Moses rejects God's commandment to kill all Canaanites expresses a radical theological motif found elsewhere in the Torah and rabbinic tradition. When Moses refused to comply with God's command on moral grounds, he placed himself in the tradition of Abraham who argued with and won the argument against God: "Far be it from You to do such a thing, to bring death upon the innocent as well as the guilty!" (Gen. 18:24) Evidently for both Abraham and Moses, the God of the covenant cannot command humans to violate the moral rule prohibiting murdering innocent people and committing injustice. "Will the judge of the earth not act justly?"

The God who covenanted with Abraham and Moses cannot be an immoral God, and hence for their covenantal descendants any teleological suspension of the ethical[24] is not a legitimate religious option for a believer of the God of Abraham and Moses. This is the most important moral lesson of Genesis 22,

21. The Jewish moral and legal teaching is, "If one comes to kill you, you may kill him first."

22. "My handiwork is drowning in the sea, and you are singing songs?" BT *Sanhedrin* 39b.

23. See *Midrash Tanna'im* cited earlier. Deut. 21:23 prescribes execution for blasphemers, but rabbinic tradition effectively eliminated all capital punishment in practice out of the belief in the ultimate sanctity and potential redemption of all human beings. Thus the only theological warrant for destroying human life is to save lives – and then only when the person to be killed is a belligerent threat to others. Jewish theology is consistent with violence in self-defense and humanitarian intervention, not with pacifism.

24. Chapter Three explores this idea in detail.

whose revolutionary theology occurs not at the beginning of the drama (as Kierkegaard thought), but at its end: Abraham's God is revealed as essentially different from the pagan idols of the surrounding cultures because the God of the covenant does not allow human sacrifice or murder done in His name.

The *Akedah* teaching is a theological rejection of the Canaanite cult of child sacrifice and taking innocent life for God; the high drama was necessary to shock Abraham out of the acceptance of this practice so dominant in his cultural setting.[25] The sanctity of human life is primary to the covenantal God and to *halakhah*, and any alleged "divine voice" counseling violence against another must be rejected both theologically and morally.[26] Sanctifying God's name in the world entails preserving life, not promoting death or violating fundamental moral norms. Thus the operative faith of a covenantal believer is the conviction that there is always a legitimate interpretation of each sacred text or teaching consistent with the sanctity of the Divine Image implanted within each human being. For him, the immoral imperative can never be normative.

The rejection of Pinḥas' zealotry as a legitimate religious model is an extension of this fundamental theological value of the sanctity of human life. There is no possibility of "redeeming God's shame" or "defending God's honor" by zealously taking law into one's own hands and harming others – however evil they

25. Thus the purpose of the "test" was not for God to verify something that the divine did not previously know, but in consonance with the connotation of the Hebrew "*nisah*" (v. 1), "to provide Abraham an experience that would make him aware of something new. See Eccles.2:1 and Judges 3:1. See also Roland De Vaux, *Ancient Israel: Its Life and Institutions* (New York: McGraw-Hill), 442f.

26. Jewish law precludes the validity of action stemming from any private revelation to murder another. Appeals to "divine voices" are inadmissible in religious courts and overridden by the general legal prohibition against homicide – again consistent with the conclusion of Gen. 22. Someone killing in God's name is more legally culpable than one who kills for profit or advantage because the former desecrates the Name of God.

may appear to be.[27] This is true not only theologically, but also empirically: contemporary Jewish, Muslim and Christian zealots have brought only shame to the God of their faith in the eyes of the human community.

For the philosophical believer, the idea of divine "shame" or "honor" is untenable. Indeed, it smacks of idolatry since it attributes transient emotions to God.[28] Rather than a correct description of God, this conception points instead only to the wounded feelings of the zealot, who uses it to justify taking vengeance on others for his own perceived humiliation.

But is there not a deeper theological consideration regarding religious zealotry? The Torah insists that the Master of the universe is "a jealous God" (Ex. 20:5 & 34:14, Deut. 6:15), who vents His anger and punishes those who reject His will.[29] And as creatures fashioned in the Divine Image, are we not obligated to engage in imitating God and following all God's ways? Should we also not be a "devouring fire," punishing those who we understand are disobeying God?

This is an old problem, one that directly speaks to the ambivalence of faith and the simultaneous creative and destructive implications of living life as a God-centered creature. The God who created the world is also the God who punishes the sinner, wreaks violence upon the wicked and destroys the disbeliever.

27. This coheres with Ex. 33: 18–23 in which God denies Moses' plea to "show me Your honor." The conclusion of that text is that a human being can never know "God's honor," but only intimations of it. ("You will see my back, but My face cannot be seen.") It follows that one may not take action toward others based upon a knowledge of the honor of God. I thank Don Seeman for indicating the relevance of this passage. See his "Violence, Ethics and Divine Honor in Jewish Thought." In *Journal of Jewish Thought and Philosophy* 16 (2008), 195–252.

28. For instance, Maimonides, *Guide of the Perplexed*, 1:29, I:52.

29. Divine "jealousy" in the Bible refers exclusively to God's reaction to idolatry, i.e. it is provoked only by humans accepting false gods. This accords well with human jealousy, which is engendered by the presence of competitors. Importantly, human zealousness as *imitatio dei* would hence apply only as a response to full-fledged idolators, not people committing other sins or crimes.

Moreover, punishment is essential to our concept of justice – particularly divine justice. Indeed, isolated radical Jewish thinkers like Yitzhak Ginzburg have spun a theology of violence and vengeance on this model of *imitatio dei*.[30]

Yet this theology is forcefully rejected by normative rabbinic tradition. Here is the rabbinic articulation and resolution of the problem:

> The children of Israel asked Moses, "Who can walk in His ways? Is it not written, 'The Lord is a whirlwind and in the story is His way' (Nah. 1:3)? And is it not written, 'Thy way was in the sea and Thy path is the great waters, and Thy footsteps were not known' (Ps. 77:20)? Is it not also written, 'A fire devours before Him and round about Him it storms mightily (ibid 50:3)?'
>
> Moses answered, "I was not speaking of these ways. His ways are loving-kindness, truth and the works of charity, as it is written, 'All the paths of the Lord are mercy and truth. (ibid 25:10)'"[31]

This is another sweeping move with crucial implications for religious behavior. While acknowledging divine wrath and punishment, Jewish tradition rejected *apriori* any human imitation of these attributes. The reason is critical: Only God can know the exact amount of justice to apply and how to employ measured punishment for beneficent ends. Because vengeance is intrinsically destructive, unmeasured punishment would engulf the world in chaos, thus undoing creation. Hence our essential human fallibility bars us from imitating God's jealousy, vengeance and punitive actions.

30. For greater elaboration on thought of Ginzburg, see Sprinzak, 258–262. See also Shlomo Fischer, "State Crisis and the Potential for Uncontrollable Violence in Israel-Palestine," and Don Seeman, "God's Honor, Violence and the State," in *Plows into Swords? Reflections on Religion and Violence,* edited by Robert W. Jenson and Eugene Korn. Center for Jewish-Christian Understanding and Cooperation, 2014. Kindle edition.

31. *Midrash Tanhuma, Va-yishlach* 10.

By contrast, loving-kindness is the building-block of the cosmos. "The world is built on mercy (*ḥesed*)," proclaimed King David the Psalmist. (Psalms 89:3) God's mercy is limitless and so there is no impediment to imitating God's compassion and mercy toward others. Thus the Jewish normative teaching of imitating God is: Just as God is merciful, so you shall be merciful; just as God is compassionate, so shall you be compassionate; just as God practices acts of loving-kindness (*ḥesed*) toward others, so shall you practice loving-kindness toward others.[32]

Of course, understanding God's mercy (*ḥesed*) raises theological problems similar to ascribing shame to God. Realizing this, Maimonides explained divine *ḥesed* as overflow ("*haflagah*") of Divine Self and hence the cause of all existence.[33] In doing so, he divested the divine attributes of mercy and compassion of emotional content, transforming them from essentially moral and psychological categories into metaphysical concepts – yet ones with profound moral implications nevertheless. God is the Ground of Being and the Sustainer of Life, and human religious perfection entails sustaining life in the emulation of the Creator of all.[34]

The rabbinical hermeneutics regarding zealotry (and, as we saw, Kierkegaard's Abraham) as well as the theological argument rejecting any human imitation of God's destructive wrath introduces a morally and theologically critical factor in thinking about God and divine will: human uncertainty. As stated, theological certainty about God and His will is another essential characteristic of religious extremism. Few religious ideas have wreaked more destruction upon the world than a person believing with

32. BT *Sotah* 14a and *Sifri, Eikev*. Cf. Maimonides, *Laws of Dispositions*, 1:6. For a fuller treatment of *imitatio Dei* and its implications for Jewish ethics and religious extremism, see David Shapiro, "The Doctrine of the Image of God and *Imitatio Dei*." In Kellner, *Contemporary Jewish Ethics* (New York: Sanhedrin Press, 1978), 127–151.

33. *Guide of the Perplexed*, III:53.

34. Ibid III: 54.

certainty that he knows the full and exclusive truth about what God wants. Isaiah Berlin describes the general problem well:

> It is a terrible and dangerous arrogance to believe that you have a magical eye that sees the truth, and that others cannot be right if they disagree. This makes one certain that there is one goal and only one for one's nation or church or the whole of humanity, and that it is worth any amount of suffering (particularly on the part of other people) if only that goal is attained – even "through an ocean of blood to the Kingdom of Love", as Robespierre said. . . . Leaders in the religious wars of Christian versus Muslim or Catholics versus Protestants sincerely believed this: "There is one and only one true answer and that one has it oneself – or one's Leader has it. This belief was responsible for the oceans of blood. But no Kingdom of Love ever sprang from it, nor could it.[35]

Berlin correctly refers to the evils of both religious and secular certainty. Yet there is a particularly acute problem with pluralism and epistemic humility for religious thinking. There, absolute faith is considered a virtue and lack of conviction and doubt are vices – hence the door is always open to extremism born of absolute belief. The need to justify and set parameters on uncertainty is theologically complex, yet it is an essential pre-condition for our understanding of God in order to bar religious fanaticism and to preclude destructive violence. Like faith itself, uncertainty is both a blessing and a curse, and more hard theological reflection needs to be devoted to this phenomenon as a religious virtue. The rabbinic use of "virtuous" uncertainty can be a start to this necessary enterprise.

To become a partner with human beings, God had to limit His infinite power and grant His human partners the power to make their own choices and act freely. This is the old Jewish mystical doctrine of *tsimtsum* – divine contraction. To make room for the

35. *Liberty* (Oxford: Oxford University Press, 2002), 345.

world, God had to voluntarily "withdraw" and cede absolute control over the universe.

Divine self-limitation that grants control to human beings includes allowing freedom of choice and action even to sinners and people perpetrating evil. Although an infinite God has the power to prevent evil and destroy sinners, according to the rabbinic understanding of Jewish historical tragedies, the God who covenants with free human beings chooses instead to exercise self-restraint:

> "Who is like You, O Strong One, God?" (Ps. 89:9) – [read] "Who is like You, strong and firm, for You hear the insult and blasphemy of evil and remain silent?" . . . "Who is like You among the mighty ones [original Hebrew: *eilim*], God?" (Ex. 15:11) – [read] "Who is like you among the silent ones [*ilmim*]?"[36]

The covenantal God of history chooses not to act, giving evil people throughout history the opportunity to repent, waiting silently for sinners to find their way back to their divine image and humanity. Self-restraint is the new understanding of divine power – an understanding that emphasizes God's limitation and tolerance, rather than divine absoluteness and omnipotence.[37]

Nor is this restricted to divine metaphysics. It has profound implications for the human-God relationship and, by extension,

36. BT, *Gittin* 56b. See also BT *Yoma* 69b.

37. For more elaboration on this idea, see Moses Cordovero's explication of Micah 7:18 in *The Palm of Deborah*, translated by Louis Jacobs (London: Vallentine, Mitchel, 1960). Basing these values on covenantal theology has more resonance in Christianity and Judaism than in Islam, which sees God more dominantly as impervious to human influence and hence does not admit of a reciprocal covenant between God and human beings. See also David Hartman, *A Living Covenant* (New York: The Free Press, 1985), 204–228.

Interestingly, Maimonides had a similar theology and was forced to relegate mutual covenantal relations to social covenants between persons. See *Guide of the Perplexed*, I:11 and III:49. In this matter, Maimonides is unrepresentative of rabbinic tradition.

all interpersonal relations. As one political thinker observed, "covenant stresses acceptance of limitations of power by both parties."[38] If so, as agents created in the Divine Image who are challenged to "walk in His footsteps," are we not also required to practice divine self-restraint and toleration of sinners? As God's covenantal partners, we may not allow ourselves to disappear as a result of violence directed against us collectively or individually. We are witnesses to the *Shekhinah* (Divine Presence) and therefore we have a covenantal obligation to survive. Yet self-defense does not allow us to exercise wrath or violence against those who do not pose a physical threat against us. And if in practice this distinction is sometimes difficult to determine, in principle it is not.

IV. THE PRACTICAL IMPORTANCE OF THEOLOGICAL VALUES

Neither nuanced hermeneutical strategies, nor our commitment to the sanctity of all persons, nor the inviolability of innocent life, nor moral norms in religious obedience, nor human self-restraint as *Imitatio Dei,* nor epistemic uncertainty, are strong enough to quell the rage that burns in extremists. Nor will they succeed in moderating extremists' behavior, since their zeal is dominated by the very opposite ideals. Violent zealots put certainty, absolute obedience, nationalism, land, uniformity and revenge at the top of their religious worldview. In addition, when fanatics reject the self-restraining covenantal God "Who must do justice" in the world, their extremist logic is not formally inconsistent. As a result, there is no "knock-out argument" against religious or any other type of fanaticism.

Yet religious extremism does not grow out of a vacuum.

38. Daniel Elazar, *Covenant and Polity in Biblical Israel.* (New York: Routledge, 1995), 1.

Fanatics are nurtured by religious authorities and peers. It takes a community to create a fanatic. Once again, the testimony of Yigal Amir bears out this crucial influence:

> "If not for a rabbinic legal ruling of *din rodef*, it would have been very difficult for me to murder. If I did not get the backing and I had not been representing many more people, I would not have acted."[39]

In the end, legal theorists, philosophers and moralists will not dissuade religious fanatics from their violence. However their own religious authorities and more sober colleagues who are open to reason and the ethical values of their traditions can be influenced away from violence. The path to curing the scourge of religious fanaticism goes through the larger community and its teachers, those armed with the tools to understand faith and holy texts in ways that exclude the legitimacy of religious violence. The cited hermeneutical examples, their methodologies and their governing values are models for understanding sacred scriptures and nurturing moral values without sacrificing either theological legitimacy or religious commitment.

The solution to religious violence is not logical, but pedagogical; not philosophical, but theological: Only personal modeling and teaching the covenantal God Who refuses to strip his human partners of their moral will and critical intelligence, Who is the God of justice, compassion and love for His creatures, can cure the world of religious fanaticism and its violence.

When we are honest, we must admit that we cannot know with certainty what God demands of us in our particular situations. True religious life is a dialectical journey that threads carefully between faith and imperfect knowledge. This is legitimately unsettling for many who seek certainty and grounding for their religious quests. We all seek secure foundations upon which to

39. Sprinzak, 277.

build our theological worlds and clear our religious paths.

I have argued for the primacy of ethical values over any religious imperatives demanding violence – even when we perceive their source as divine. While privileging the moral choice is not a logically necessary truth, history and contemporary events have proven two empirical truths that should help provide near-certainty in our religious quests: Acting through violence to glorify God has in fact achieved the very opposite result: It has profaned, not glorified, God before the world. Human history has shown that nothing so readily falsifies religious testimony as does the justification of extremism with its denial of moral norms; and nothing so effectively "pushes God out of the world,"[40] as does violence and murder. Indeed the fanatic's god is seen by others not as God, but only an evil and loathsome personal obsession. Far from bringing a recognition of God, religious violence functions as a contemporary negative witness that demonstrates the heinous error of those practicing violence. Both the religious extremist and his god stand rejected before all reasonable persons, and only the irrational apocalyptic messianist can deny these facts.

In wreaking havoc and destruction, religious violence murders the Divine Image implanted on earth, reverses divine creation, and plunges human society into chaos. Far from ushering in spiritual or messianic ideals, violence has led only to hatred and "oceans of blood."

So if we must pave our religious journey with certainty, these two empirical truths should suffice. Choosing moral values as the ground of our theology leads us down the path to the Creator Who nurtures His creation, to the God of the Bible Who continues to covenant with His creatures and Who is the source of blessing and human flourishing.

40. In Hebrew, *Ḥilul ha-Shem* usually translated as "profanation of the divine name," literally means "emptying [the world] of the divine name."

Frequently I ask myself why the Torah considers idolatry to be the worst and unforgivable sin. It is a distressing question. Misidentifying God and misrepresenting what Heaven demands of us are surely not virtues, but neither do these cognitive mistakes appear to warrant the extreme vigilance and categorical condemnation that the Bible attaches to idolatry. And what meaning can idolatry have for us today, now that the worship of stars, trees, emperors and other material objects is rarely practiced?

Our idea of a supreme and demanding God is a sublime idea. Due to this power, it can be the source of unbounded goodness or unlimited curse. If we do not understand that the God of the universe demands His children to be carriers of divine blessing and sustainers of life, to complete creation rather than to destroy it with pious fury, we are blind to the difference between faith and idolatry. Indeed, if idolatry holds any meaning in today's world, it is surely the worship of a god of vengeance and violence who does not bind his worshippers to moral values and the sanctity of life.[41]

The long history of religious violence teaches us that the infinitude of God and the ultimate claims the Divine makes on His creatures makes "getting God right" a matter of ultimate significance – metaphysically or cognitively, but more importantly, morally and existentially. God is our most powerful human conception, and how we understand Heaven will determine whether we create a world suffused with harmony, friendship and progress or plunge the world back to its primordial chaos by unleashing unlimited destruction on the human family and its civilization.

On this religious understanding, the future of faith, humanity – and God – rests.

41. This is the conception of idolatry formulated by the thirteenth century rabbinic authority, Menachem ha-Meiri. He transformed the concept of idolatry from metaphysical error to a religion that abandons morality and the laws of civility. See Chapter Three, note 5.

Chapter Nine

Judaism and the Religious Other

"Why was Adam created alone? [i.e. Why did all humanity emerge from one person?] . . . To tell of the glory of The Holy One, for when a person mints many coins from the same die, all the coins are identical. But while the King of Kings, The Holy One, mints all persons from the same die, no person is identical to another."
(Mishnah Sanhedrin 4:5)

I. INTRODUCTION

The above statement of the *mishna* announces that human diversity is an undeniable fact. Further, it insists that our diversity is not merely a *de facto* reality, but also a theological *desideratum* that testifies to the uniqueness and glory of God. And this diversity the *mishna* extols is not limited to differences in physical appearance, but includes all dimensions of human personhood.

Yet does this affirmation of diversity also extend to *theological* pluralism, i.e., the acknowledgement of a number of valid religions? Is the multiplicity of religious beliefs a value we should celebrate or a lamentable condition to be overcome at some point in the natural future? Or is religious uniformity one of the goals reserved only for the *eschaton,* when human life will be mysteriously transformed into the ideal? These are the more crucial and complex questions.

Like the Christian and Muslim thinkers who shaped their own

religious traditions, Jewish prophets, rabbis, philosophers, poets and pietists also prized theological agreement and endowed it with a powerful thrust throughout Jewish thought. In the words of Zechariah, "The Lord shall be King over all the earth; and in that day shall the Lord be One, and His name one." (Zech. 14:9) The *Aleinu* prayer that religious Jews recite three times each day is another central Jewish text that proclaims not religious diversity, but uniformity:

> We place our hope in you, Lord our God, that we may soon see your glory when . . . all humanity will call on Your name . . . and all the world's inhabitants will realize that to You every knee must bow and every tongue must swear loyalty.

In the face of these potent visions of religious uniformity, it is not self-evident that the idea of religious diversity is an important Jewish *desideratum.* Can traditional Jews see the Image of God in the face of the religious Other? In the contemporary Western world where people interact daily with others of different faiths, these questions are of momentous theological, moral and social significance.

How does Jewish thought regard religious diversity and evaluate the religious Other? I want to analyze these general subjects by considering a number of more specific questions:

1. Does Judaism have a fundamental position of tolerance, pluralism or indifference toward other faiths and their worshippers?

2. Is the endorsement of tolerance and religious pluralism an ideal or merely a pragmatic concession?

3. What are the limits of legitimate religious diversity?

4. Is religious uniformity a value to be actively pursued in history or an ideal reserved only for *yimot ha-mashiaḥ*, the messianic era at the end of history?

5. If religious uniformity is an ideal, what are legitimate methods for achieving that consensus?

II. SOME CLARIFICATIONS

Before analyzing these questions, it will help to state a number of preliminary observations about the nature of Jewish theological, legal and philosophic traditions.

In referring to Judaism or Jewish tradition, I am relating to sacred Jewish Scriptures (The Torah) and their rabbinic commentaries, the Talmud and the corpus of post-talmudic rabbinic commentary on Talmud, medieval and modern Jewish philosophical writings as well as the living experience of the Jewish people throughout history. This is a vast field consisting of many voices, and rarely is there unanimity on any given issue. Judaism's intellectual tradition is a culture of dialectic and disagreement, where dissent is present on issues both large and small. Even axiomatic principles and foundational texts often give rise to diverse and conflicting interpretations.

For example, consider the following question that, as we soon will see, has extensive implications for our study: Is the Torah directed exclusively at Jews or is it ideally a divine code for all humanity?

One popular rabbinic opinion announces,

> The Torah was given in a free place [the desert of Sinai], for had the Torah been given in the land of Israel, the Israelites could have said to the nations of the world, "You have no share in it." But now that it was given in the wilderness publicly and openly, in a place that is free for all, everyone wishing to accept it could come and accept it.[1]

This rabbinic statement claims that the Torah was given in the desert to demonstrate that it is not exclusively directed at Jews. Quite the contrary: the giving of the Torah in no-man's land

1. *Mekhilta De-Rabbi Ishmael, Ba-Hodesh.*

was a clear signal that the Torah was intended for all peoples. Implicitly, then, "Torah is available to all those who come into the world. It remains in place, available for anyone to take it. The Torah is the litmus test for all humanity, not just Jews."[2]

Conversely, the talmudic authority Rabbi Yohanan declared that, "a non-Jew who studies the Torah deserves death, for it is written, 'Moses commanded us with the Torah, [it is] the inheritance of the congregation of Jacob' (Deut. 33:4) – it is our inheritance, not theirs;" and R. Simeon ben Lakish taught that "a non-Jew who keeps a day of rest deserves death."[3]

These are two absolutely incompatible rabbinic positions. Which is correct? Is God's revelation to the Jewish people universal, or limited only to that people? The answer is "both," depending on time, context and inquiry. Jewish tradition and theology are in their essence dialectical and pluralistic, with few absolutely categorical truths: "These and these are the words of the living God," concluded the talmudic rabbis.[4] One should hesitate, therefore, to infer conclusions simplistically from isolated scriptural verses or individual rabbinic pronouncements. Understanding Jewish teachings demands working diligently to ferret out normatively accepted positions from minority or non-normative claims.

Closely related to the above methodological point is the fact

2. Marc Hirshman, "Rabbinic Universalism in the Second and Third Centuries." *Harvard Theological Review* 93 (2000), 101–115. For other rabbinic statements implying this, see *Sifrei*, Numbers 119.

3. BT *Sanhedrin* 58b–59a. It is undetermined whether "deserves death" is to be taken literally, or is only hyperbole, meant to signify harsh condemnation. Such rhetorical hyperbole is common in rabbinic statements. Whether literal or only hyperbole, it was, of course, never practiced.

4. BT *Eruvin* 13b. Another bold rabbinic expression of Jewish pluralism and its problematics is: "This one prohibits and this one permits. How, then, can I learn Torah? . . . All the words have been given by a single shepherd, one God created them, one Provider gave them, the Lord of all deeds, Blessed be He, has spoken them. So make yourself a heart of many rooms and bring into it the words of the House of Shammai and the words of the House of Hillel" (*Tosefta*, Jerusalem Talmud *Sotah* 7:12).

that neither Jewish theology, nor law nor philosophy are strictly deductive disciplines that yield logically necessary conclusions.[5] Halakhic rulings and conclusions are influenced by historical experience, time and place. In other words, Jewish theology places a premium on the lived experience of the Jewish people rather than on dogma and theoretical first principles. As our human experience and conceptions of God evolve, so has Jewish theology.

One highly relevant example for our study is how *halakhah* evaluated Christianity over time. In the first and second centuries, Jewish Christians were considered *minim* – intolerable heretics. After Christianity broke from Judaism and became primarily a gentile religion, rabbis considered Christian belief in the trinity and incarnation to be unacceptable violations of the belief in the One Creator of the universe because those beliefs violated pure monotheism and divine incorporeality. Later during the late Middle Ages, rabbis living in Christian Europe staked out a position that Jewish law required only Jews to believe in pure monotheism, and validated belief in the trinity for Christians because the triune Christian conception included the true Creator of heaven and earth. This position became normative Jewish teaching for European Jews from the late Middle Ages into modernity, primarily because of the social, economic and political changes in relations between Jews and Christians.[6] In other words, the normative Jewish legal and theological positions shifted. In fact, very few positions in Judaism are absolute dogma that are immune to reconsideration and change.[7]

The debate about what constitutes core unchangeable belief in Judaism is robust, yet few maintain that recognition of other

5. See Chapter One.

6. See Jacob Katz, *Exclusiveness and Tolerance* (Jerusalem: Schocken, 1962), Ch. X, and Eugene Korn, "Rethinking Christianity" in *Jewish Theology and World Religions* (Littman Library of World Civilization, 2012), 203–204.

7. Minority opinions in Jewish law were preserved and studied because under different circumstances or eras, they might become normative opinions to be followed (*Mishna Eduyot*, Ch. 1).

religions, tolerance and legitimate religious pluralism are included in this small subset.[8] On the contrary, attitudes to gentiles and their faiths are among the subjects in Jewish tradition that were most influenced by the fluctuating Jewish experience with gentiles throughout history.

In Jewish tradition, *halakhah* plays the dominant role in rabbinic thought, while philosophy and theology play secondary roles. While law does not exhaust rabbinic tradition (as the harsh polemical Christian and secular antagonists of Judaism have incorrectly asserted), theological principles and concepts are frequently derived from case law or legal categories, rather than the reverse, Hence halakhic texts and legal analysis are often indispensable to determining Jewish theological, philosophic and ethical ideas.

III. THE COVENANT

Judaism is a covenantal faith. At its foundation, Judaism is the expression of the biblical covenant between God and the Jewish people. The sacred pact was initiated with Abraham (Gen. 12–15) and was in turn later bequeathed to Isaac, Jacob and their progeny. The family covenant later blossomed into a national covenant when the Israelite nation experienced the exodus from Egyptian slavery and accepted Mosaic revelation at Sinai (Ex. 19–20). Since that revelation, the starting point of rabbinic theology has been that each Jew is bound by the 613 divine commandments of the Mosaic covenant, whose details are defined by Jewish law. Indeed, responsibility to this covenant and the sense of "commandedness" is the traditional definition of

8. For an extensive treatment of the debate on the content of Jewish dogma, see Marc Shapiro, *The Limits of Orthodox Theology* (London: Littman Library of Jewish Civilization, 2004), and Menachem Kellner, *Must a Jew Believe Anything?* (London: Littman Library of Jewish Civilization, 2006).

Jewish identity. The most prominent sign of male Jewish identity is circumcision, whose Hebrew term is *berit* – covenant.

As we have just seen, some rabbinic speculation pointed in the direction of this covenant (Torah) having relevance for all humanity, but in practice Jewish tradition limited the obligations of the Abrahamic/Mosaic covenant to the Jewish people. At best, the Torah of Moses might apply to all humanity only in the distant future of the messianic era, after history as we know it has ended. But prior to the *eschaton*, the Jewish covenant remains particularistic: The Torah addresses the Jewish people uniquely, and in normative Jewish thought, the people of Israel remain singularly elected by God. The biblical prophets and the talmudic rabbis poetically conceptualized the covenant as an intimate partnership between God and the Jewish people, and the private and exclusive nature of the relationship is why the prophets Isaiah, Zechariah, Jeremiah and Hosea repeatedly use the metaphor of marriage in referring to the covenantal relationship between God and the Jewish people.

Judaism has taken much unkind and unfair criticism from Christian polemicists and Enlightenment rationalists for its particularist conception of the biblical covenant. It was, to use Kierkegaard's phrase, "a scandal of particularity." Those critics were seduced by "Plato's ghost," who insisted that truth was universal, so that what is true for one person must be true for all persons at all times.[9] Judaism resisted the urge to universalize the biblical covenant, and it is precisely the particularistic nature of the Sinai covenant that provides Jewish theology and law with the logical opening for acknowledging valid non-Jewish religions and conceptions, i.e. theological pluralism. Because it is particular to Jews, the covenant created space for other modes

9. I owe this formulation of Plato to Jonathan Sacks, *Dignity of Difference*. (London: Continuum, 2002), 49.

of human-divine contact, and for different theological conditions that bestow dignity and legitimacy upon the gentile Other.

Universalism has an ambivalent logic. Universal theological schemes possess the virtue of providing all people with the possibility of a relationship of love, grace, and salvation before God. However, universal doctrines are also imperialistic. By their very nature they deny valid alternative schema, and so they lead easily to delegitimizing those who do not subscribe or submit to the universal vision. They seek to eliminate differences by imposing one faith, one regime or one empire on all humanity. In the end, all universal doctrines are the logical opposite of pluralism and often the natural opponents of tolerance.

As we saw in the previous chapter, Isaiah Berlin articulated the grave danger of universal theological monism. Believers inevitably try to impose their belief system on all humanity, and history has proven the truth of Berlin's tragic conclusion: "This belief was responsible for the oceans of blood. No Kingdom of Love ever sprang from it, nor could it."[10]

From the Christian apostle Paul onward, Christian theology universalized the biblical covenant, expanding the original biblical view from the descendants of Abraham to all humanity. The consequences of this universalizing logic were the dogmatic insistence on a single universal redeeming covenant, and that belief in Christianity was the exclusive path to theological truth. Thus the Catholic Church has taught since medieval times "*Extra ecclesiam nulla salus*" – There is no salvation outside the Church. Perhaps more critically for our study, those outside the church were deemed inferior and barely tolerated *in this world* also.[11] As the only non-Christians in medieval Europe,

10. *Liberty* (Oxford: Oxford University Press, 2002), 345.

11. The second century Church father, Irenaeus, explained the original import of the principle: "[The Church] is the entrance to life; all others are thieves and robbers. On this account we are bound to avoid them . . . We hear it declared of the unbelieving and the blinded of this world that they shall not inherit the world

Jews experienced this intolerance in their flesh. Christians considered Judaism blasphemous and illegitimate, and saw Jews as unbelievers to be treated as social and spiritual outcasts. Jewish stubbornness and "blindness" to universal Christian truth were grounds for imposing humiliation, discrimination, conversion and physical persecution upon them. Some of this hostility was defended on the grounds that it expressed love and concern, for without conversion to Christianity, Jews were "lost." In other words, the claim of universality by the Catholic Church led directly to a denial of religious pluralism in principle and only minimal toleration in fact.

IV. THE NOAHIDE COVENANT

In addition to the Mosaic covenant at Sinai, a universal covenant known in rabbinic language as the Noahide covenant is a core element of Jewish tradition. The necessity of this covenant is eminently logical, since as we have seen, a cardinal Jewish theological and moral principle is that God created every human being *b'Tselem Elokim* – in the Image of God. Hence all humans are endowed with intrinsic dignity and spiritual capacities. If so, the Creator of all humanity could not possibly restrict divine love to one people. God must in some way relate to all His children with love and responsibility. The God of the first eleven chapters of the Torah, the Creator of the cosmos, cannot be an ethnic, tribal God.

The Bible (Gen. 9) relates that after the great flood, God established a covenant with Noah and his descendants, i.e. all

---

of life which is to come . . . Resist them in defense of the only true and life-giving faith, which the Church has received from the Apostles and imparted to her sons." (*Against Heresies*, Book III) After the Second Vatican Council and its document, *Lumen Gentium,* the Catholic Church accepted a more expansive interpretation that allowed salvation to some outside the Church. This is the official Catholic Church position today.

humanity. According to Jewish teachings, this covenant contains exactly seven commandments: the six prohibitions against murder, theft, sexual wildness, idolatry, eating a limb of a live animal (symbolizing cruelty and disdain for life) and blasphemy, as well as the one positive injunction to establish courts of law to justly enforce those six prohibitions to ensure that people do not live in a pre-civilized brutal and lawless Hobbesian jungle.[12] The rabbis understood blasphemy in this context to mean intolerance directed toward any true religion teaching about the universal Creator. Thus the Noahide covenant is the vehicle that enables non-Jews to stand responsible before God, and it is this theological principle that grants them social, moral and theological legitimacy in Jewish thought.

It is important to note that technically the Noahide covenant does not require a gentile Noahide to believe in God.[13] The obligations associated with this covenant are primarily, if not exclusively, moral. At most, Noahides might be required to believe in a generic creator who implanted a moral order in the world and who ensures punishment to people who violate that order.[14] That is, Noahides might be required to believe in a transcendent authority, that "God is," but not in any more specific theology or particular way to worship God.

In effect, the rabbis subscribed to a double covenant theory. Jews have a covenant of 613 commandments, while all gentiles are members of the seven commandment Noahide covenant. It

12. *Tosefta Avodah Zarah* 8:4 and Maimonides, MT, *The Laws of Kings and their Wars* (*Hilkhot Melakhim*), 9:1.

13. Maimonides may have thought that theological knowledge was necessary, but the content of that knowledge is in question. See Steven Schwarzschild, "Do Noahides Have to Believe in Revelation?" *Jewish Quarterly Review* 58 (1962), and Eugene Korn, "Gentiles, The World to Come and Judaism: The Odyssey of a Rabbinic Text" *Modern Judaism*, October 1994.

14. The rabbis who formulated the concept of the universal Noahide covenant believed that one could not lead a coherent moral life without believing in a divine authority who punished the guilty and rewarded the innocent. Like other pre-moderns, a secular ethic was unthinkable.

is crucial to understand that each covenant is theologically valid for its respective adherents, and Noahides are not expected to convert to the Jewish covenant or Judaism. All gentiles who live faithfully by these basic laws of civilization are considered to be worthy gentiles, *benei Noaḥ* ("children of Noah") in rabbinic parlance.[15] Their covenant is independent and authentic, and observing the Noahide covenant is a valid way of life in the eyes of both God and the rabbis.[16]

In summary, we may say that Jewish theology divides humanity into three categories: Jews, righteous Noahides whose valid beliefs dictate that they obey the moral Noahide commandments, and pagans whose beliefs do not respect the Noahide obligations and were therefore deemed illicit.

V. IDOLATRY AS THE LIMIT OF TOLERANCE

In theory Judaism's double covenant theology creates a wide opportunity for acknowledging the legitimacy of religious diversity, the validity of non-Jewish religious forms and respect for gentiles, all without Jews sacrificing the primacy of their unique status in God's economy or their particularistic Jewish theological convictions.

Yet a thorny problem lurks behind this simple picture. It turns on defining the criteria for violating Noahide commandments, and, more specifically, what constitutes the Noahide prohibition against idolatry. Jewish Scriptures, the Talmud and Jewish law all insist upon intolerance toward idolatry and its worshippers

15. Maimonides, MT, *The Laws of Kings and their Wars*, 8:10.

16. Noahides are accorded positive status in this worldview. According to some rabbinic opinions gentiles who faithfully keep the Noahide commandments are even regarded by God as more beloved than Jews who violate the fundamentals of their covenant of 613 commandments. See Jacob Emden, *Seder Olam Rabah Vezuta*, cited in Oscar Z. Fasman, "An Epistle on Tolerance by a 'Rabbinic Zealot.'" In Leo Jung, (ed.). *Judaism in a Changing World* (New York: 1939), 121–139.

– sometimes to the point of annihilation.[17] The definition of idolatry and the delineation of who falls within the idolatrous domain is thus the key to determining Judaism's acceptance of non-Jews and the limits of legitimate religious pluralism.

Throughout the Bible idolatry represents the morally and spiritually intolerable, and numerous religious texts require its destruction. So harshly did the sacred Jewish Scriptures assess idolatry that they teach that God commanded the Israelites to "let no [idolatrous] soul remain alive" (Deut. 20:16) when entering the Promised Land.[18] In later rabbinic legal, ethical and theological discourse too, idolatry represented the line where tolerance ends and intolerance is warranted.[19] The covenant of Noah allowed for theological pluralism and practical tolerance, yet only within limits.

The Hebrew term most frequently employed for idolatry in rabbinic and Jewish legal literature is *avodah zarah,* literally "foreign worship." Technically, *avodah zarah* means all worship deemed illicit by Jewish law, both in its idolatrous and non-idolatrous manifestations.[20] While often identified with the pagan idolatry that the Torah so loudly condemns, it is in fact a

17. Since the demand to exterminate the Canaanite and Amalekite nations appears repeatedly and insistently in the books of Deuteronomy, Joshua, and Samuel, and because King Saul lost his kingship due to his failure to execute this commandment literally, the harsh requirement of annihilation was understood literally by Jewish legal tradition. See Chapter Four for how rabbinic tradition interpreted these *mitsvot.*

18. This refers to the seven idolatrous Canaanite nations inhabiting the land. The biblical accounts of the actual conquests found in the Book of Joshua reiterate that his army did not leave any idolatrous Canaanite alive when possible. There is extensive discussion in Jewish literature of the moral problematics of this command. See Chapter Four, as well as *The Gift of the Land and the Fate of the Canaanites in Jewish Thought,* Katell Berthelot, ed. Menachem Hirshman and Josef David, (Oxford U., 2014) and Avi Sagi, "The Punishment of Amalek in Jewish Tradition: Coping with the Moral Problem," *Harvard Theological Review* 87,3 (1994), 323–346.

19. See the trenchant analysis of idolatry and its function in *Idolatry* by Moshe Halbertal and Avishai Margolit, (Cambridge, MA: Harvard U., 1994).

20. For further elaboration, see Eugene Korn, "Rethinking Christianity" *op. cit,* p. 201.

wider category that also includes non-pagan but still illegitimate worship.

Rabbinic thinkers understand the category of *avodah zarah* and who falls under the rubric of an intolerable idolator differently. Fundamentally, two competing conceptions are dominant in Jewish thought, and both are inferred from biblical texts. The Torah (e.g. Deut. 4,12,16) sometimes describes idolators as people who worship celestial bodies, stars and trees (i.e. any finite physical object) because they mistakenly understand them to be divine. In other places (e.g. Lev. 18; Deut. 12) the Bible portrays idolators as people or cultures with abominable immoral practices. The first more cognitive conception was emphasized by rabbis with philosophic bents, most prominently the twelfth century halakhist, doctor and philosopher, Maimonides, who lived in Muslim Spain and Egypt. As the greatest Jewish legal authority in Jewish history, Maimonides exerts a prodigious influence over the Jewish canon. And as rationalist philosopher steeped in the metaphysics of Aristotle, he understood idolatry as any conceptual error that identifies God with something that is in fact not divine,[21] specifically anything that is physical, plural, has emotions or is subject to change.

Maimonides thus considered not only ancient sun worship, star worship and polytheism to constitute idolatry, but also judged Christianity to be idolatrous because of its doctrines of the incarnation and the trinity. He considered Christians who held these beliefs to be idolators and subject to all the same strictures of alienation and intolerance as were the biblical Canaanites and other ancient pagans. Driven by intellectual consistency, Maimonides was no Jewish chauvinist: He considered Jews who harbored personalistic conceptions of God, i.e. that God has human emotions of anger, love and regret, to be worse offenders

21. This is why Maimonides placed the laws regarding idolatry in his legal code, *Mishneh Torah* in the Book of Knowledge (*Sefer Madda*).

than gentiles who believed that God was physical.[22] By contrast, Islam's conception of Allah, is free of any corporeal dimension and insists on absolute monotheism (similar to Judaism in that respect). Hence Maimonides considered Muslims to be observant Noahides and Islamic theology regarding God to be legitimate.

It is clear that Maimonides' life experiences influenced his legal views. He never lived with Christians and learned about Christianity only from books. Except for his brief stay in Crusader Palestine, he resided all his life in Muslim societies. It was thus not difficult psychologically for him to categorize Christianity as idolatry and see Christians as the intolerable Other. Nor did he have to grapple in his society with the practical difficulties that Jewish law would impose on Jewish interactions with Christians should Christians be considered to be idolators halakhically.

Rabbi Menachem Meiri, who lived in thirteenth century Christian Provence, emphasized the other biblical identification of idolators as primitive immoral pagans with abominable ethical, religious and sexual practices. He conceptualized idolatry in moral terms: Idolatry is cultic worship whose primary character is the absence of moral demands upon its worshipers. *Avodah zarah* is any religion that does not impose on its adherents the fundamental ethical restraints against murder, theft, sexual wildness, lawlessness, that is, the foundation of orderly civilized society.[23] Thus according to Meiri, even polytheists and corporealists who subscribed to fundamental moral values could belong to the domain of valid believers. The Torah requires pure monotheism of Jews, but not of gentiles. Meiri had no theological or practical problem with Christianity or any other civilizing religion of which he could possibly be aware. In fact, he relegated illegitimate idolatry of his day to the far-flung corners of the

22. *Guide of the Perplexed*, I:36.

23. See his commentary on the Talmud, *Beit ha-Beḥirah*, BT *Sanhedrin* 57a and *Avodah Zarah* 20a.

earth – i.e. only to places where no Jews lived. In doing so he consigned Judaism's mandatory intolerance of idolators to the realm of theory alone.[24]

Thus Jewish limits of tolerance, diversity and theological pluralism will vary significantly depending on how "foreign worship" is understood. In practice, while a number of contemporary religious Jews claim to accept Maimonides' harsh ruling against Christianity, this is merely rhetorical since no Jew consistently follows Maimonides' ruling in practice.[25]

Both the Torah and Jewish law affirmed the residency and civil rights of gentiles in an ideal Jewish polity governed by Jewish religious law. The Bible denotes such a person as a *ger toshav* ("resident alien") and repeatedly (Ex. 22:21, 23:9; Lev. 19:33; Deut. 24:17, 27:19) warns Jews not to oppress or take advantage of this stranger in their midst.

Under Jewish law, Jews have rigorous religious obligations to support and sustain this gentile stranger economically, and ensure that he not dwell "close to the border [due to danger of an enemy attack] or in an unseemly place; rather, he should reside in a goodly dwelling in the midst of the Land of Israel, in a place where his business or artisanship can prosper."[26] This is the rabbinic expansion of Jewish civil obligations toward the religious Other that is derived from the biblical commandment, "He [the gentile] shall dwell in your midst, in whatever place he will choose, in any one of your cities, wherever it is beneficial to him; you must not taunt him." (Deut. 23:16)

It is important to note that the insistence on legitimate religious

24. How Meiri would assess modern moral atheists is an important and complicated issue. I am convinced that Meiri required belief in and submission to a transcendent God because like nearly every other thinker in the Middle Ages he assumed that any moral code lacking a punitive and rewarding divine authority could not be sustained. Nor is this idea confined to the Middle Ages. In *The Brothers Karamazov*, Dostoevsky claimed that "without God, all is permitted."

25. See Eugene Korn, "Rethinking Christianity" *op. cit.* p. 197.

26. BT, *Gerim*, 3:3,4.

diversity and the religious obligations devolving upon Jews to protect the safety, dignity and economic health of the religious Other in their midst, are present even in *the ideal* Jewish polity where Jews are sovereign. This indicates that acceptance and protection of the gentile are not practical concessions to *realpolitik*, but obligatory values that religious Jews must implement when they possess political power and social dominance. While the status of the *ger toshav* is technically applicable only in the Jewish homeland under Jewish sovereignty, the concept is rich in general implications for the values of pluralism, tolerance and obligations toward the religious Other in Judaism. The Bible, Jewish law and the Talmud could have constructed the ideal as a monolithically Jewish polity in which there was no religious diversity and no need to extend recognition or protection of gentiles. Pointedly, they did not.

Who qualifies as a *ger toshav,* with rights of residency and protection in this ideal Jewish polity? The Talmud decided that it is any non-Jew who foreswears idolatry and accepts the ethical requirements of the Noahide commandments.[27] Given that this status is a civil and social one, it is reasonable to assume that the renunciation of idolatry required of the resident stranger is achieved by his commitment to obey the fundamental moral responsibilities required for membership in a stable and just society – that is, Meiri's conception of idolatry. Testing the stranger for the purity of his metaphysical understanding of God (i.e. Maimonides' understanding of idolatry) makes no sense in this context. It is more logical for the residency requirement to provide warrant that the would-be resident be a law-abiding civilized member of Jewish society than that he be a sophisticated theologian.

Similarly, it would seem that in our pluralistic modern and post-modern societies where people of different Abrahamic and

27. *Ibid.* See also Maimonides, MT, *The Laws of Kings and their Wars*, 8:10.

Asian religions interact regularly, where theological ideas play a less significant role than in the past, where democracy is a dominant ethos, where atheists exhibit social and moral responsibility no less than believers, and where the concept of universal human rights is an intrinsic part of our Western worldview, Meiri's conception of idolatry as behavior bereft of civil and moral restraint stakes out the proper conception of Jewish tolerance of gentiles and its limits.[28] This conception grants legitimacy to anyone committed to ethical principles, social responsibility, compassion for others and improving the world that God created for his creatures to flourish. In practice, most Jews – religious and secular, lay and rabbinic – adhere to this policy, whether conscious of Meiri's theory or not. In other words, it has become Judaism's normative approach today.

VI. THE AFTERLIFE AND THE MESSIANIC ERA

Thus far I have analyzed Jewish law and theology's approach to religious diversity in the empirical world as we know it. What of the afterlife, known as *olam ha-ba* ("the world to come") in Jewish tradition? Who is entitled to such exalted status? The reward of eternal life is a fundamental principle of Judaism, but unlike Christian theology, Jewish religious thought devotes little time to eschatology and the nature of life after death. Its focus is life on earth and the responsibilities of Jews while alive in this world. Also unlike Christians, Jews do not talk of "eternal salvation," rather of "a share in the world to come." Nor is this a purely distant metaphysical concern. In all theological traditions, as in Judaism, earning eternal afterlife is an indicator of what

28. While Meiri thought that idolatry was found only in the far-flung corners of the earth, today that is not so. A Muslim or Jewish terrorist – should not be tolerated because of his behavior, even though his theology may be monotheistic. See also Alon Goshen-Gottstein, "Concluding Reflections" in *World Religions and Jewish Theology*, op. cit.

is understood to be a meritorious life in this world, both for ourselves and others.

Yet there are significant Jewish texts that speculate about the after-life. The talmudic and medieval rabbis paid some gentiles the ultimate theological compliment by teaching that "righteous gentiles have a share in the world to come."[29] Again it was Maimonides who set the normative Jewish position on this question. He ruled in accordance with the talmudic opinion that righteous gentiles do participate in the world to come, and rejected the rival talmudic opinion that such salvation was confined to Jews.[30] Even after accepting this broad principle, two critical questions remain: (1) What earthly life qualifies a person to gain a share in the world to come? and (2) What, if any, religious belief is required to merit this eternal life? If theological belief *is* necessary and that required belief is the acceptance of all Mosaic revelation at Sinai, then *de facto* the only gentiles with a share in the world to come would be those few who subscribe to Orthodox Jewish theology. Thus potential universal salvation could easily be denuded of its breadth – in other words, *Extra Synagogam nulla salus* – "Outside the synagogue there is no salvation."

A few Jewish particularists took this extreme position based on an idiosyncratic reading of a key Maimonidean text on the question,[31] yet nothing suggests that Maimonides himself subscribed to this restrictive particularist view. He was a philosophical and theological universalist who believed that metaphysical knowledge was necessary for eternal life and that this knowledge was not contingent on any particular national history. While Jewish tradition gives Jews some advantage over others because

29. BT *Sanhedrin* 105a and Maimonides, MT, *Laws of Repentance* 3:5, *Laws of Testimony* 2:10 and *The Laws of Kings and their Wars*, 8:11. For an extended discussion of salvation for righteous gentiles, see Schwarzschild, *op. cit.* and Korn, "Gentiles, The World to Come and Judaism: The Odyssey of a Rabbinic Text," *op. cit.*

30. Maimonides, MT, *The Laws of Kings and their Wars*, 8:11.

31. See Eugene Korn, "Gentiles, the World to Come as and Judaism," *op. cit.*

of their possession of divine revelation, Maimonides taught that true knowledge of God is a rational capability that is open to any dedicated human being.[32] This is also the position of modern Jewish rationalist philosophers, foremost among them Moses Mendelssohn.[33]

Most rabbinic thinkers were not as philosophically oriented as was Maimonides, and hewed close to the explicit requirements of the Noahide covenant. They insisted that gentiles merited eternal life when they scrupulously commit themselves to the moral life of social responsibility and restraint required by the seven practical Noahide commandments.[34]

In other words, the majority rationalist Jewish position regarding salvation is close to Meiri's ethical interpretation of idolatry and the Noahide covenant. It is important to understand, however, that whether we accept Maimonides' metaphysically oriented requirement of eternal salvation or Meiri's more ethical conception, the "world to come" is a religiously diverse community. The difference lies primarily in the density of its population: Maimonides' world to come was a sparsely populated realm of metaphysically sophisticated Jewish and gentile souls (i.e. intelligences), while Meiri's was a more populous diverse community of beings who had lived a morally committed and ethically responsible life.

What of the messianic era, not the eternal metaphysical realm of the after-life but the culmination of sacred history when the

32. Maimonides, MT, *Laws of Jubilee* 13:13; *Guide of the Perplexed* I; 1–2 and III: 51. For a full explanation of this point in Maimonides, see Menachem Kellner, "We Are Not Alone." In *Radical Responsibility: Celebrating the Thought of Chief Rabbi Lord Jonathan Sacks.* (Jerusalem: Koren, 2012), 139–154; Menachem Kellner, *Maimonides' the Universalist* (London: Littman Library of Jewish Civilization, 2020), and his *Gam Hem Keruyim Adam: Ha-Nohkri Be-Einei Ha-Rambam* [Heb.] ("*They also are Called Human: The Gentile in the Eyes of Maimonides*") (Ramat Gan, Israel: Bar-Ilan U., 2016).

33. See Alexander Altmann, *Moses Mendelssohn: A Biographical Study.* (Tuscaloosa, AL: University of Alabama, 1973), 217–218.

34. See, for instance, Rabbi Abraham Kook, *Letters*, [Heb.] Vol. 1, 100.

divine covenant is fulfilled?[35] This conception is actually more significant for our study, since Jewish thinkers have understood the messianic era to represent the ideal state of human affairs of our social and religious orders. The messianic ideal also highlights the relationship between the theological mission of the Jewish people and the rest of humanity.

The central paradox of the Bible is that the universal God of all creation enters a covenant with a particular people (the Jews) that is ideally situated in a limited particular geography (Canaan/Land of Israel). The tension between the universal God and the particularist covenant is resolved by Abraham's and his descendants' universal mission. The Torah insists that the purpose of God's election of the Jewish people is for the Jewish nation to serve all humanity, since at the first moment of covenant God tells Abraham, "You shall be a blessing. . . . Through you [and your progeny] all the nations of the earth shall be blessed." (Gen. 12:2–3) The Jewish covenantal mission is delineated further when God informs Abraham that to fulfill his covenantal mission he is to "instruct his children and his posterity to keep the way of the Lord, by doing *tsedaqah u'mishpat*, what is right and just." (Gen. 18:19)

This universal covenantal purpose is so essential in the Torah, that it is repeated four additional times to Abraham, his son Isaac and his grandson Jacob as heirs to the covenant. (Gen. 18:18; 22:18; 26:4; 28:13–14)

Later the Torah indicates that Jewish covenantal mission connects to humanity when it demands that the Jewish people be "a kingdom of priests" (Ex. 19:6), i.e. the entire Jewish people is charged with the priestly function of bestowing divine blessing upon the other nations of the world.[36] Later still, this universal

35. While some early rabbinic opinions identified the messianic era with the afterlife, Maimonides sharply distinguished between the two. Owing to his prodigious influence, most post-Maimonidean rabbinic opinions accepted his distinction.

36. See Eugene Korn, "The People Israel, Christianity and the Covenantal

mission is repeated in different formulation by the Jewish prophets: "I will make you a light of the nations, that My salvation may reach the ends of the earth." (Isa. 49:6) Thus, the world was not created for the Jewish people, but the converse: the Jewish people were created for the world.[37] It is this universal dimension of the Jewish covenant that rescues the coherence of the Torah's narrative. It bridges the disparity between God's cosmic concern in the Bible's first eleven chapters, and the intensely particularistic focus on the Jewish people that dominates the remainder of the Bible.[38]

Rabbinic authorities understood these covenantal goals of blessing and instruction to refer to bearing witness to and informing all humanity of the one transcendent Creator as well as to demonstrating commitment to the divine ethic of righteousness and justice – what one prominent contemporary rabbi has termed "ethical monotheism."[39] Abraham was primarily a model and teacher, and the rabbinic stories contend that he converted others through rational persuasion and modeling a life of compassionate ethical witness. Significantly, however, Abraham's faith was not the particular faith of Judaism, but a more generic faith in the single Creator of the universe and His moral law.[40] Since Abraham lived generations before the Mosaic revelation that provides the foundation for Judaism as we know it today, technically Abraham was a theological Noahide, not a Jew

---

Responsibility to History." In *Covenant and Hope*. Edited by Jenson Robert W and Eugene Korn. (Grand Rapids, MI: Eerdmans, 2012), 145–172.

37. Naftali Zvi Berliner, Commentary on the Torah (*Ha-emeq Davar*). Introduction to the Book of Exodus.

38. For further elaboration on the paradoxical particularistic/universalistic character of the biblical covenant see Jon D. Levenson, "The Universal Horizon of Biblical Particularism" in *Ethnicity and the Bible,* edited by Mark R. Brett. Leiden, (Netherlands: Brill, 2002), 143–169.

39. Shlomo Riskin, "Covenant and Conversion: The United Mission to Redeem the World" in *Covenant and Hope, op. cit.* 99–128.

40. Maimonides, MT, *Laws of Idolatry*, 1:1–3, *The Laws of Kings and their Wars,* 9:1, *Book of Commandments*, positive commandment 3.

commanded by the particularistic law given to Moses at Sinai.[41]

Abraham is the prototype of covenantal responsibility in Jewish tradition. His model together with the independent validity of the Noahide covenant are the primary reasons that for nearly all of Jewish history, Jews eschewed attempts to convert others to Judaism. There simply was no theological need to do so. Even today, there is a distinct aversion to proselytizing gentiles. However according to *halakhah*, Jews have the religious obligation to influence gentiles toward the universal Noahide moral code without any hint of making them Jews.[42] In this way the rabbinic theology of religious diversity entails a sensitive dialectic between the Noahide and Mosaic covenants: The responsibility to maintain concern for the welfare of all human beings and to teach ethical commitment whenever possible emanates from the Noahide covenant, while the aversion to forcing upon others unique Jewish religious requirements and commitments emerges from the particularistic Mosaic covenant.

The biblical prophets provide a stunning picture of what human society will look like when the Jewish covenantal mission is achieved. Isaiah, Micah, Amos, Zechariah and Jeremiah portray the messianic era as a human society committed to ethical monotheism, one shorn of violence and suffused with harmony, peace and human flourishing. This ideal is at once both unified and diverse: All peoples have come to accept the moral authority of

41. This is a critical, but not widely appreciated point. It is however, the consensus of the majority of medieval Jewish biblical commentators. See commentaries on Genesis 26:5 by Rabbis David Kimkhi (Radak), Obadiah Seforno, Moses ben Nahman (Naḥmanides), Abraham Ibn Ezra, Samuel ben Meir (Rashbam), and Chizkiya bar Manoach (Ḥizkuni). See also Maimonides, *MT, Laws of Kings*, 9:1. For a contemporary expression of this position by a traditionalist rabbinic authority, see Joseph Soloveitchik, *Abraham's Journey*, ed. David Shatz, Joel B. Wolowelsky, and Reuven Ziegler (Ktav, 2008), 58; for further elaboration of Abraham as a theological Noahide, see Korn, "The People Israel, Christianity and the Covenantal Responsibility to History," *op. cit.*, 155–156.

42. Maimonides, MT, *The Laws of Kings and their Wars*, 8:10 and Riskin, op cit.

the God and fundamental moral values, yet the diverse nations of humanity retain their separate religious identities and worship the one Creator of the universe in their own ways. Micah's vision explicitly states this pluralism as part of this messianic ideal:

> It shall be in the end of days that the mountain of the Lord shall be established on top of all mountains and shall be exalted above the hills. And (many) peoples shall stream onto it. Many nations shall come, and say, "Come let us go up to the mountain of the Lord and to the house of the God of Jacob; and He will teach us His ways and walk in His paths. For the Torah shall go forth from Zion, and the word of the Lord from Jerusalem." They shall beat their swords into plowshares and their spears into pruning hooks. Nation shall not lift up sword against nation, nor shall they learn war anymore. But every man shall sit under his vine and his fig tree; and none shall make him afraid. . . . For let all people walk, *each in the name of his God* [emphasis added, EK] and we will walk in the name of the Lord our God for ever and ever." (4:1–5)[43]

As we saw earlier, Maimonides also understands this idyllic messianic picture as the culmination of Jewish covenantal life, and he emphasized its importance by concluding his *Mishneh Torah* with his vision of the messianic era.[44] His message is clear: The entire corpus of Jewish law that he codified in the work are designed to produce this supreme theological ideal.

Whether Maimonides believed that all people will subscribe to the same theological truths and religion at that time is subject to scholarly debate,[45] yet even those who claim that Maimonides envisaged religious unity in the messianic era understand that

43. The parallel passage in Isaiah 2:1–4 does not include "For let all people walk, each in the name of his God and we will walk in the name of the Lord our God for ever and ever." See commentaries of Shlomo ben Yitzhak (Rashi) and David Kimchi (Radak) on Micah 4:5, who interpret the verse not as *de jure* pluralism, but as *de facto* toleration of all who accept ethical monotheism.

44. End MT, *The Laws of Kings and their Wars*, 12:5.

45. See debate between Menachem Kellner and Chaim Rapoport on this

for him this ultimate universal religion would be a theologically pure worship unlike the specific religious form of worship today. This unity will be achieved by teaching fundamental theological truth, not by forcing particularist forms of religion or ethnic religious policies upon others. If there is conversion, it is neither to any single type of synagogue, church, mosque or ashram, nor to one particular liturgy, but to varying forms of commitment to the Creator of Heaven and Earth that allow for non-idolatrous differences in worship and practice.[46]

VII. THE OPEN FUTURE

The Torah principle that all persons are created in the Image of God, the rabbinic doctrine of the Noahide covenant with all humanity, and the particularistic Mosaic covenant together provide the legal and theological framework for the normative Jewish attitudes regarding religious diversity. These Jewish theological elements naturally give rise to an approach of tolerance toward the non-idolatrous gentiles. Jewish law and ethics can go further still: the category of *ger toshav*, the alien resident in a Jewish polity whom Jews are obligated to sustain and protect, establishes the basis for more than mere toleration. It is the theological and legal foundation for Jewish engagement with and taking responsibility for peaceful gentiles.

Of course there are perils to unbounded particularism also. A particularistic covenant can lead – and at times has led – to arrogance and narrow chauvinism. If Jews are uniquely loved

question in *Meorot,* Vol. 13 (2008), found at http://www.yctorah.org/content/view/436/10, accessed on February 7, 2020.

46. Maimonides maintained that pure monotheism without a hint of ethnic or Mosaic ritual was the ideal form of religion and that Mosaic ritual was a result of contingent (and therefore probably temporary) historical circumstances. (MT, Laws of Idolatry 1:3) In addition, he believed that contemplation constituted a higher form of worship than verbal prayer. Hence we can assume for him this silent meditation would be the common form of worship in the ideal messianic era.

and elected by God, as the particularistic Mosaic covenant asserts, Jews can come to regard gentiles as theologically and ontologically inferior, as mere background noise to the central biblical drama played out in religious history between God and the Jewish people. Such particularism leads not to the unmitigating pressure on the Other that so often characterizes theological universalism, but to its opposite – indifference and hostility.

The key to constructive religious pluralism is a sensitive dialectic that navigates carefully between the poles of particularistic and universalistic theological claims. This dialectic accepts the Jewish universal concern for all people and particularism's virtue of not absolutizing my own faith, which allows me to accept the differences of others. This dialectic should balance the two opposing religious sensibilities, with each pole exercising a constraint on the other.

Only today can Jews truly test this dialectic. When Jews were a weak minority scattered throughout Europe, Northern Africa and the Middle East for nearly two thousand years, they rarely practiced active intolerance toward the majority gentile populations in whose midst they lived, whether Christians or Muslims. Yet as Yehudah Halevi already noticed in the tenth century, perhaps it was only because they lacked the means to do so.[47] Were exilic Jews pluralists out of religious principle and Jewish teachings, or were they only tolerant due to their weakness?

Tolerance as a value and pluralism as a principal can be demonstrated only with the ability to exercise control and intolerance. The sovereign and majority status of approximately half of all Jews in the world today in the State of Israel are now testing the Jewish commitment to tolerance and acceptable religious diversity on moral, political and social levels. As a pluralistic democracy, Israel is legally committed to the rights of non-Jewish minorities. Yet neither pluralism nor tolerance is an absolute

47. *The Kuzari* I: sections 113–115.

value, and the proper limits of those values is being vigorously debated today among Israeli politicians and religious authorities alike. At stake is whether the sovereign Jewish majority in Israel can express its national integrity without falling prey to a narrow chauvinism that overlooks the dignity, equal rights and religious integrity of non-Jews and their beliefs.

The new Israeli conditions of independence, majority status and national sovereignty create the possibility for both liberal pluralism and particularism to express themselves. Yet under this freedom, narrow particularism runs unchecked among some insulated and hypernationalistic Israelis. Counter to national Israeli values and policies, at times these extremists deny the legitimacy of religious pluralism, advocate restricting the freedom of Israeli gentiles and limiting their residency rights, and even physically assault those in their midst – all on allegedly halakhic and theological grounds.[48] Tragically, God's particularist covenant with the Jewish people granting it election and title to the Land of Israel has led these particularists to deny the universal human equality endowed by the Image of God, the rights of gentile Israeli citizens and the legitimacy of religious diversity that the Noahide covenant entails.

As we have seen, absolute universalism can easily lead to a harmful doctrine of forced imperial inclusion, while the opposite ideology of extreme particularism can also evolve into a troublesome doctrine of religious exclusion. The latter one-sided parochialism leaves the God of all creation and the universal mission of the Jewish people in the deep background. Its proponents are

48. In 2009 the extremist rabbis Yitzhak Shapira and Yosef Elitzur published *Torat Hamelekh* ("The Teaching of the King"), *op. cit.*, which justifies killing innocent gentiles in war. In 2010, a number of Israeli nationalist rabbis wrote a public letter prohibiting selling Israeli land to gentiles. In 2015 Jewish nationalists set fire to the Church of Loaves and Fishes in the Galilee, claiming it to be a house of idolatry. And frequent incidents continue today of Jewish religious extremists defacing church properties in the ancient part of Jerusalem and assaulting Armenian priests living there.

led to absolutize the Jewish covenant for everyone on the Land and support a policy of religious imperialism and intolerance. The most extreme Jewish particularists have seized on elements of Jewish mysticism (*kabbalah*) and begun to advocate ethnic superiority, maintaining that Jews are ontologically superior to gentiles – in contradiction to the biblical and Jewish rationalist theological tradition.[49] They come morally close to the very anti-Semitic universalist enemies who victimized Jews in the medieval and modern Diaspora. They have become the enemies they hate.

Importantly, the prominent contemporary Jewish theologian Irving Greenberg has defined contemporary idolatry as all absolute monistic theological doctrines – whether universalist or particularist – that deny religious pluralism. They are idolatrous both because they mistake the finite human for the infinite Divine and because they inevitably lead to conflict, destruction and death.[50]

This phenomenon points to another truth about religion. As

49. One example is the mystic Rabbi Yitzhak Ginsburg, who has a significant following including Yitzhak Shapira and Yosef Elitzur (see previous note). His racial theory of Jewish ontological superiority is directly opposed to the rationalist strain of Jewish thought and ethics, again most clearly exemplified by Maimonides, as explained in Chapter Seven. For more on Ginsburg, see Don Seeman, "God's Honor, Violence, and the State" *op. cit.* Much of the impetus for the assertion of Jewish ontological distinctiveness and superiority comes from the medieval foundational text of Jewish mysticism, the *Zohar* and its subsequent commentators in the kabbalistic tradition.

50. "This pseudo-infinite cannot contain the infinity of life (or of human dignity). In fact, we know that idolatry is the god of death and that it creates a realm of death. . . . All human systems (even those that are given by divine revelation) that claim to be absolute, exercise no self-limitation and leave no room for the other turn into idolatry, i.e. into sources of death. . . . It is no accident that Nazism which sought perfection and eliminated all restrictions and limitations created a realm of total death – the kingdom of night. . . . All political systems and all religions that allow themselves to make unlimited absolute claims are led to idolatrous behaviors. They often generate death-dealing believers. . . . All social systems that "other" the other and absolutize their own host culture turn idolatrous and then degrade or destroy others." Irving Greenberg, "Pluralism and Partnership." In *For the Sake of Heaven and Earth.* (Philadelphia: Jewish Publication Society, 2004), 210.

mentioned earlier, no religion is intrinsically pacifistic or tolerant; nor is any religion violent and intolerant in its essence. Each religion's sacred texts and theologies at times counsel peace and tolerance, and at other times display intolerance and hostility. Which is essential and which marginal? What are the limits of its tolerance?

As noted, Christianity is mostly tolerant and accepting of diversity today, but in the Middle Ages it was intolerant of religious diversity. Islam was largely tolerant and comfortable with religious pluralism in some countries during the late Middle Ages, but today its Middle East varieties commonly exhibit intolerance and violent extremism. While Jews were largely pacifistic and tolerant in exile and most continue to be so today, the phenomenon of Jewish intolerance has begun to rise in Israel. Religious intolerance and violence have stained, and continues to stain, religious Muslim, Christian, Jewish, Hindu and even normally pacifist Buddhist communities. If so, while in a given time some religions tend more than others toward intolerance, extremism and violence, there is no "essential nature" of any faith – only the actions, thoughts, and testimonies that a living community of believers manifests at a given time in history. As we saw in the previous chapter, it is not sacred texts or theology that define a religion's essence or its character; it is, rather, how the believing community interprets, prioritizes and lives the meanings of those sacred texts and theologies that defines that community's religion.

In light of this truth it is clear that there is no single permanent Jewish theological position on religious diversity and tolerance of others. At some times Jewish particularism emphasizing gentile otherness and an expansive definition of idolatry that frowns on religious diversity gains ascendency. At other times a more open universalistic position may prevail built around the ideas of all people created in the Image of God, the Noahide covenant and Jewish obligations toward the *ger toshav*. In the best of times a dialectic balance operates, one that sustains Jewish identity and helps shape a constructive theological respect for diversity and acceptance of the Other. Like God Himself, who the Bible names, "I will be Who I will be," (Ex. 3:14) the future of Jewish theology is not determined. The responsibility for its future is in our human hands.

The nature of emerging Jewish doctrines regarding gentiles will depend greatly on the quality of Jewish relations with non-Jewish religions, persons and nations. When Jews feel oppressed and victimized, the former particularistic motif will naturally gain prominence. When Jews experience more security, tolerance and acceptance, they will feel sufficiently secure to open themselves to principled theological diversity and mutual religious appreciation. During those times Jewish thinkers and rabbis may begin to tackle the challenges that contemporary pluralistic life poses for Jewish theology and ethics.

Will Jewish tradition be used creatively to refashion the legal category of *ger toshav* to all peace-loving gentiles both inside and outside of sovereign Israel, emphasize the intrinsic dignity and equality of each person derived from his divine image, and reformulate Jewish legal and theological categories to better understand Asian religions and their believers? Will it develop a positive appreciation of ethical secularism?

Out of the ideals of tolerance, *de jure* pluralism and appreciation of human difference, a bold comprehensive Jewish ethic of religious diversity awaits us. This understanding will encompass Jews, Christians, Muslims, Asian believers and ethical secularists; it will be borne of freedom, principle and independence.

Afterword

Jewish Ethics & the Future

How future Jewish ethics are refashioned around the basic values of justice and compassion, how they play out in the pluralistic world of Diaspora Jewry and the more insulated world of Israeli Jews, and how they meet the unprecedented contemporary challenges of science, equality, democratic politics, military power, pluralism and new conceptions of gender will not be determined by any heteronomous revelation from above. It will emerge from below, out of the everyday deliberations, ethos and principles of Jews as they live their lives, interact with others, and build their future communities.

Like the Torah itself, Jewish ethics may have started at Sinai, but it no longer resides there. The Torah and our talmudic rabbis tell us *Lo ba'shamayim hi* – "It is not in heaven."[1] Jewish life, and the possibilities of holiness and ethics are in our hands. While the fundamental Jewish values of *tsedeq* and *ḥesed* are eternal, how and if they are realized are up to us.

If lived correctly, Jewish ethics of the future can reflect the ancient dream of the biblical patriarchs, Israel's prophets and traditional rabbis alike. This is the covenantal dream of peace achieved and harmony experienced among all God's human children. Whether Jews live out the ethical ideals of *tsedeq* and

1. Deuteronomy 30:12.

ḥesed and whether they work to fulfill their moral responsibilities will determine whether the Jewish people realize the Torah's challenge for the nation of Israel to be a holy people and a light to the world.

Bibliography

BOOKS

Amital, R. Yehuda. *Jewish Values in a Changing World.* Jersey City, NJ: Ktav, 2005.

______.*Commitment and Complexity: Jewish Wisdom in an Age of Upheaval.* Jersey City, NJ:Ktav, 2008.

Angel, Marc, editor. *Conversations*, Autumn 2013. New York: Institute for Jewish Ideas and Ideals, 2013.

Auerbach, Shlomo Zalman. *Minhat Shlomo*, II.

Berger, Peter. *The Heretical Imperative.* Garden City, NY: Doubleday, 1979.

Berkovits, Eliezer. *Essential Essays on Judaism by Eliezer Berkovits*, edited by David Hazony. Jerusalem: Shalem Press, 2002.

Berlin, Isaiah. *Four Essays on Liberty.* New York: Oxford U., 1969.

______. *Freedom and Its Betrayal: Six Enemies of Human Liberty.* Princeton, NJ: Princeton

University, 2002.

______. *Liberty.* Oxford: Oxford University Press, 2002.

Berliner, Naftali Zvi Yehudah. *Ha`ameq Davar* [Heb.]. Jerusalem: 1969.

Berthelot, Katell; David, Joseph E.; Hirschman, Marc editors. *The Gift of Land and the Fate of the Canaanites in Jewish Thought.* New York: Oxford U., 2016.

Black, Max. *Critical Thinking.* New York: Prentice Hall, 1952.

Blackburn, S. *Ethics, A Very Short Introduction.* Oxford, UK: Oxford U., 2001.

Bornstein, Abraham. *Avnei Netser* [Heb.]. Lodz: 1926.

Cherlow, Yuval. *In His Image.* Jerusalem: Maggid, 2015

Cordovero, Moses. *The Palm of Deborah*, translated by Louis Jacobs. London: Vallentine, Mitchel, 1960.

Cowdrey, H.E.J. *The Genesis of the Crusades in Holy War.* Columbus, OH: Ohio State U., 1976.

De Vaux, Roland. *Ancient Israel: Its Life and Institutions.* New York: McGraw-Hill.

Dessler, R. Eliyahu. *Mikhtav Eliyahu,* translated by Aryeh Carmell as *Strive for Truth.* Nanuet, NY: Feldheim, 2016.

Elazar, Daniel. *Covenant and Polity in Biblical Israel.* New York: Routledge, 1995.

Epstein, Barukh Ha-Levi. *Torah Temimah* [Heb.]. Tel Aviv: Sifrei Kodesh.

Ewing, C. *The Morality of Punishment.* London: K. Paul, Trench, Trubner and Co., 1929.

Fackenheim, Emil, *Quest for Past and Future.* Bloomington, Indiana: Indiana U.; 1968.

Feinstein, Moshe. *Iggrot Moshe.* New York: 1961.

Fuchs, Camille and Rosner, Shmuel. *#IsraeliJudaism: Portrait of a Cultural Revolution.* Jerusalem: Jewish People Policy Institute, 2019.

Gaon, Sa'adya. *Book of Beliefs and Opinions*, translated by Samuel Rosenblatt. New Haven: Yale U., 1955.

Glasner, R. Shmuel. *Dor Revi'i.* Jerusalem, 1977.

Goldman, Eliezer/Gellman, Yehuda/Heyd, David/Ravitsky, Aviezer/ Ross, Yaakov, editors. *Between Religion and Ethics* [Heb.]. Ramat Gan, Israel: Bar Ilan University, 1993.

Goren, R. Shlomo. *Meshiv Milhamah* [Heb.] Jerusalem 1996.

Goshen-Gottstein, Alon and Korn, Eugene, editors. *World Religions and Jewish Theology.* London: Littman Library of Jewish Civilization, 2012.

Green, Ronald M. *Religion and Moral Reason.* New York: Oxford U., 1988.

Greenberg, Irving. *For the Sake of Heaven and Earth.* Philadelphia: Jewish Publication Society, 2004.

———. *Living in the Image of God.* Lanham, MD: Rowman and Littlefield, 1998.

Haidt, Jonathan. *The Righteous Mind.* New York: Random House, 2012.

Ha-Kohen, Meir Simcha. *Meshekh Ḥokhmah* [Heb.]

Halbertal, M. *Bein torah v'ḥokhmah* [Heb]. Jerusalem: Magnus, 1997.

______. *Interpretative Revolutions in the Making* [Heb.]. Jerusalem: Magnes, 1997.

Halbertal, Moshe and Margolit, Avishai. *Idolatry*. Cambridge, MA: Harvard U., 1994.

Halevi, Judah. *The Kuzari: An Argument for the Faith of Israel*. New York: Schocken Books, 1987.

Hare, R.M. *Freedom and Reason*. New York: Oxford University, 1965.

Harris, Michael J/ Rynhold, Daniel/Wright, Tamra, editors, *Radical Responsibility: Celebrating the Thought of Chief Rabbi Lord Jonathan Sacks*. Jerusalem: Koren, 2012.

Hartman, David. *A Living Covenant*. New York: The Free Press, 1985.

Heschel, Abraham. *The Prophets*. New York: Burning Bush Press, 1962.

Heyd, David, ed. *Toleration: An Elusive Virtue*. Princeton NJ: Princeton U., 1996.

Hirsch, R. Samson Raphael. *Horeb*, Translated by Grunfeld I. New York: Judaica Press, 2002.

Ibn Paquda, Bahya ibn. *Duties of the Heart*. Nanuet, NY: Feldheim, 1996.

Jenson, Robert W. and Korn, Eugene, editors. *Covenant and Hope*. Grand Rapids, MI: Eerdmans, 2012.

Jenson, Robert W. and Korn, Eugene, editors. *Plowshares into Swords? Reflections on Religion and Violence*. Center for Jewish-Christian Understanding and Cooperation, 2014. Kindle edition.

Juergensmeyer, Mark. *Terror in the Mind of God*. Berkeley, CA: University of California, 2000.

Kant, Immanuel. *Groundwork of the Metaphysic of Morals*, translated by H.J. Paton. New York: Harper and Row, 1956.

Karelits, Avraham Yeshaya. *Ḥazon Ish* [Heb.]. Jerusalem: 1994.

Kariv, A. *Me-sod Ḥakhamim* [Heb.]. Jerusalem: Mossad Harav Kook: 1976.

Kellner, Menachem and Gillis, David. *Maimonides the Universalist: The Ethical Horizons of the Mishneh Torah*. London: Littman Library of Jewish Civilization, 2020.

Kellner, Menachem, editor. *Contemporary Jewish Ethics*. New York: Sanhedrin, 1978.

______. *Must a Jew Believe Anything?* London: Littman Library of Jewish Civilization, 2006.

______. *Maimonides on Judaism and the Jewish People*. Albany, NY: SUNY Press, 1991.

———. *Maimonides' Confrontation with Mysticism*. London: Littman Library of Jewish Civilization, 2006. 229–264.

———. *Gam Hem Keruyim Adam: Ha-Nohkri Be-Einei Ha-Rambam* [Heb.] (*They also are Called Human: The Gentile in the Eyes of Maimonides*). Ramat Gan, Israel: Bar-Ilan U., 2016.

Kierkegaard, Soren. *Fear and Trembling*. London: Penguin Books, 1986.

Kook, R. Avraham Yitzḥak Hakohen [Heb.]. *Orot Ha-kodesh*. Jerusalem: 1938.

———. *Iggerot Re'iyah* [Heb.]. Jerusalem: 1946

Loerberbaum, Yair. *The Image of God: Halakhah and Aggadah* [Heb.]. Tel Aviv: Schocken, 2004.

Loewe, Judah. *Gur Ayeh*. Jerusalem: 1987.

———. *Netivot Olam*. Jerusalem: 1961.

Maimonides, Moses. *Perush Ha-Mishnayot* [Heb.], In *Mishneh im Perush ha-Rambam,* [Heb.] trans. and ed. Yosef Kapach. Jerusalem: Mosad ha-Rav Kook, 1964.

———. *Mishneh Torah* [Heb.]. Jerusalem. Mossad Ha-Rav Kook.

———. *Guide for the Perplexed,* translated by Shlomo Pines. Chicago: University of Chicago, 1963.

———. *Epistles of Maimonides: Crisis and Leadership*, translated by Abraham Halkin. Jerusalem: Jewish Publication Society, 1985.

Malino, Jonathan. *Judaism and Modernity: The Religious Philosophy of David Hartman*. Burlington, VT: Ashgate, 2004.

McTernan, Oliver. *Violence in God's Name*. Maryknoll, NY: Orbis, 2003.

Me'iri, R. Menachem, *Bet HaBeḥirah* [Heb.] Sofer edition. Jerusalem.

Moore, G.E. *Principia Ethica*. London: Cambridge U., 1903.

Nardin, Terry, editor. *The Ethics of War and Peace*. Princeton, NJ: Princeton U. 1998.

Plato, *Euthyphro*. In *Plato, Complete Works*. John M. Cooper, ed. Indianapolis. Hackett Publishing Co. 1997.

Putnam, Robert, *Bowling Alone*. New York: Simon & Schuster, 2001.

Rosenberg, B. and Heuman, F., editors. *Theological and Halakhic Reflections on the Holocaust,* edited by Hoboken: Rabbinical Council of America, 1992.

Roth, Leon. *Is There a Jewish Philosophy?* Littman: London, 1999.

Rousseau, J.J. Social Contract. London: Penguin, 1968.

Sacks, Jonathan. *The Dignity of Difference*. London: Continuum, 2002.

______. *Morality: Restoring the Common Good in Divided Times*. Jerusalem: Maggid, 2020.

______. *Not in God's Name: Confronting Religious Violence*. New York: Schocken Books, 2015.

Scholem, Gershom, *Major Trends in Jewish Mysticism*. Jerusalem: Schocken, 1941.

Selengut, Charles. *Sacred Fury*. Walnut Creek, CA: AltraMira, 2003.

Shapira, Yitzhak and Elitsur, Yosef. *Torat Hamelekh* [Heb.]. Israel, 2010. In English: http://torathamelech.blogspot.com/.

Shapiro, Marc, *The Limits of Orthodox Theology*. London: Littman Library of Jewish Civilization, 2004.

Shilat, Ya'akov, *Iggerot ha-Rambam* [Heb.]. Jerusalem: Ma'aliyot, 1988) Vol. 1.

Singer, Marcus George. *Generalization in Ethics*. New York: Atheneum, 1971. 36–46.

Soloveitchik, Joseph B. *Halakhic Man*, translated by Lawrence Kaplan. Philadelphia: JPS 1983.

______. *From There You Shall Seek*, translated by Naomi Goldblum. Jersey City, NJ: KTAV, 2008.

______. *Abraham's Journey*, edited by David Shatz, Joel Wolowelsky and Reuven Ziegler. Jersey City, NJ: Ktav, 2008.

______. *Days of Remembrance* [Heb.]. Jerusalem: World Zionist Organization. 1986.

______. *B'sod Hayaḥid Vehayaḥad*, edited by Pinchas Peli. Jerusalem: Orot, 224.

Spero, Shubert. *Morality, Halakha and the Jewish Tradition*. New York: Ktav, 1988.

Spiegel, Shalom. *The Last Trial: On the Legends and Love of the Command to Abraham to Offer Isaac as a Sacrifice: The Akedah*. New York: Jewish Theological Seminary, 1950.

Spinoza, Baruch, *Spinoza's Critique of Religion*. NY: Schocken, 1965.

Sprinzak, Ehud. *Brother Against Brother*. New York: Free Press, 1999.

The Koren Siddur, American Edition. Jerusalem: Koren, 2009.

Twersky, Isadore *Introduction to the Code of Maimonides (Mishneh Torah)*. New Haven, CT: Yale U, 1980.

Uziel, Ben-Zion Meir, *Mishpatei Uziel* [Heb.]. Jerusalem: 1968.

Weiss, Raymond L., editor. *The Ethical Writings of Maimonides*, NY: Dover 1983.

Wood, Allen W. and DiGiovanni, George, editors. *Religion and Rational Theology*. Cambridge, UK: Cambridge U., 1996.

Wurzburger, Walter. *Ethics of Responsibility*. Philadelphia: Jewish Publication Society, 1994.

ARTICLES

Berlin, Isaiah. "Two Concepts of Liberty. In *Four Essays on Liberty*. New York: Oxford U. 1969.

Blau, Yitzhak. "Biblical Narratives and the Status of Enemy Civilians in Wartime" *Tradition* (39:4).

Block, Yitzchok. "G-d and Morality." *B'Or Ha'Torah* (12). 2006.

Boylan, Stanley. "A Halakhic Perspective on the Holocaust. In *Theological and Halakhic Reflections on the Holocaust*." Edited by B. Rosenberg and F. Heuman. Hoboken: Rabbinical Council of America, 1992.

Crocker, Richard L. "Early Crusader Songs." In Cowdrey, H.E.J. *The Genesis of the Crusades in Holy War*. Columbus, OH: Ohio State U., 1976.

Ephraim E. Urbach. "All who Save One Life' – Development of the Version, Vicissitudes of Censorship and the Manipulations of Printers" [Heb.]. In *Tarbiz* 40:3, 1971.

Fischer, Shlomo. "State Crisis and the Potential for Uncontrollable Violence in Israel-Palestine." In *Plowshares into Swords? Reflections on Religion and Violence*, edited by Robert W. Jenson and Eugene Korn. Center for Jewish-Christian Understanding and Cooperation, 2014. Kindle edition.

Goshen-Gottstein, Alon. "Concluding Reflections." In *World Religions and Jewish Theology*, edited by Alon Goshen-Gottstein and Eugene Korn. London: Littman Library of Jewish Civilization, 2012.

______. "The Body as Image of God in Rabbinic Literature." In *The Harvard Theological Review* 87 (1994).

Greenberg, Irving. "Pluralism and Partnership." In Greenberg, Irving. *For the Sake of Heaven and Earth*. Philadelphia: Jewish Publication Society, 2004.

Halbertal, Moshe. "Ones Possessed of Religion: Religious Tolerance in the Teachings of the Meiri." *The Edah Journal* 1:1, *Marheshvan* 5761 at http://edah.org/backend/JournalArticle/halbertal.pdf.

Hirshman, Marc. "Rabbinic Universalism in the Second and Third Centuries." *Harvard Theological Review* 93 (2000).

Horowitz, Elimelech (Elliot) "From the Generation of Moses to the Generation of the Messiah: Jews against Amalek and his Descendants," [Heb.]. *Zion* 64 (5759/1999).

Kant, Immanuel. "The Conflict of the Faculties," 7:63. In *Religion and Rational Theology*, trans. and ed. Allen W. Wood and George DiGiovanni. Cambridge, UK: Cambridge U., 1996.

Kellner, Menachem, "*Farteitcht un Farbessert* – On Correcting Maimonides." *Meorot* 6:2 at http://www.yctorah.org/content/view/330/10.

______. We Are Not Alone." In *Radical Responsibility: Celebrating the Thought of Chief Rabbi Lord Jonathan Sacks,* edited by Michael J. Harris, Daniel Rynhold and Tamra Wright. Jerusalem: Koren, 2012.

Knopf, Anthony. "Moral Intuition and Jewish Ethics," *Hakirah* 23 (2017).

Korn, Eugene, "The People Israel, Christianity and the Covenantal Responsibility to History." In *Covenant and Hope,* edited by Robert W. Jenson and Eugene Korn. Grand Rapids, MI: Eerdmans, 2012.

______. "Legal Floors and Moral Ceilings: A Jewish Conception of Law and Ethics." *The Edah Journal, Tammuz* 7562 (2002) at https://library.yctorah.org/files/2016/09/Legal-Floors-and-Moral-Ceilings-A-Jewish-Understanding-Of-Law-and-Ethics.pdf.

______. "Rethinking Christianity." In *World Religions and Jewish Theology,* edited by Alon Goshen-Gottstein and Eugene Korn. London: Littman Library of Jewish Civilization, 2012.

Lamm, Norman, Amalek and the Seven Nations: A Case of Law vs. Morality. In *War and Peace in the Jewish Tradition*, edited by Lawrence Schiffman, Joel Wolowelsky. New York: Yeshiva University Press, 2007.

______. "Loving and Hating Jews as Halakhic Categories," *Tradition* 24:2 (1989).

Lau, Benjamin, "A Reflection of Truth: The Rabbinate and the Academy in the Writings of A. S. Rosenthal on Violating the Sabbath to Save Gentile Life." *Meorot* 10, Tevet 5773 found at https://library.yctorah.org/files/2016/07/meorot-10-tevet-5773.pdf.

Leibnitz, Gottfried Wilhelm, "Reflections on the Common Concept of Justice." In *Philosophical Papers and Letters*, edited by Leroy E. Loemker. Dordrecht, Netherlands: Kluwer Academic Publishers, 1989.

Levenson, Jon D. "The Universal Horizon of Biblical Particularism." In *Ethnicity and the Bible,* edited by Mark R. Brett. Leiden, Netherlands: Brill, 2002.

Lichtenstein, R. Aharon. "Does Jewish Tradition Recognize an Ethic Independent of Halakha." In *Contemporary Jewish Ethics,* edited by Menachem Marc Kellner. New York: Sanhedrin Press, 1978.

Lior, Dov. "Jewish Ethics" In *Book of Hagi* [Heb.].

Lubitch, Ronen. "The Extermination of Amalek and the Arab Enemy: Between Biblical Commentators and Contemporary Rabbis [Heb.]. In *Shanon* 22 (1977).

Mabbott, J.D. "Punishment." *Mind*, 48:190 (1939).

Maimonides, Moses. "Eight Chapters. In *The Ethical Writings of Maimonides,* edited by Raymond L. Weiss. NY: Dover 1983.

———. "Epistle to Yemen." In *Epistles of Maimonides: Crisis and Leadership*, translated by Abraham Halkin. Philadelphia: Jewish Publication Society, 1985.

Rabinovitch, R. Nahum. "*Darkhah shel Torah*" [Heb.]. *Me'aliyot.* In English: "The Way of Torah." *The Edah Journal* (Tevet 5763 (2002) at https://library.yctorah.org/files/2016/09/The-Way-of-Torah.pdf.

Ravitsky, Aviezer. "Prohibited Wars in Jewish Tradition." In *The Ethics of War and Peace*, edited by Terry Nardin. Princeton, NJ: Princeton U. 1998.

Riskin, R. Shlomo. "Covenant and Conversion: The United Mission to Redeem the World." In *Covenant and Hope*, edited by Robert W. Jenson and Eugene Korn, Grand Rapids, MI: Eerdmans, 2012.

———. "Selling Land in Israel to Gentiles." *Meorot* 2011, found at https://library.yctorah.org/files/2016/07/Riskin-Selling-land-in-Israel.pdf.

Sagi, A. & Statman, Daniel. "Dependency of Ethics on Religion in Jewish Tradition," in *Between Religion and Ethics*, [Heb.] Ramat Gan, Israel: Bar Ilan University, 1993. In English: "Divine Command Morality and the Jewish Tradition." *Journal of Religious Ethics* 23 (1995).

Sagi, Avi. "The Punishment of Amalek in Jewish Tradition: Coping with the Moral Problem. *Harvard Theological Review* 87:3 (1994) 323–346.

Schwarzschild, Steven. "Do Noahides Have to Believe in Revelation?" *Jewish Quarterly Review* 58 (1962).

Seeman, Don. "God's Honor, Violence and the State." In In *Plows into Swords? Reflections on Religion and Violence,* edited by Robert W. Jenson and Eugene Korn. Center for Jewish-Christian Understanding and Cooperation, 2014. Kindle edition.

———. "Violence, Ethics and Divine Honor in Jewish Thought." In *Journal of Jewish Thought and Philosophy* 16 (2008).

Shapiro, David. "The Doctrine of the Image of God and *Imitatio Dei.*" *Judaism* 13:1 (1963).

Soloveitchik, Haym. "Religious Law and Change: The Medieval Ashkenazic Example." *AJS Review*, 12, (1987).

Soloveitchik, R. Joseph B. "Catharsis." *Tradition* 17:2 (1978).

______. "Surrendering to the Almighty," address to the Rabbinical Council of America, 1998.

______. "*Mah Dodeikh Midod*" [Heb.]. In *B'sod Hayaḥid Vehayaḥad*, edited by Pinchas Peli. Jerusalem: Orot, 224.

______. "Lonely Man of Faith." *Tradition* 7:2 (1965).

______. "*Kol Dodi Dofeq.*" In *Theological and Halakhic Reflections on the Holocaust.* edited by B. Rosenberg and F. Heuman. Translation by Lawrence Kaplan.

Stern, Josef. "Maimonides on Amalek, Self-Corrective Mechanisms, and the War against Idolatry." In Malino, Jonathan. *Judaism and Modernity: The Religious Philosophy of David Hartman.* Burlington, VT: Ashgate, 2004.

Weiss, Avraham. "*Shelo Asani Ishah*: An Orthodox Rabbi Reflects on Integrity, Continuity and Inclusivity." *Conversations*, Autumn 2013. New York: Institute for Jewish Ideas and Ideals, 2013.

Williams, Bernard. "Toleration: An Impossible Virtue." In *Toleration: An Elusive Virtue,* edited by David Heyd. Princeton NJ: Princeton U., 1996.

Wurzburger, Walter. "Covenantal Imperatives." In *Samuel K. Mirsky Memorial Volume.* New York: 1970.

WEB PAGES

Choose Life, at http://www.jpost.com/Jerusalem-Report/Choose-life-412588. Accessed on February 18, 2020.

Declaration on the Torah Approach to Homosexuality (2011), found at www.torahdec.org. Accessed on August 6, 2016. (Removed 2018).

Depression in the LGBT Population, at https://www.healthline.com/health/depression/gay. Accessed on February 17, 2020.

Hundreds of Orthodox Rabbis Carry Organ Donor Cards, at https://hods.org/about-hods/orthodox-rabbis. Accessed on February 17, 2020.

Jachter, Howard. *Halachic Perspectives on Civilian Casualties – Part 3, Parashat Toledot*, (24:9) at www.koltorah.org/index2.html. Accessed on February 17, 2020.

Karoll, Dov. *Laws of Medical Treatment on Shabbat*, at https://www.yutorah.org/lectures/lecture.cfm/756185/_Dov_Karoll/Laws_of_Medical_Treatment. Accessed on February 17, 2020.

Memorandum of Understanding on Conversion Therapy in the UK, at https://www.psychotherapy.org.uk/wp-content/uploads/2016/12/MoU-conversiontherapy.pdf. Accessed on February 17, 2020.

Nishmat Avraham, at http://www.medethics.org.il/articles/NA2/NishmatAbraham.yd.339.asp. *A Portrait of Jewish Americans*. https://www.pewforum.org/2013/10/01/jewish-american-beliefs-attitudes-culture-survey. Accessed on February 17, 2020.

Orthodox Rabbi Benny Lau's Powerful Denunciation Of Homophobia Justified In The Name Of God, at http://www.tabletmag.com/scroll/192649/watch-orthodox-rabbi-benny-laus-powerful-denunciation-of-homophobia-justified-in-the-name-of-god. Accessed on February 18, 2020.

Rabbinic Statement Regarding Organ Donation and Brain Death, at http://organdonationstatement.blogspot.com. Accessed on February 17, 2020.

Rabbinical Council of America. *Halachic Issues in the Determination of Death and in Organ Transplantation Including an Evaluation of the Neurological "Brain Death" Standard*. June 2010. At http://www.rabbis.org/pdfs/Halachi_%20Issues_the_Determination.pdf. Accessed December 22, 2020.

Responsum: The Congregation and People with Homosexual Tendencies, at https://eng.beithillel.org.il/responsa/the-concgregation-and-people-with-homosexual-tendencies. Accessed on February 18, 2020.

Statement of Principles, at http://statementofprinciplesnya.blogspot.co.il/. Accessed on February 17, 2020.

The Lies and Dangers of Efforts to Change Sexual Orientation or Gender Identity, found at https://www/hrc.org/resources/tje-lies-and-dangers-of-reparative-therapy. Accessed on February 17, 2020. Accessed on February 17, 2020.

The Growing Regulation of Conversion Therapy, at https://www.ncbi.nlm.nih.gov/pmc/articles/PMC5040471. Accessed on February 17, 2020.

Index of Terms / Names

About the Author

Rabbi Dr. Eugene Korn holds a doctorate in moral philosophy from Columbia University and Orthodox rabbinic ordination from *Pirchei Shoshanim* in Israel. He was founding editor of *The Edah Journal*. His books include *Jewish Theology and World Religions; Plowshares in Swords? Reflections on Religion and Violence; Covenant and Hope; Two Faiths, One Covenant?;* and *The Jewish Connection to Israel*. His English writings have been translated into Hebrew, German, Italian and Spanish. He and his wife, Lila Magnus Korn, live in Jerusalem.